Whiskers on K

a celebratory romp through the Stourbridge Glass industry

from the perspective of a few of my favourite things

- Stourbridge Glass; then and now
- the people and their stories
- my favourites; an appreciation
- bringing it all together
- hidden gems; raid that loft!
- the future's bright

Graham Fisher MBE

with a foreword by Ian Dury

(A talk by Ian to Bidford W.I. on 11/10/18.)

SPARROW PUBLISHING

A Spug Book
First published in UK by Sparrow Publishing 2015
Drovers Barn
Whitney-on-Wye
Herefordshire HR3 6EU

ISBN 978-0-9548781-7-7

Printed and bound in UK by Acanthus, Wellington, Somerset TA21 9PZ

COVER:

Rupert James Bartholomew poses in a magnificent bowl by Allister Malcolm
Photo: Graham Dale Photography Ltd

Contents

Foreword

HAVING BEEN PRIVILEGED to contribute in a small way to Whiskers on Kittens as Editorial Consultant, I have also been asked to proof the draft manuscript and offer comment.

Once again, as with his other writings, Graham has managed to tease out knowledge and inform his audience with a combination of the factual details and the importance of the social heritage within the Stourbridge Glass industry, so often ignored by other writers in our world of glass.

One feels immensely privileged through the medium of this book to go into Graham's family home, to share the joy that these treasures bring him and to learn of the importance they play within his life as he explores the journey of the manufacturing process, a process that has involved generations of craftsmanship and has been passed on through families or the skilled practices that have been honed within the factories over many decades and which have been applied to each piece of glass.

This journey that he takes will also help evoke yearnings within ourselves to question the importance of objects within our own homes that we may learn to treasure, and to offer an opportunity to share with others the stories of why these items mean so much to us.

Treasures don't necessary have to relate to financial values but their appreciation may lie more in an understanding of the craftsmanship, love, sentiment, style or design of the piece. Looked after well and cared for these *mementos* will often outlive us but hopefully they will then become cherished memories for the next generation.

Graham has become a brilliant ambassador for the 21st century Stourbridge Glass industry and those of us who still work within the trade owe a tremendous debt of gratitude to him for the work that he undertakes so enthusiastically on our behalf, promoting at every opportunity the fact that there is still life left in our glass trade; changed from previous glories of mass production, yes, but now awaiting new horizons just around the corner.

Ian Dury

Glass Heritage Officer
Webb Corbett Visitor Centre
http://ruskinglasscentre.co.uk/history-heritage/

In loving memory of Frederick Robson Montgomery

6th April 2013 - 30th March 2014
'Fast Freddie but not quite fast enough'

Forever remembered.

'The preservation of our heritage involves a handing over of the flame as much as a fanning of the ashes.'

A Writer Explains

the *raison d'être* behind this book and that rather curious title ...

ALRIGHT, I CONFESS; I must be one of the few people in the known universe who has not sat through *The Sound of Music*. Yet despite this glaring deficiency in my erudition even I can identify *'Raindrops on roses and whiskers on kittens'* as the first line of *My Favourite Things*. Perhaps this is some sort of subliminal reflection that I do keep Pedigree puddy-tats or maybe it's just an indicator that I should get out more, but when I decided to compile a book that would demonstrate from a lay perspective the history, achievements and sheer majesty of the Stourbridge Glass industry, well, for some reason all I could hear in my head was Julie Andrews a'warbling. And why not?

Thus did foment the idea of taking a few of *my* favourite things, examining their significance to me personally and then extrapolating their connotations to offer a more detailed appraisal of a once-mighty enterprise; an industry that still not only survives - albeit in curtailed form - but which is once more beginning to thrive as it adapts to life in the 21st century. Admittedly the glory days of huge glass factories employing hundreds of people may have gone, but Stourbridge is still universally acknowledged for the quality of its traditional glassware, its innovative new practitioners especially in the Studio Glass movement, cutting-edge developments in scientific applications, the preservation of its heritage and an evolving vision toward its future sustainability.

The *acme* of this last point is encapsulated in proposals by the British Glass Foundation (BGF) **www.britishglassfoundation.org.uk** to create a world-class glass facility on the site of the former Stuart Crystal works at Wordsley. By the time this book reaches print the Trustees of the BGF, of which I am one, are hopeful that work should be well under way towards its construction. The aim of the BGF is to create a fitting home for the word-renowned Stourbridge Glass collection that will show not only the history of Stourbridge Glass but which may also act as a beacon, even a catalyst, for its perpetuation.

The items described here serve the purpose of illustrating these attributes and collectively will offer a bespoke overview that should provide a compelling case for keeping the faith in Stourbridge Glass. I undertake this by first describing the object before then relating why it is of significance to me. The *denouement* is my punch-line in which I explain how and where the techniques or attributes of each object, or collection of objects, relate to the broader picture. I follow this with a section in which I bring all the *denouements* together in a holistic summation of the industry that should remove all doubt. Gosh, that all sounds cleverly convincing stuff to me; let us see if I can similarly convince you.

All are from our family collection and are lying around my house right now, where they are enjoyed and treasured for what they are. They are an eclectic bunch and I emphasize their significance, as will become evident, is entirely personal. I do not particularly promote their monetary value, their quality or their aesthetic appeal. Some of them are broken or not even completed. In each instance they are used here to express a point. However, it is inspiring to realize that these, or something like them, are the sort of bits and bobs that could be lying around anyone's - your - household right now. Ignored, unremarkable, unloved; yet how a scratch below the surface could reveal a mine of information that elevates them way above the mere commonplace.

Whiskers on Kittens is intended as a celebratory romp through the wonders of Stourbridge Glass past and present yet very much with a nod to the future. The objectivity accrued in my youth as a science student has never deserted me, or perhaps more accurately I have found difficulty in shaking it off, and so it is almost with a sense of breaking the shackles that I revel here in yomping through my own suppressed subjectivity; this is unashamedly opinionated and doubtless reflective of my own biases and preferences. Yet how ultimately rewarding it would be for me as a glass enthusiast to feel that it helps stimulate interest in others to find deeper meaning in their own *objets* that may be lodged unappreciated in attics, sideboards or out in the shed. There is something deeply therapeutic in the realization that some old piece of glass might not only be worth a few bob, but more intriguingly may *per se* be an intrinsic part of a richer tapestry that transcends mere cash. As the lady herself famously sang: *'When I'm feeling sad; I simply remember my favorite things; And then I don't feel so bad.'* Yep, works for me.

Happy hunting.

Graham Fisher
Herefordshire
May 2015

A Few Clarifications

... that may assist in your enjoyment of this book

Stourbridge Glass; then and now

Throughout this work reference is made to *Stourbridge Glass*. A mighty industry that once dominated the world and from which the area prospered well into the 20th century may be no more, but 'reports of its death are greatly exaggerated' (see FAVOURITE 10) and the industry has not only survived but is in some respects once more beginning to emerge as a potent force.

The closure of Stuart Crystal in 2001 with the loss of 220 jobs saw the last of the glassmaking 'heavyweights' succumb to forces that are beyond our purview here (my 2010 book JEWELS ON THE CUT, Sparrow Publishing 2010, explains more) but from such ashes promising new shoots are arising. Nowhere is this better exemplified than in the burgeoning Studio Glass movement, described later (Allister Malcolm, FAVOURITE 3; Webb decanter, FAVOURITE 7). There are also those who managed to survive the decline and who are still manufacturing glass products ranging from beautiful fancy-ware to high-spec technical equipment, together with numerous practitioners in the 'cold' fields of *decorating*, which is the generic term for any form of cutting, engraving or otherwise adorning the blank piece.

Nowadays the *Stourbridge Glass Quarter* is generally taken to include Broadfield House Glass Museum, Red House Glass Cone and Ruskin Glass Centre/Glasshouse College, together with various manufacturing facilities, decorators and retail outlets. At the time of writing, a new home is being sought for the Stourbridge Glass collection and the British Glass Foundation (see below) is an independent body that acts as a facilitator between the relevant parties in seeking to bring this about.

Crystal; an explanation

Whilst some of the items herein are referred to simply as 'glass' the term 'crystal' is also used, so an interpretation of the distinction may be helpful. Where other types of glass are referred to a brief explanation may be found in the accompanying text.

Although others well before him had used lead in glass - the white layer of the Roman Portland Vase contains 12% lead oxide - it was George Ravenscroft who, in 1674, applied for a patent to be the sole manufacturer of lead glass in England. He replaced calcium oxide, extracted from limestone, with lead oxide. Unlike old saucepans, the lead is locked into the chemical structure. The modification allowed for a softer glass that could be bleached and which could take a deep cut. It also rendered the glass softer to work. Stourbridge glassmakers eventually specialized in this technique and the area became synonymous with high-quality cut and engraved glassware.

To be considered *full lead crystal* the mix must contain at least 30% lead oxide. Most English manufacturers used at least 33% until the 1960s; samples from the 2014 archeological dig at Coalbourn Brook, Amblecote dating to the 1700s were analyzed at 40%. Over 24% can be referred to as *lead crystal*, anything less than 24% is simply known as *crystal*. Non-lead glass can be referred to as *crystalline*.

Lead gives the glass its celebrated 'ping', a brilliant crisp resonance when flicked with the fingernail that helps even the most unappreciative lay observer differentiate between a quality wine glass and a 'free with 5 gallons' version from their local petrol station. It is also an essential component that allows the glass to be acid or hand-polished. A proportion over 65%, not generally used in decorative glassware, absorbs radioactivity and can be used as radiation shielding.

The British Glass Foundation; what is it?

Some of the items mentioned herein, notably the 2012 Portland Vase Project artifacts, are destined to spend their days in the protectorate of the British Glass Foundation (BGF). It may thus be helpful to explain what the BGF is.

Since the 1980s Broadfield House, Kingswinford has been home to the world-renowned Stourbridge Glass collection. BGF arose from uncertainties over the future of the site as a Glass Museum and rapidly matured from a fledgling group of enthusiasts of disparate backgrounds into a cohesive body that has since established its credentials as a serious player *inter alia*. BGF is independent, apolitical and purely philanthropic. The Foundation's primary aim remains to secure a suitable and permanent home for the Stourbridge Glass collection.

For an organization that did not even exist prior to November 2010, the BGF has in the interim amassed an impressive portfolio of achievements. 2012 will go down as a pivotal year. The splendid Gala Afternoon held at Hagley Hall near Stourbridge; its associations with, and support of, the International Festival of Glass; the 2012 Portland Vase Project, the World's Longest Glassmaking Demonstration - to name but a few, and with more since - have all helped propel BGF to a position of prominence in the world of glass, a position from where it continues to promote glass in general, and Stourbridge Glass in particular.

GlassCuts, an *ad hoc* email bulletin sent free to subscribers, is the public voice of the BGF. It is distributed by a dedicated team *'here in the shimmering opulence that is the Editorial Suite of GlassCuts Towers'* that is, in reality, the respective desks of BGF Secretary Lynn Boleyn and me. Yet we are all justifiably very proud of *GlassCuts*. Envisaged as an occasional information broadsheet it quickly blossomed into a multi-page newsletter with colour imagery, bulletin board and diary dates offering support across the spectrum and has carved its own unique niche at the forefront of contemporary news in the world of glass. From a modest first issue in October 2011, just three years later came the publication of *GlassCuts@50*, a sumptuous hard-bound compendium featuring 'a selection of the best bits from the first 50 issues'.

As Whiskers on Kittens approaches publication the BGF and its partners are seeking to create a world-class glass facility on the site of the former Stuart Crystal works in Wordsley. Stuart was home to the White House Cone that sadly is no longer extant, although its counterpart Red House Cone still stands directly on the other side of the road.

To learn more about BGF and receive its regular free information output, offer support or make a donation visit **www.britishglassfoundation.org.uk**.

Acknowledgements

I AM INDEBTED to various quadrupeds who have been of assistance or inspiration. It has been all most enjoyable, which is how it should be. Special mention to our stars William Arthur Montgomery and Rupert James Bartholomew - fancy cats deserve fancy names - but not forgetting the regal Charlotte Henrietta Arabella, *aka* the debonair Cha-Puss, happy to be bridesmaid yet ne'er the bride. Also the twins, bearded collies Angus and Douglas, not quite stars yet but their turn will come.

Fine work too from various bipeds, as acknowledged throughout the text, but particular thanks go to fellow broadcaster Cockney Ken Frances who, in the day-job as a photographer, is adept at capturing a fine shot, is he not? Although his name isn't actually Ken Frances, it's Graham Dale. And he's not quite a Cockney. No, I don't either; sometimes it's just best not to ask. History will be the final arbiter as to how we ever got away with those Breakfast Shows; happy days.

To Ian Dury, formerly of Stourbridge Glass Engravers and now Heritage Officer at Webb Corbett Visitor Centre; a glass-man for all of his working life, who has offered me his invaluable counsel and undertaken sub-editorial duties above and beyond the call. The titular accolade of Editorial Consultant here barely begins to repay my gratitude. I am singularly grateful for both his support and his continuing friendship, both of which seem to know no bounds.

Very special thanks of course, to Spug and Mrs Chipmunk, affectionate *sobriquets* that refer respectively - and respectfully - to my other half and my mother, without whom none of this would have been remotely possible. I am blessed that they continue to support my flights of fancy with a combination of consummate grace and endless patience. It was the former who cleverly suggested I change my original working title of *Raindrops on Roses* to the infinitely more apposite *Whiskers on Kittens*. She was right.

Leonardo and the Art of Glassmaking is an extension of an article that first appeared in *The Blackcountryman*, the magazine of the Black Country Society **www.blackcountrysociety.co.uk** Spring 2015 edition, vol 48 no2. I am obliged to Editor Mike Pearson for his indulgence and support.

Finally in recognition of those wonderful people who comprise the Stourbridge Glass industry, some of whom have become dear friends but numerous others I will never even know, for making, decorating or otherwise having a hand in fashioning my favourite things.

Photographs of the FAVOURITES and other pieces where indicated are by Graham Dale.
Graham Dale Photography Ltd
Kingsley Studios
52 - 53 High Street
Stourbridge DY8 1DE
01384 444846
www.kingsleystudios.co.uk

Whilst Graham Dale was commissioned to furnish many of the photographs used herein I am grateful to other sources who are credited where appropriate.

All items are from author's collection unless otherwise indicated.
Items marked SIC are courtesy of Sheila Iris Chapman, the aforementioned Mrs Chipmunk.

Layout, publication and other clever stuff is all courtesy of Mary Spence MBE of Sparrow Publishing, the aforementioned Spug.

No animals or humans were harmed in the making of this book. Although it did nearly drive me nuts, but I don't suppose that counts.

Thank you, thank you and nay thrice times thank you all. Meow, woof and cheers.
GF

GRAHAM FISHER is a writer and presenter who has over many years of diverse output carved a niche as an astute observer of the lateral and the arcane. A devoted son of the Black Country, where he has lived all of his life, in 2013 he 'took a step outside for a while' and relocated to the Welsh borders. He frequently returns to the area where he pursues his principal passions as a waterways specialist with an interest in glass. A regular contributor in both fields he sits on the West Midlands Waterways Partnership and is a Trustee of the British Glass Foundation. He was invested for services to inland waterways in 2001 and in 2005 was voted by his peers as Inland Waterways Personality of the Year, assuming the mantle from previous recipients that include John Craven OBE, David Suchet CBE and Timothy West CBE. In 2015 he sat as a jury member for the International Festival of Glass Biennale.

By the same author:
GlassCuts@50 (Sparrow Publishing/British Glass Foundation, 2014)
In our Time (Sparrow Publishing/British Glass Foundation, 2013)
The 2012 Portland Vase Project (Sparrow Publishing, 2012)
Jewels on the Cut (Sparrow Publishing, 2010)
Out of The Chair (Sparrow Publishing, 2009)
The Sweet Life (Sparrow Publishing, 2004)

OPPOSITE:
Our kittens; the inspiration
Photos: Mary Spence

Whiskers on Kittens

a celebratory romp through the Stourbridge Glass industry

from the perspective of a few of my favourite things

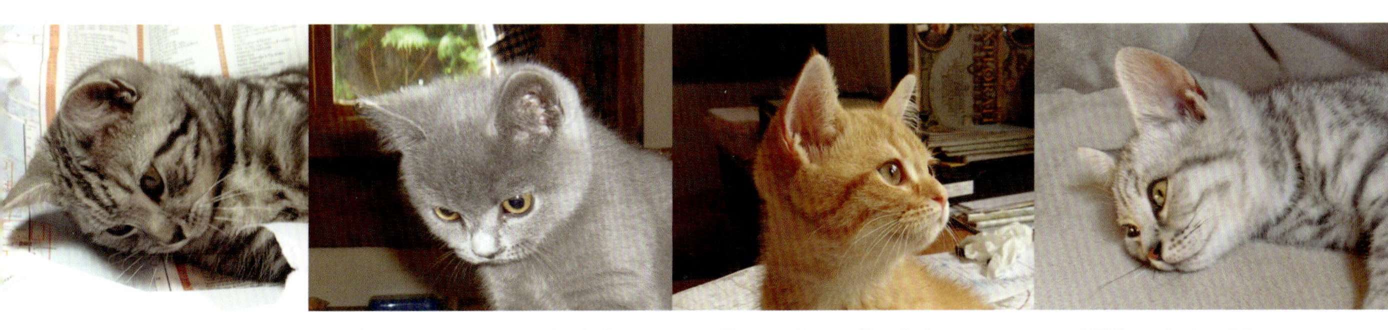

rederick Robson Montgomery
Freddie

Charlotte Henrietta Arabella
Cha-Puss

Rupert James Bartholomew
Roops

William Arthur Montgomery
Will-I-Um

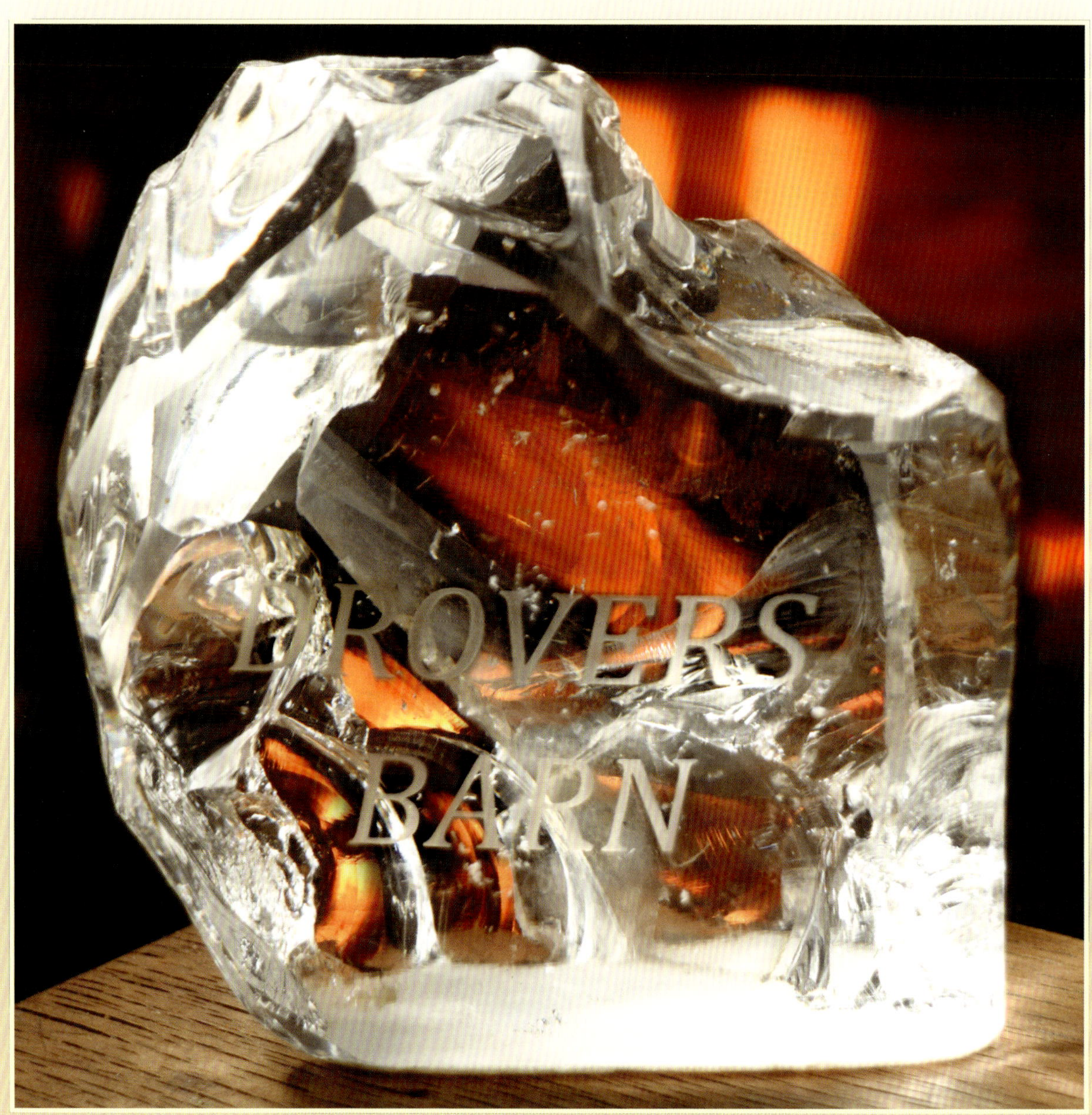

Favourite 1 : Cullet Block

Favourite 1 : Cullet Block

Description and aspects

CHUNK OF CLEAR GLASS 6.5kg, irregular shape with flat base and faces, height 18cm, width 16cm, depth 12cm, marked *DROVERS BARN* (no apostrophe)

Personal significance

I open with something of a dichotomy. This item is ostensibly one of the plainest of my favourite things yet it has inordinate personal significance since it denotes the transition from my apprenticeship as enthusiastic newcomer to an acknowledged contributor within the glass establishment, an attainment of which I am immensely proud.

For an explanation of all this I need to go back almost a lifetime to when I first became fascinated by inland waterways. I needn't detain the reader too long here other than to suggest that after close on half a century of being involved in some way or other with canals and rivers, I could be forgiven for becoming perhaps slightly jaded or *blasé* in my efforts to find increasingly innovative ways in which to appreciate them and maintain my enthusiasm. There are only a finite number of ways one can describe a waterway before a pernicious form of writer's lethargy sets in. Salvation in the guise of a refreshing new direction came in 2008 when I was appointed as an Outreach Worker for Broadfield House Glass Museum, Kingswinford and was invited to develop a remit to promote Stourbridge Glass.

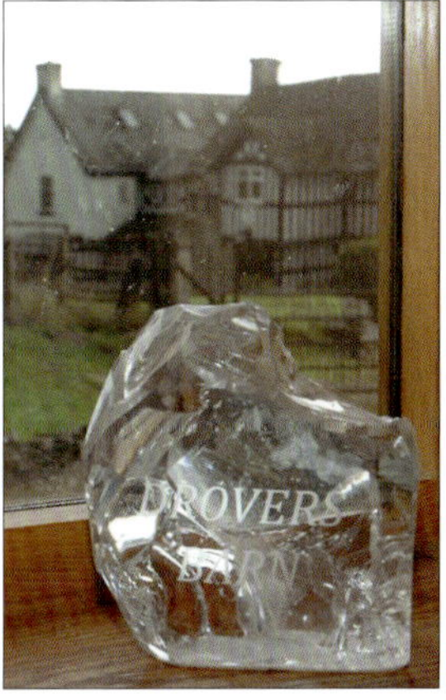

Favourite 1 on the window ledge in Drovers Barn
Photo: Graham Fisher

My palette was spread large in front of me; the Stourbridge Canal, where I had moored various narrowboats for the best part of three decades, passes right through the very heart of the once-mighty Stourbridge Glass industry. This is all now part of the tourist trail denoted by 'The Crystal Mile' but which is more usually accessed *via* the A491 trunk road between Stourbridge and Kingswinford. Examining it from a novel perspective that I had not previously considered, in 2010 I published JEWELS ON THE CUT, *an exploration of the Stourbridge Canal and the local glass Industry.*

Part of this work had, of necessity, referred to the recreation of the Portland Vase, an iconic piece of Roman cameo glass that was reproduced not once but twice in the 19th century in glassworks directly adjacent to the canal. Other than recording this as part of the Grand Journey I thought nothing more of it until 2011 when I was asked to attend Ruskin Glass Centre for a meeting with the Centre Manager of the time, Leigh White, and the then proprietor of Stourbridge Glass Engravers, based in the centre, Ian Dury.

Having read my work and noting my reference to the Portland Vase, they took me into their confidence regarding a project to bring the requisite

Opposite:
Cullet Block
Photo: Graham Dale

talent together at Ruskin for an initiative to recreate the Portland Vase for the 21st century; an initiative that would demonstrate to the world the skills still surviving in Stourbridge and which would set a beacon of excellence to which prospective glass artisans could aspire for decades to come.

I shadowed the project from start to finish and my book, The 2012 Portland Vase Project: Recreation of a Masterpiece, became the official account of this remarkable story. Job done, I thought no more of this until I was politely summoned one day in 2013 to Ian's office.

By this time he had also assumed responsibility for the Webb Corbett Visitor Centre, the Ruskin Centre being the former home of Webb Corbett, latterly Royal Doulton, before its closure and subsequent renaissance under the auspices of Glasshouse College. Part of the refurbishment involved the clearing of the old glass furnaces.

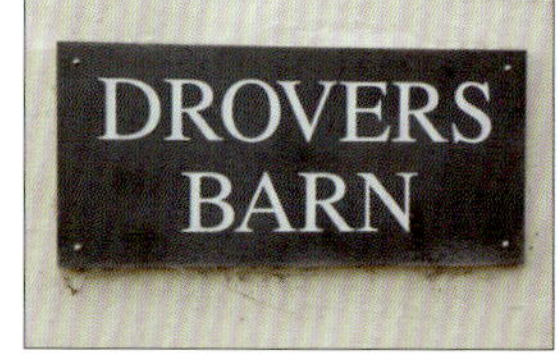

This was all commensurate with my family and I deciding to drop off the edge of the known world for a while, which led to our relocation from the Black Country to Drovers Barn, a 17th century timber building which, as the name suggests, was a former barn on the drovers' trails across the Welsh borders. This cullet block sits in pride of place in my eponymous home - is fashioned from one of the very last pieces of cullet (see below) removed from the old furnaces at Webb Corbett. It has been annealed and burnished to remove imperfections before being personalized by means of sandblasting with *DROVERS BARN*. And yes, the absence of an apostrophe is deliberate, although perplexing to the purist, the name being inherited with the house.

Presented to me as a 'thank you' by Ian for my support, to the casual onlooker it may just appear a lump of glass cullet. But the provenance of its origins combined with Ian's nomination of me as his favoured *ad hoc* ambassador for the Stourbridge Glass

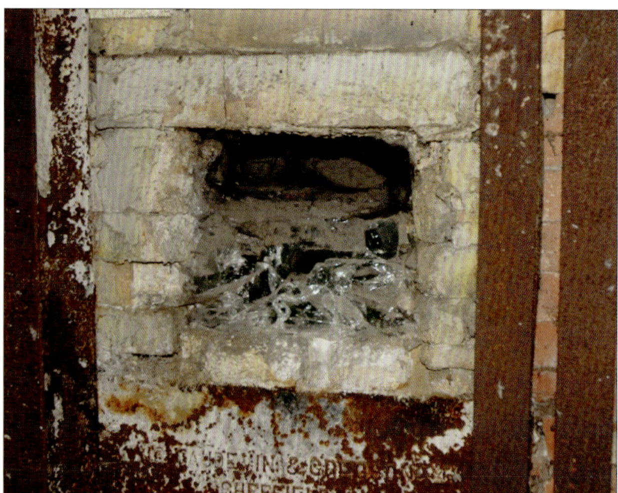

Right:
Old glass furnace at Webb Corbett
Photo: Graham Fisher

Cullet

Scraps of broken or waste glass that can be remelted as part of a new mix. The term possibly derives from the French *collet*, describing the collar-like neck of glass left on a blowing iron.

industry elevates this to the realms of a treasured item. I would not part with it for all the tea in China. More importantly it represents to me the acceptance of a greenhorn into a wonderfully arcane world of which, just a few years previously, I had precious little knowledge. Its monetary worth may be limited; its intrinsic value is incalculable.

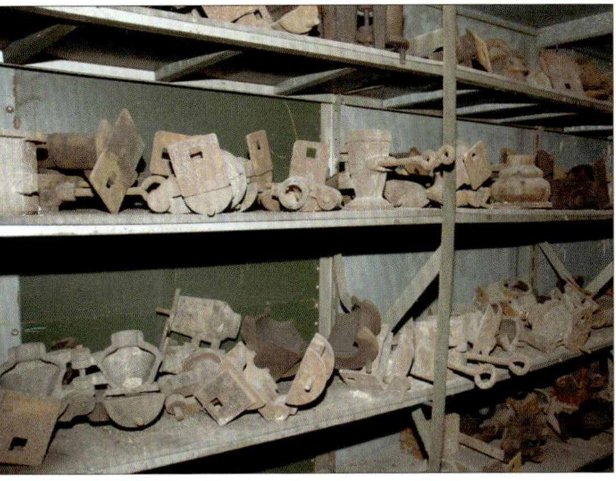

Cup moulds in the Webb Corbett store room before it became part of the new Visitor Centre
Photo: Graham Fisher

The denouement

The Drovers Barn cullet block is an example that epitomises the skills that still survive in Stourbridge; skills that enable a lump of featureless waste glass to be annealed, burnished and sandblasted to create an item of aesthetic presence and sentiment that also has a practical functionality. Lest one imagines this to be easy it should be remembered that many of the craftsmen, glassmakers and glass decorators served an apprenticeship of at least five years.

It is also representative of the numerous instances of modesty and lack of pretension that characterises the vast majority of those working in the industry. As will be seen in other examples of my favourite things the workers in the industry are, from my experiences, typically characterised - and, I understand, historically were also - by an understated appreciation of their own abilities. To the outsider looking in, glassmaking invokes the most extraordinary skills and talents. To those displaying such talents with routine regularity and consummate ease, it is 'just a job' (see Favourite 4).

Paradoxically, it may be this genuine humility and niceness, the general restraint and the lack of aggression in self-promotion that were amongst the factors contributing to the industry's demise.

References and Further Information

Webb Corbett Visitor Centre
Ruskin Glass Centre, Wollaston Road, Amblecote. Stourbridge, West Midlands DY8 4HF
01384 399419
http://ruskinglasscentre.co.uk/history-heritage/

Broadfield House Glass Museum
Compton Drive, Kingswinford, West Midlands DY6 9NS
01384 812745
www.dudley.gov.uk/see-and-do/museums/glass-museum

Jewels on the Cut; An exploration of the Stourbridge Canal and the local glass industry
Sparrow Publishing 2010 ISBN 978-0-9548781-2-2)

The 2012 Portland Vase Project; Recreation of a Masterpiece
Sparrow Publishing 2012 ISBN 978-0-9548781-4-6

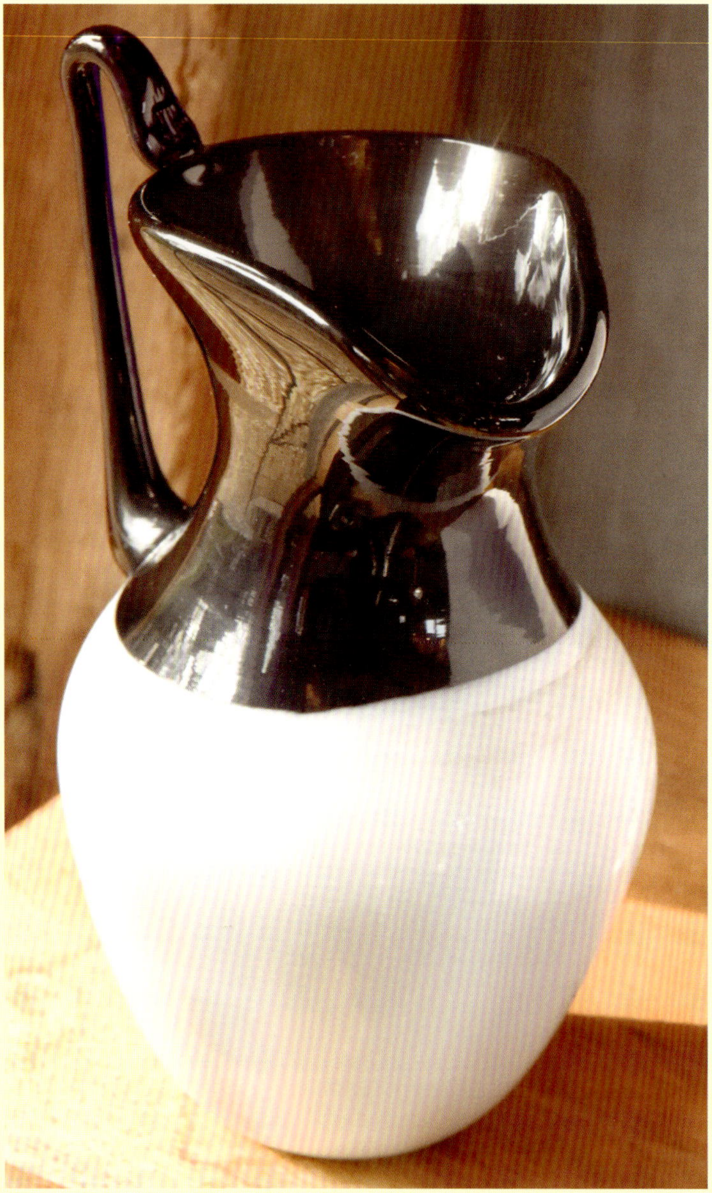

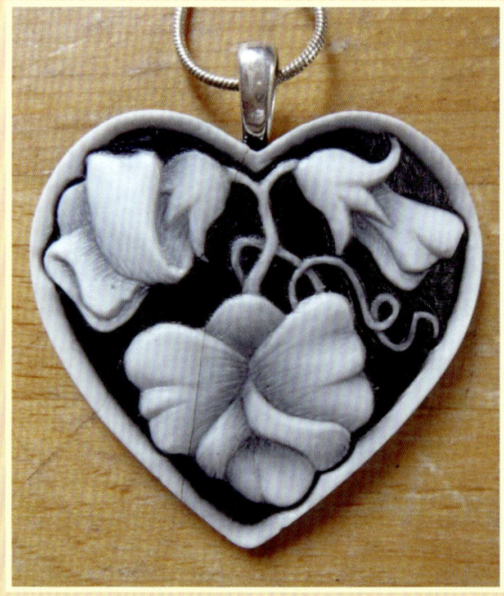

Favourite 2 : Jug and Pendant

Favourite 2 : Jug and Pendant

Description and aspects

JUG opal over cobalt blue cameo glass, height 13cm, width at widest point (6cm up from base) 8cm, circumference at base 3cm opening to 5cm at mouth. Slender handle 7cm rinsing 1.5cm above mouth.

PENDANT opal over blue cameo carved with stylized flower imagery, heart shape, 4cm at highest, 4cm at widest, 0.3 cm thick.

Personal significance

In a pattern that will be repeated throughout I confess that I have begun to go slightly off message already here since I have lumped two of my favourite things together as one item. But it's not really cheating since they are inextricably linked - even the more so that they were both made from precisely the same batch of opal and cobalt blue mixes.

They emanate from the 2012 Portland Vase Project (2012 PVP) and the small jug was a trial undertaken by master glassblower Richard Golding before the blowing proper got under way. Richard is proprietor of Station Glass which is situated in the former Shenton Railway Station near Nuneaton; he has long-standing connections with Stourbridge and his talents were re-imported back here for the duration. I am always at pains to point out on his behalf that this diminutive sample was a test piece to evaluate aspects such as the colour, ductility and flow of the melt and should in no way be seen as representative of any other work by Richard - least of all the completed vase - and who may be assured that I would never deign to represent it as anything other than what it is. Notwithstanding, I believe this tiny work, which was presented to me by Project Coordinator Ian Dury as an aid to my subsequent speaking presentations,

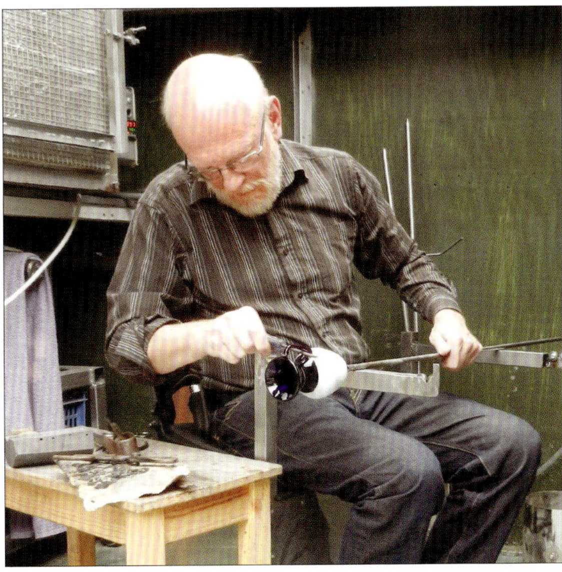

OPPOSITE:
JUG (left)
Photo: Graham Dale
PENDANT (right)
Photo: Mary Spence

LEFT:
Richard making the test piece, FAVOURITE 2
Photo: Ian Dury

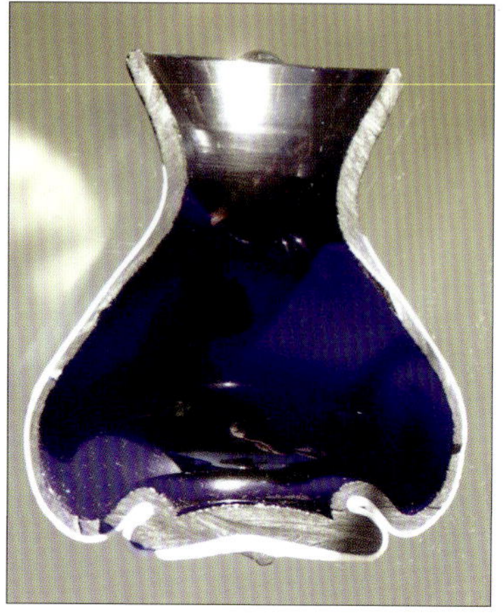

Cross-section of a sample piece to show the structure of the cameo
Photos: Ian Dury

will one day become of great significance *per se*, if it is not already, as an artifact that has its place and tells its own story as part of the project.

Nothing went to waste from 2012 PVP and the pendant is part of a limited edition collection of 100 carved by cameo engraver Terri-Louise Colledge, who also carved the replica Portland Vase and associated items, from blows of glass that didn't survive the full journey. This particular one I bought for my dear ol' mom, who wears it with pride. Noticing a work of true artistry when I see it, in fact I acquired several. These also serve to remind me of my acquaintance with a lady who is almost certainly the first woman in history to carve a cameo glass Portland Vase. There is more on the role of women in glassmaking at Favourite 7.

The denouement

This simple jug and exquisite pendant are in themselves of great significance but together they represent the expression of talents by a team of twelve craftsmen

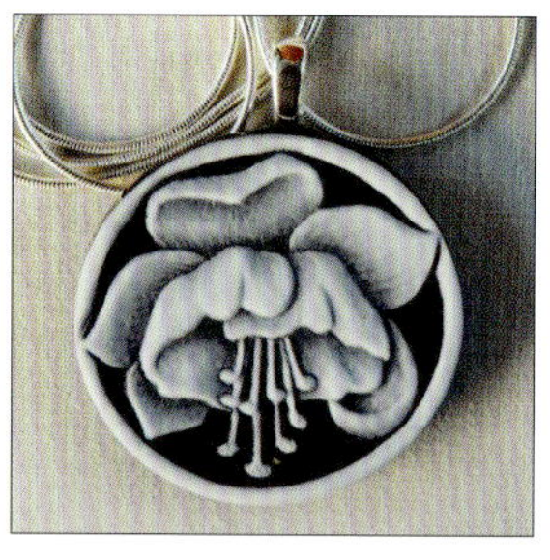

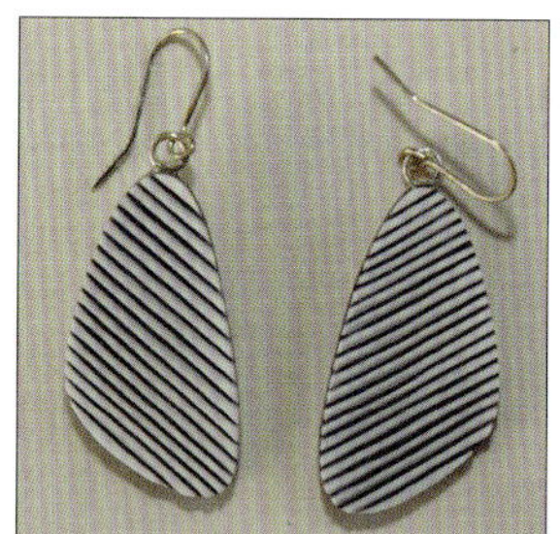

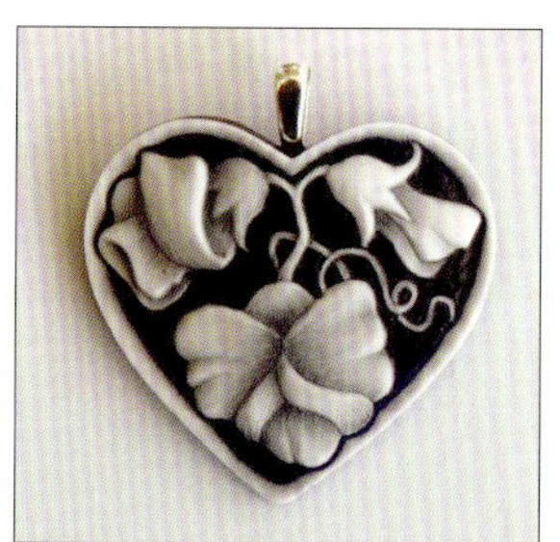

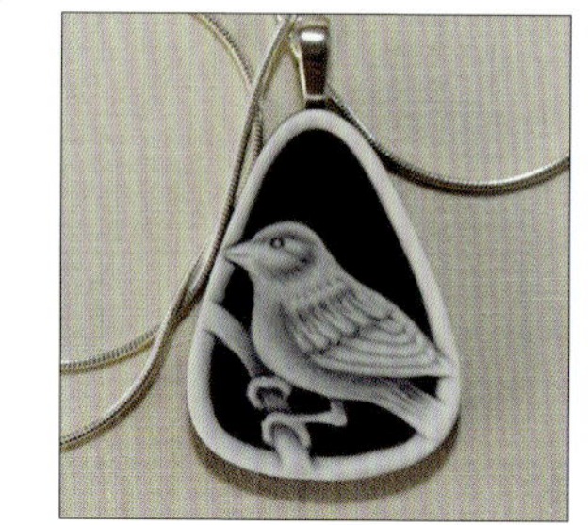

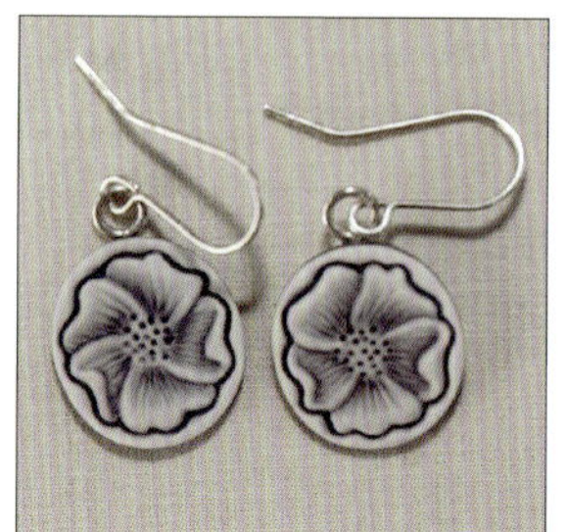

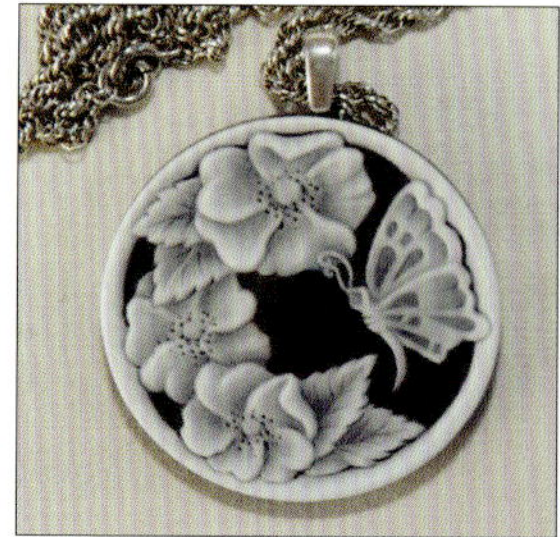

Pieces that survived: jewellery made from fragments left from the Portland Vase Project
Photos: Graham Fisher

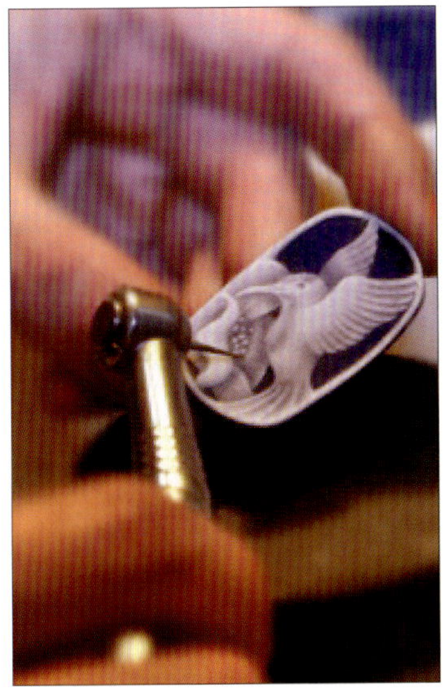

and women who physically worked on a project that has already become woven into glassmaking history.

The primary purpose of 2012 PVP was to demonstrate to the world that Stourbridge still has the requisite abilities to produce such a masterpiece. In this it succeeded admirably and will be recalled as truly epic for generations to come. However, in an extraordinary act of magnanimity Project Coordinator Ian Dury, who also owns the artifacts, has gifted them on permanent loan to the British Glass Foundation as the centerpiece of the proposed new glass facility in Wordsley. This tremendous gesture will offer a lasting validation to the people of Stourbridge and beyond as to our glassmaking capabilities and status.

There are also repercussions here for the development of friendships and associations elsewhere within the glass world. The interplay between Plowden & Thompson, who supplied the materials for 2012 PVP, Friends of Broadfield House Glass Museum, the Stourbridge Canal and various other seemingly disparate, elements will all become the clearer by the time Favourite 10 is reached.

Left:
Terri-Louise Colledge engraves a fragment
Photo: Ian Dury

Each limited edition piece comes with a Certificate of Authenticity
Image: Mary Spence

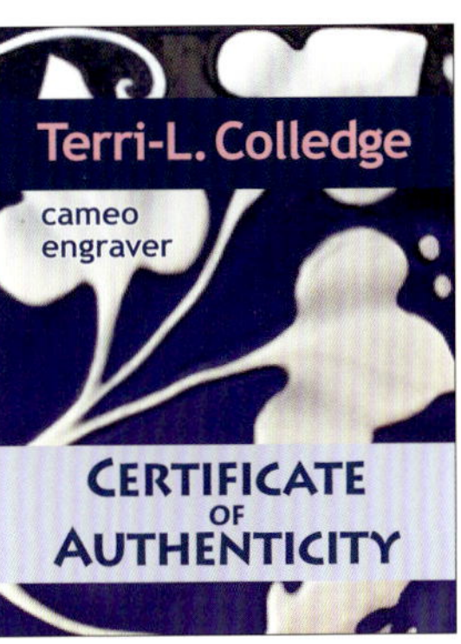

References and Further Information

Richard Golding
Station Glass, Shenton Station, Dadlington Lane, Shenton CV13 6DJ
01455 213929
www.stationglass.com

Terri-Louise Colledge
www.terricolledgeglass.com

Terri-Louise Colledge and the 2012 Portland Vase base disc
Time-lapse video of Terri carving the base disc by Tom Southall
www.youtube.com/watch?v=i2X7ykQ5Flc

Ian Dury, Heritage Officer
Webb Corbett Visitor Centre
Ruskin Glass Centre, Wollaston Road, Amblecote. Stourbridge, West Midlands DY8 4HF
01384 399419
http://ruskinglasscentre.co.uk/history-heritage/

The Portland Vase - An Enigma in Glass
Video account courtesy of History West Midlands **www.historywm.com** narrated by author
www.youtube.com/watch?v=GccdpXZKMUo

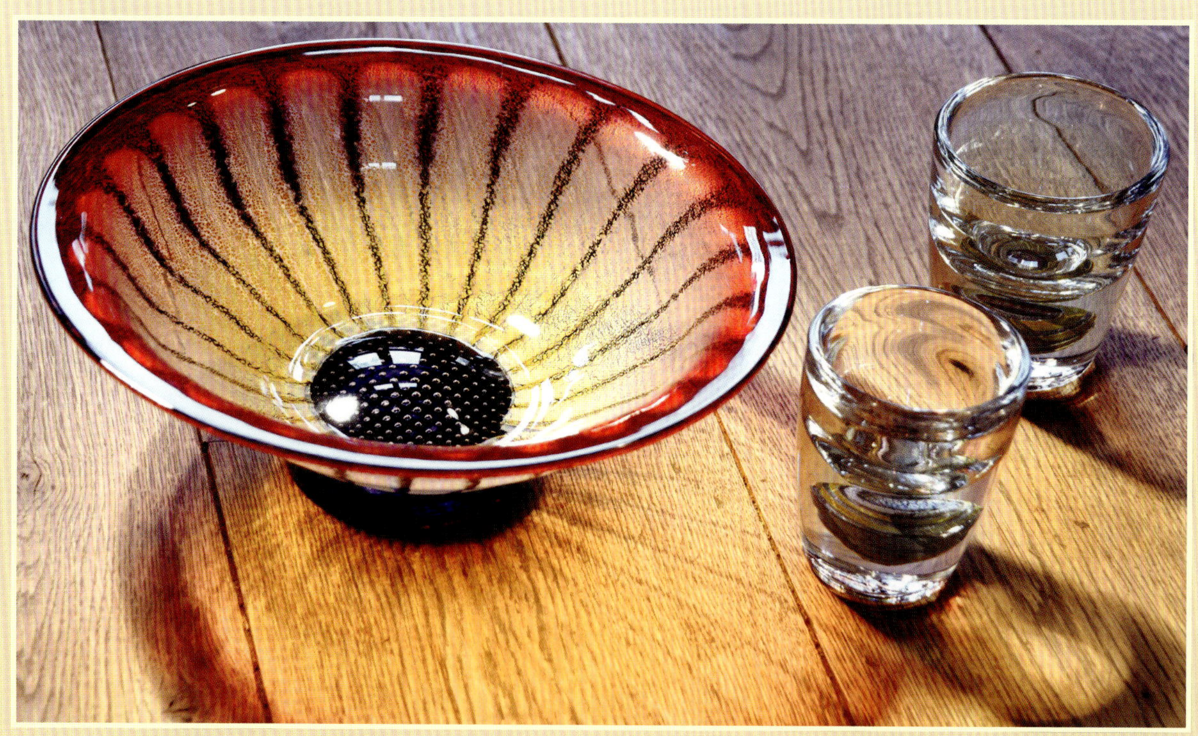

Favourite 3 : Bowl and Tumblers

Favourite 3 : Bowl and Tumblers

Description and aspects

DECORATIVE BOWL in hand-fashioned blown glass, multicoloured but predominantly red, silver and blue, 28cm diameter x 10cm depth; circular base plate in blue of 2cm thickness with signature engraved by artist and dated 2014.

'HIS AND HERS' TUMBLERS both of heavy hand-fashioned blown glass with multicolour 'conch shell' swirl embedded in base, one at 962gm and 9cm diameter by 11cm tall, capacity 200ml, the other at 902gm, nominally smaller in stature and with a capacity of 140ml. Both engraved by artist on base; smaller one reads: *'This one is to be used after a Bitch of a day'* and larger one:*'This one is to be used after a Serious bitch of a day.'*

All items by Allister Malcolm.

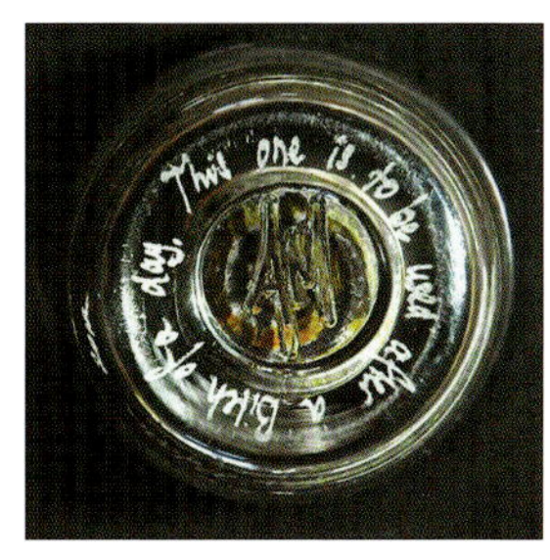

Inscription on the base of the smaller tumbler
Photo: Graham Fisher

Personal significance

Fellow British Glass Foundation Trustee Allister Malcolm is resident glass *artiste* at Broadfield House Glass Museum and now enjoys an international reputation that he has forged over the best part of a decade and a half of professional creativity. He is also a dab hand at coming up with fundraising ideas for the BGF's coffers and his World's Longest Glassmaking Demonstration was just one in an impressive list of such initiatives that attracted widespread sponsorship. Held as part of the International Festival of Glass 2012, the challenge saw him taking to his kiln through the night over a hot August weekend at Broadfield House to go head-to-head with his colleague Elliot Walker at Red House Glass Cone, both 'contestants' being supported and assisted by a catalogue of luminaries from the glass world including Lynn Baker, Jonathan Harris, Helen Millard, Darren Weed, Laura Birsdall and many more. The array of pieces accumulated during the marathon was subsequently auctioned by Fieldings of Stourbridge, with all proceeds going to the BGF.

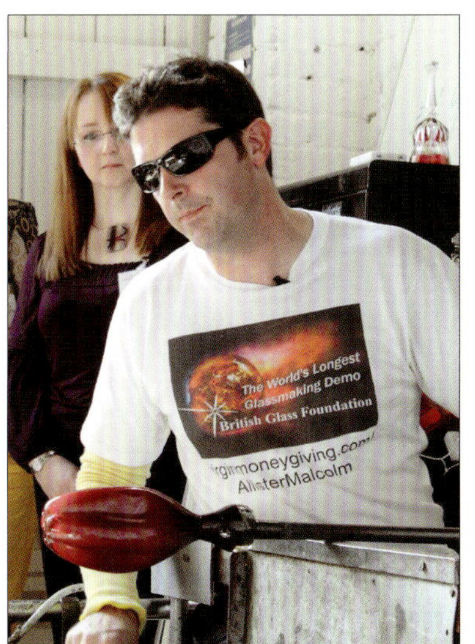

My association with this, apart from my support as a BGF Trustee, was to assist with the PR drive by liaising with local media and to compose text for a commemorative brochure. My publisher,

Opposite:
Bowl and Tumblers
Photo: Graham Dale

Left:
Allister at the World's Longest Glassmaking Demonstration
Photo: Darren Weed

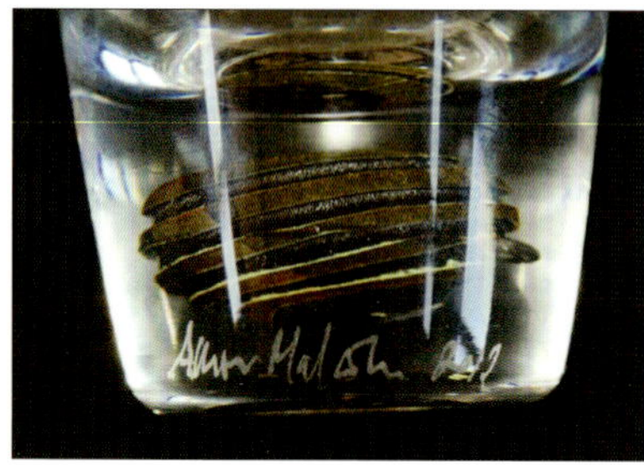

Detail in tumbler base
Photo: Gaham Fisher

who also happens to be my other half, produced a stunning little 'flyer' that neatly surmised the occasion and the participants. As a 'thank you' Allister subsequently, and unexpectedly, presented us with these tumblers which will endure as a reminder of our involvement with a gloriously madcap weekend that not only elevated the profile of the BGF at a crucial time in its development but also raised a significant amount of cash.

It is in a totally separate context that I describe my acquisition of the glass bowl, which was given to me following my presentation to the AGM of Pedmore Sporting Club (PSC) on 21st May 2014. BGF Chairman Graham Knowles also happens to serve on the committee of PSC, a philanthropic group that raises funds for local worthy causes. During his round-robin tenure as Chairman of PSC he kindly invited me to offer a talk illustrating the significance of glass to the area, at the end of which I was presented with the bowl. Lovely.

The connection between the glasses and the bowl, although relating to entirely separate events, is obvious - they were all made by Allister Malcolm. Plus they all now enjoy a prominent place in my home, where they are commented

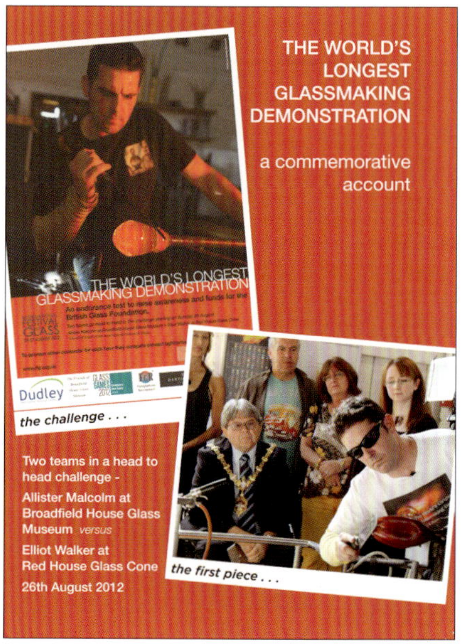

RIGHT:
The commemorative brochure from the World's Longest Glassmaking Demonstration
Image: Mary Spence

IAN DURY COMMENTS . . .

Fred Bridges was one of the founders of the former International Glass Centre in Brierley Hill. He recruited top craftsmen from the local crystal companies, such as father-and-son team Stan and Colin Gill, cutter John Davies and master glassmaker Malcolm Andrews, to teach their skills to the next generation of glassworkers. Their trainees are now amongst the most respected of contemporary glassmakers and I would venture to suggest that a visit to just about any glassmaking studio in the UK would reveal artists who were trained by, or have some direct connection with, these doyens of their craft.

The translation of skills from traditional techniques to contemporary applications is remarkable but then *plus ça change plus c'est la meme chose*. (The more it changes the more it's the same thing). Molten glass remains the principal material and the tools of the glassmaker have not changed in centuries.

upon enviously by just about everyone who steps through the door. To me, they are almost akin to a photograph album in reminding me of happy and rewarding times. Not surprisingly, they also have a substantially deeper personal significance.

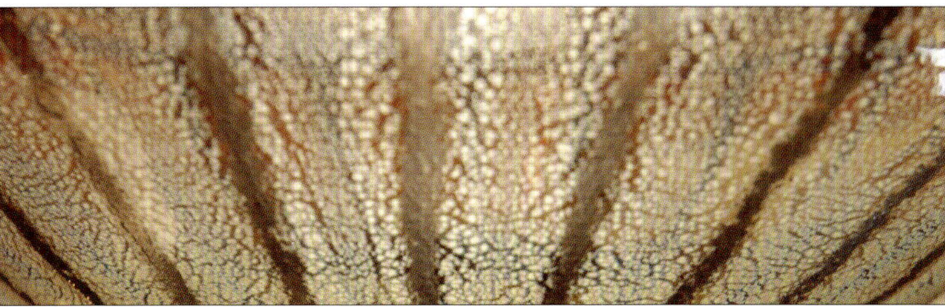

Detail of the bowl
Photo: Graham Fisher

The denouement

The 2012 International Festival of Glass was also commensurate with the 50th anniversary of the generally accepted birth date of the Studio Glass movement. In essence, Studio Glass involves the use of the medium to produce individual and highly stylized pieces, both aesthetic and functional, that are an expression of the creator's unique artistic abilities. The movement first took serious foot-hold in the USA but has since found a spiritual home in Stourbridge, which is now home to a number or recognized practitioners. Allister Malcolm is at the forefront of the Studio Glass movement and has become a celebrated craftsman within his field. The days of making thousands of identical cut glass items for the White Star Line, owners of *RMS Titanic*, may have passed but it is the likes of Allister and his fellow artisans who are helping to redefine Stourbridge Glass in a role befitting the 21st century and to secure its future for succeeding generations.

Apropos nothing in particular, in a flight of fancy that saw me examine the connection between glassmaking and the numerical Fibonacci sequence I utilized these pieces as the basis for a discussion as to whether talent could be defined by algorithms. The resulting article, which appeared in the Spring 2015 edition of *The Blackcountryma*n, the quarterly magazine of the Black Country Society, is reproduced under Leonardo and the Art of Glassmaking.

Contacts and References

British Glass Foundation
www.britishglassfoundation.org.uk

Allister Malcolm
www.allistermalcolm.com

International Festival of Glass
www.ifg.org.uk

Leonardo and the art of glassmaking ... formulaic skill or divine gift?
The Blackcountryman Spring 2015: Vol 48: No 2
www.blackcountrysociety.co.uk

Studio Glass
Numerous; browse 'Studio Glass Movement'

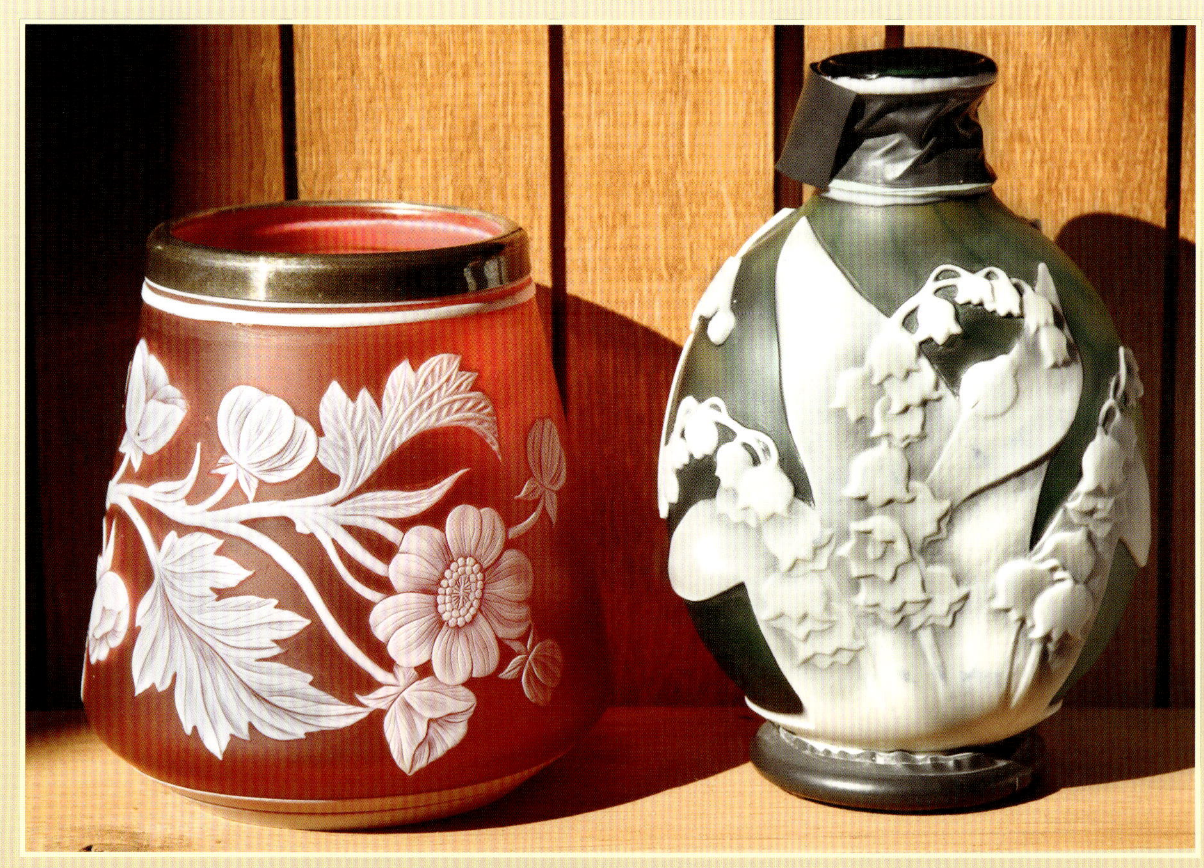

Favourite 4 : Cameo Vase and Bottle

Favourite 4 : Cameo Vase and Bottle

Description and aspects

CAMEO VASE ruby overlayed with ivory carved in floral pattern with striations around head and base and gold collaring. 10cm diameter at base tapering through a height of 11cm to rim of 7cm diameter.

CAMEO BOTTLE green overlayed with ivory in lily of the valley floral pattern (incomplete) 14cm tall with base of 5cm diameter; body 9cm at widest, 6cm deep. 'Resist' tape to base and neck.

Personal significance

I simply had to put these two together since their sum is so much than their individual parts in representing just a few of the aspects that make Stourbridge Glass so captivating. Both are cameo glass, comprising a layer of (usually) lighter glass over a (usually) darker underlayer. Both are roughly the same size and both, in their own little quirky ways, are quite delighful. But for me it is their differences that make them so worthy of being brought together on the same plinth.

The red one first; I have yet to accurately identify it but I suspect it was made either by Stevens & Williams or Stuart sometime in the mid or late 19th century. A bit of a curate's egg, it has characteristics of both and I would be grateful if someone could put me out of my misery and accurately identify its provenance; whatever it is, I think it is simply adorable. It came our way *via* auction when my astute mother, no glass expert but an admirer of fine examples, snaffled it up for a song. Truth is, no-one else was interested in it other than her and it now resides in her showcase on display and accompanied by fulsome commentary for anyone who will listen as to how she proudly beat the gavel.

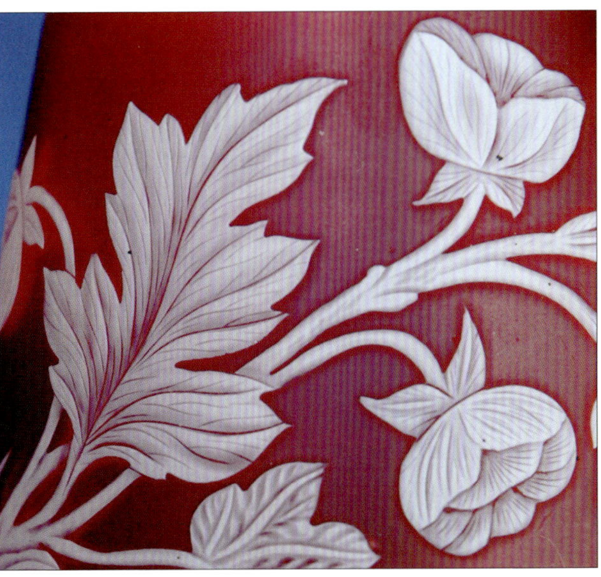

Exquisite detail on the leaves and petals
Photo: Graham Fisher

OPPOSITE:
Ruby CAMEO VASE (left) and unfinished Green CAMEO BOTTLE (right)
Photo: Graham Dale

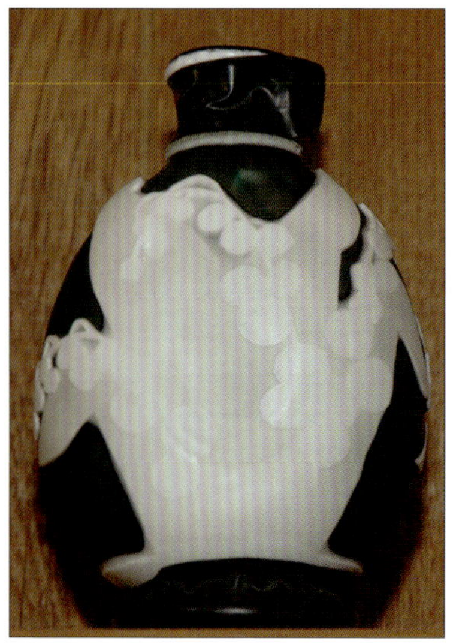

The reverse of the bottle showing the stage before detailed carving begins
Photo: Graham Fisher

The green one is a much more modern variant and is uncompleted. It came into my possession in my early days of entering the glass world when cameo engraver Terri-Louise College (the same lady who was later to carve the 2012 Portland Vase) gave it to me as a tactile aid in my speaking presentations. It is unfinished since the carving of the outer layer revealed faults in the underlayer that Terri felt detracted from the quality of the piece to the degree that it would be unsellable. The black tape is the 'resist' that has remained *in situ* since the outer layer was sandblasted away in readiness for final carving.

The piece has since been with me on numerous outings where I use it to demonstrate the nature and manufacture of cameo glass and the problems that can unexpectedly arise before the piece is completed, rendering it un-marketable. Though unfinished and unworkable, this is an example that I treasure since it came my way from a lady at the top of her game who embraced me as an associate and supporter of both her work and the industry at large. Offer me lots of money; the answer is still no.

I was subsequently proud beyond my station to shadow Terri as she carved the items for the 2012 Portland Vase Project, referred to at Favourite 2, for which I was the official biographer. By this time our friendship had blossomed and I was able to see at first hand and at close quarters the mind-blowing skills she possesses.

The denouement

I believe the green piece, though defective and incomplete, does have a monetary value but that is hardly the point since I have no intention of realizing it. I am more taken by Terri's reaction when she gave me it and told me of the several weeks of work she had undertaken on it, now to no avail. At the same time she also showed me examples of other items that, way down the line from her starting work on them, transpire to have some hitherto hidden defect. When I remarked how frustrating that must be she replied with no apparent hint of concern: *'It's just one of those things, you have to take no notice and get on with it.'* As I have commented on numerous occasions since then when I have related this tale, I have known grown men turn to drink for less and Terri's breezy uncomplicated outlook is so typical of the inherent humility and *sang froid* that, for me, characterises the men and women of the Stourbridge Glass industry and of which I have experienced numerous examples.

On another occasion, in fact the first time I met Terri, I spent an afternoon at a glass facility taking photographs for a presentation. On my leaving the staff lined up and expressed their appreciation to me. Some actually bowed slightly from the waist. When I suggested it was I who should be thanking them I was told: *'We appreciate the fact that you come here as an enthusiast and go out to tell others about what we do. To us, this is simply a job'.*

And will I ever forget the occasion on August 2012 when the press-pack that had gathered at the Hagley Hall Gala Afternoon first saw the newly completed and utterly exquisite 2012 Portland Vase that she had engraved to international acclaim. Asked by one grizzled hack how this compared with her previous work she replied with an unfazed drollness, which for that moment redefined understatement: *'I dunno; I've never actually carved human figures before'.*

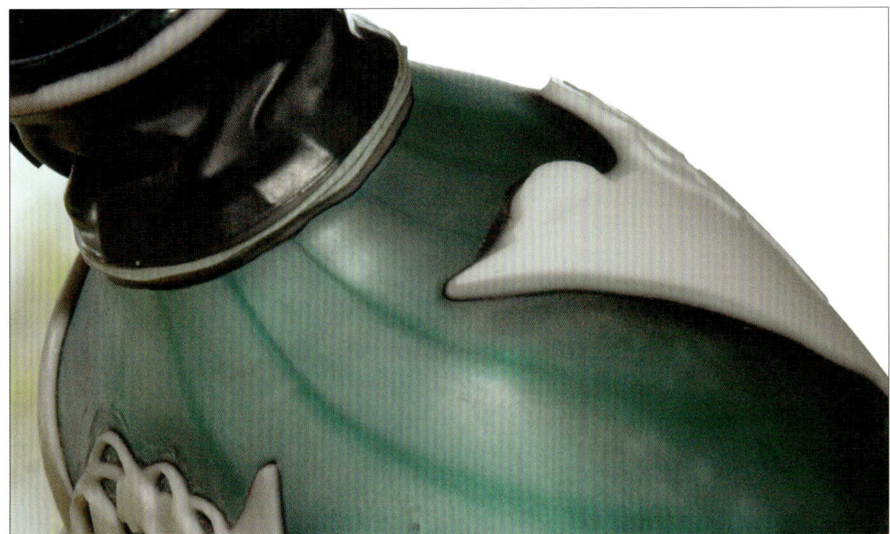

Side view showing faults in the green underlayer, not visible until the removal of the overlayer; follow the darker green trails towards the neck and note the fine grey lines along the edges of the trails - those are cracks where the two different glass mixtures have reacted against each other
Photo: Graham Fisher

Self-effacement on a grand scale; I have been privileged to meet some genuinely lovely people.

References and Further Information

Terri-Louise Colledge
www.terricolledgeglass.com

Stevens & Willliams (latterly Royal Brierley)
http://gorgeousglass.org.uk/steven-williams/
http://en.wikipedia.org/wiki/Royal_Brierley
Founded in 1846, Stevens & Williams Ltd became Royal Brierley Crystal Ltd in 1930 when the company took the name to signify its appointment as the Royal British Glassmakers. Former Chairman and Managing Director David Williams-Thomas is Patron of the British Glass Foundation **www.britishglassfoundation.org.uk**

Stuart Crystal
http://www.ehow.co.uk/about_5460458_history-stuart-crystal.html

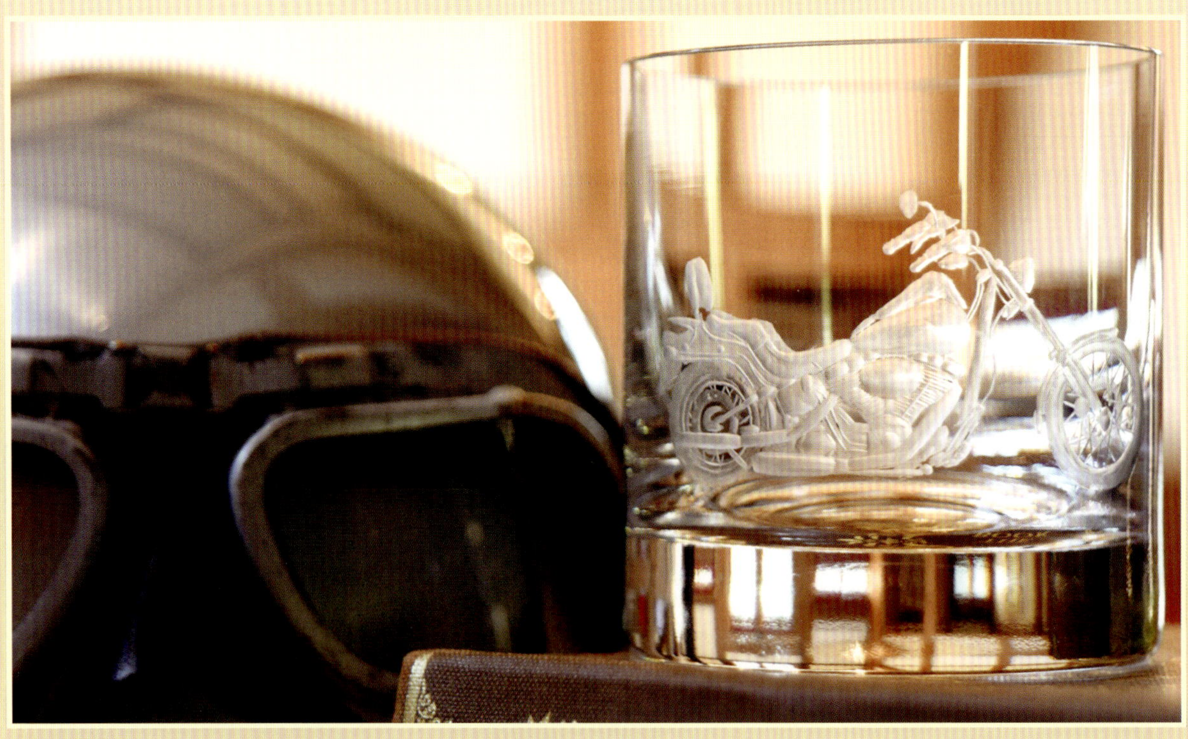

Favourite 5 : Engraved Tumbler

Favourite 5 : Engraved Tumbler

Description and aspects

CLEAR LEAD CRYSTAL TUMBLER heavy base 10cm tall x 8.5cm circumference. Decorated by copper wheel technique with detailed image of customized Harley Davidson motorcycle, model FSXTI dated 2004.

Personal significance

This is a tale of talent reinvented, talent latent and talent personified together with a bit about a footballer and a musician thrown in, all of which conspire to propel this high up the list of my favourite things.

That may need an explanation.

First, the talent reinvented. My publisher, who as mentioned at Favourite 3 also happens to be my other half, is a cartographer by trade. Makes maps. Pretty darned good at it, too. Up to just a few years ago she used Rotring mapping pens (remember them and their very thin long nibs?), magnifying glasses, French curves, that sort of low-tech stuff which up until then had done the job for hundreds of years. Then along came computers. Approaching the time of her career where she either had to adapt or be cast hopelessly adrift, she retrained herself; *Adobe InDesign, Illustrator, Photoshop* and all that technical stuff. One determined lady.

For talent latent, compare her story with the lot of one of her graphic deisgner acquaintances and take a look at the picture of my motorcycle she commissioned from him as a gift. He painted it freehand; it is by any yardstick quite superb and is accurate in every detail right down to the individual creases on the seat and backrest that identify this to me uniquely as my machine. Such ability, yet come the technological revolution and this fine illustrator couldn't, or didn't want to, hack the transition. Last I heard of him he was a security officer at Gatwick Airport.

Opposite:
Engraved Tumbler
Photo: Graham Dale

Below:
A stunning piece of artwork marked *Harley Davidson Softail Custom* by Nigel Davis, 2012.
Photo: Graham Dale

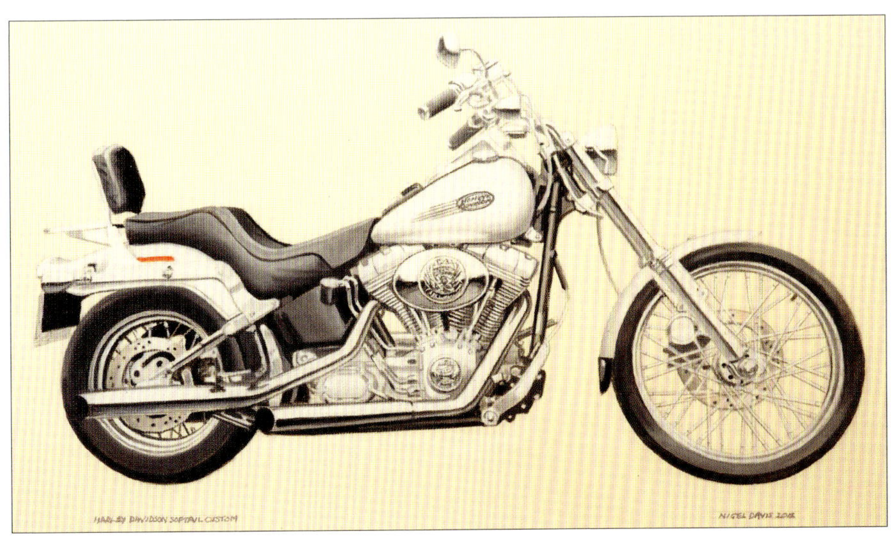

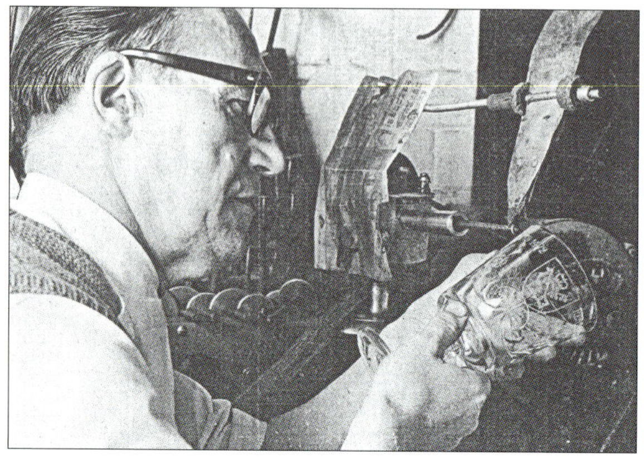

Bill Mason in the 1970s, one of Stourbridge's leading copper wheel engravers
Photo: Paul Delmar

As for talent personified, the image of the glass tumbler, presented to me by Mary as a rather special birthday gift, shows it in spades. An exact replica of the freehand picture, which is in turn the image of my machine right down to the creases in the seats and backrest, set into glass by Carl Palmer using nothing more than a small copper wheel rotating at high speed on a spindle against which he presses the glass. A former apprentice with Royal Brierley and now one of the best in his field of copper wheel engraving, Carl uses his gifts of artistic expression to create an image that, whilst actually cut into the glass, appears to stand out from it in 3D relief. Quite incredible.

Again I go somewhat off-message but I suppose I can permit myself a bit of poetic licence. Now, I appreciate David Beckham can control a ball with beauty and grace and effortlessly kick it past several other people into the back of a net. I would not question that he is a gifted footballer. But this, to me, is not genius. Sir Paul McCartney can compose a catchy tune that will sell by the millions and have us all tapping our feet. I have no doubt that he is a gifted musician. But this, to me, is not genius.

Now look closely at the image of my motorcycle, an exact replica of the picture that is in turn an exact replica of the real thing, etched into glass by a tiny wheel of copper. Go back a few pages and look again at Allister Malcolm's bowl fashioned by hand from molten glass using little more than metal tongs and wet newspaper or Terri Colledge's cameo pendant carved with just a combination of incredible precision and a dentist's drill. Or even Richard Golding's experimental 'blow' of the Portland Vase. *Those*, I suggest, are genius.

The denouement

I am as yet barely halfway through my collation of favourite things and already I have described a variety of *artistes* from the esoteric world of Stourbridge Glass whose talents almost defy belief. Yet there is so much more upon which I have yet to touch. It is therefore imperative that we identify and record that which we still have left and nurture it for future generations to marvel at and learn from.

Some, like those previously mentioned, are still practicing, teaching others and continuing the skills. Yet there are others that are becoming lost in the ether and, in a discourse on Harbridge Glass (operational for a short time in the latter part of the 20th century off Platts Crescent, Amblecote) that appeared in *The Blackcountryman*, the magazine of the Black Country (Spring 2011 Vol 44 No 2) I noted:

... the list goes on. But there is one common thread - everyone I have described herein has a passion for this thing called Stourbridge Glass and offers a direct

lineage back to the glory days when it reigned supreme. This is the sheer power of living testimony, a mere cupful of which weighs far heavier than any amount of recorded data or archive ever can. And, unlike the veterans of WWI who have only recently faded forever, and those of WWII who are rapidly following suit, there is yet so much of Stourbridge Glass that still has its practitioners in links that penetrate right back to its finest hour. Such a vibrant legacy demands per se *our fullest efforts in preserving it whilst we still have the sands of time in our grasp. To ignore this opportunity would be folly on the grandest scale, the inevitable corollary of which will bear witness to much wailing and gnashing of teeth in a milieu of unmitigated regret.*

I remain confident that the Stourbridge Glass Industry, albeit in a form unrecognizable from its heyday, will nonetheless survive and prosper. However, it should be seen in the same light as the mighty oak that shoots its leaves forward in its efforts to grow. How ultimately futile is that effort if it has no roots with which to first secure itself. The proud history of the industry is its roots and they must therefore be preserved and nurtured for their own sake if we are to employ them as the foundation from which we can continue to develop sustainably into the future.

The Webb Corbett Visitor Centre is one repository where memories are recorded, displayed and stored. I happen to know about this particular one because of my modest involvement with it. There may be others but if we are to avoid the *much wailing and gnashing of teeth in a milieu of unmitigated regret* then many more such initiatives are needed. And now.

Copper Wheel Engraving Lathe
used by Amblecote Craftsman
William Thomas Mason
1913 - 2005
Gifted by Donation, Courtesy of
Graham Fisher MBE

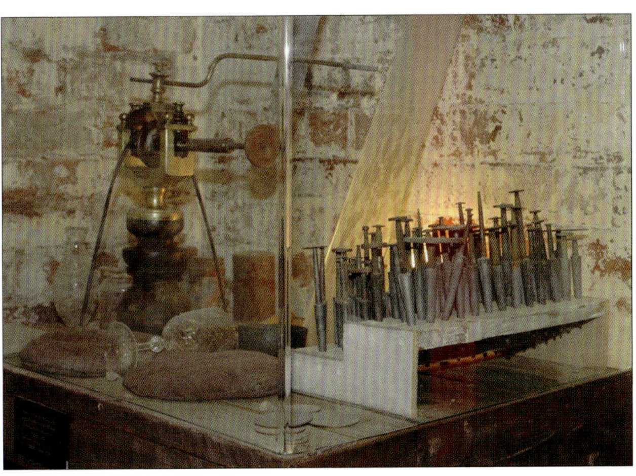

Copper wheel engraving lathe and interpretive plaque housed in the Webb Corbett Visitor Centre
Photo: Graham Fisher

References and Further Information

Carl Palmer
Based at Red House Glass Cone, High Street, Wordsley, West Midlands, DY8 4AZ
www.dudley.gov.uk/see-and-do/museums/red-house-glass-cone

Webb Corbett Visitor Centre
Ruskin Glass Centre, Wollaston Road, Amblecote. Stourbridge, West Midlands DY8 4HF
01384 399419
http://ruskinglasscentre.co.uk/history-heritage/

Wheels within wheels
'A sideways look at the Stourbridge Glass industry and some of its lesser known exponents from the perspective of the associated Stourbridge Canal'
The Blackcountryman Spring 2011: Vol 44: No 2
www.blackcountrysociety.co.uk

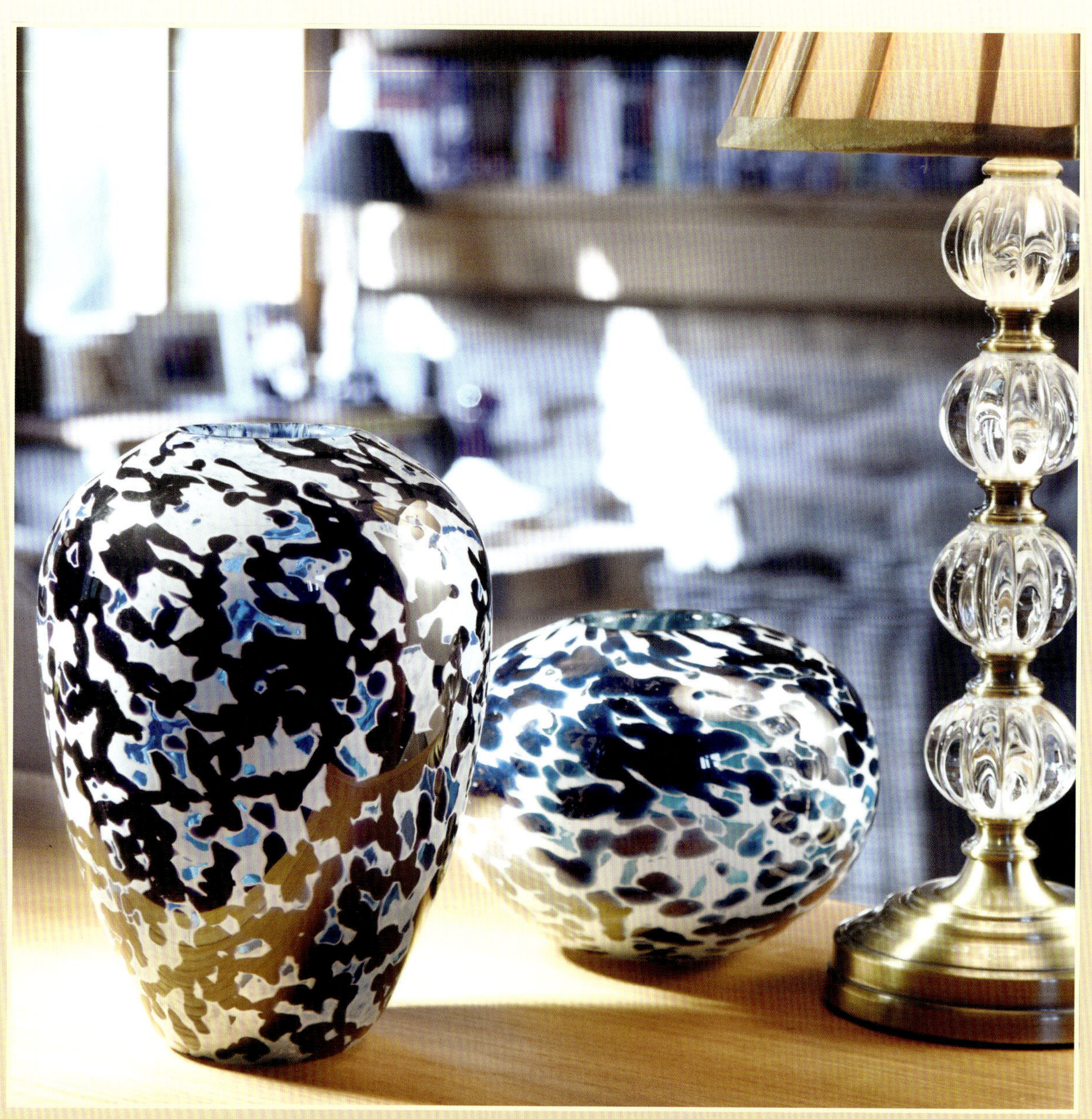

FAVOURITE 6 : VASES (ABOVE) AND PAPERWEIGHT (RIGHT)

Favourite 6 : Vases and Paperweight

Description and aspects

VASE 22cms tall opening from 6.5cm at base to 15cm at shoulders before tapering to 6cm at neck, blue glass with random white flecks, some of which are translucent.

VASE in similar pattern, 13cms tall opening from 12cm at base to 17cm at shoulders before tapering to 5cm at neck, blue glass with random white flecks, some of which are translucent.

PAPERWEIGHT multicoloured but predominantly red and gold, flattened, circular in shape, 7cm high and 13cm diameter at widest.

Personal significance

The two blue and white vases are by Lynn Baker, the red and gold paperweight by Jonathan Harris. I have a deep attachment to these insomuch that I followed them from their gestation inside the pot right through to seeing them end up on our mantelpiece, so to speak. They were made as part of the World's Longest Glassmaking Demonstration that I alluded to at Favourite 3 when, as part of the 2012 International Festival of Glass (IFoG) Allister Malcolm took to his kiln over a hot August weekend at Broadfield House Glass Museum to go head-to-head with his colleague Elliot Walker at Red House Glass Cone. In light of my various other commitments throughout IFoG I was only able to attend the Allister end of things yet even so my family and I were riveted in fascination right through into the wee hours and beyond. We were not alone and there were scores of people similarly riveted as Allister and his guests plied their skills with an increasing weariness that was superseded only by their resolute determination.

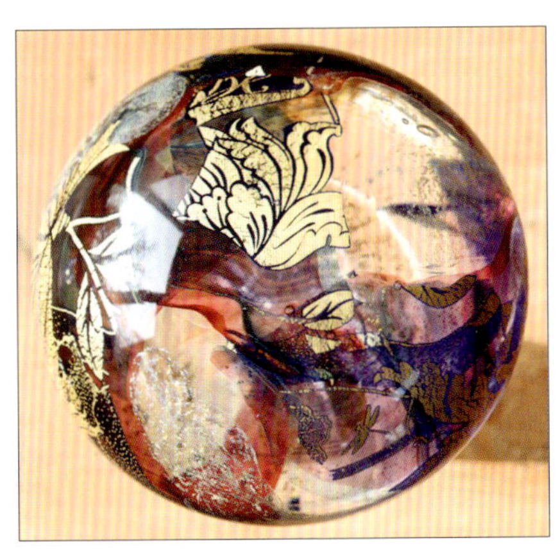

The blue vases were a relatively straightforward masterclass by Lynn Baker that went without a hitch; no problem there. Other than noting the weight of the things - a heavy lump of molten glass on the end of an iron that *per se* takes considerable skill to even handle, let alone work - they were completed well within her two-hour allocated slot with apparent consummate ease by an *artiste* at the very top of her game. The blue body of each is interspersed with white flecking, some of which is not actually

Opposite:
Vases (SIC)
Photo: Graham Dale

Left:
Paperweight (SIC)
Photo: Graham Dale

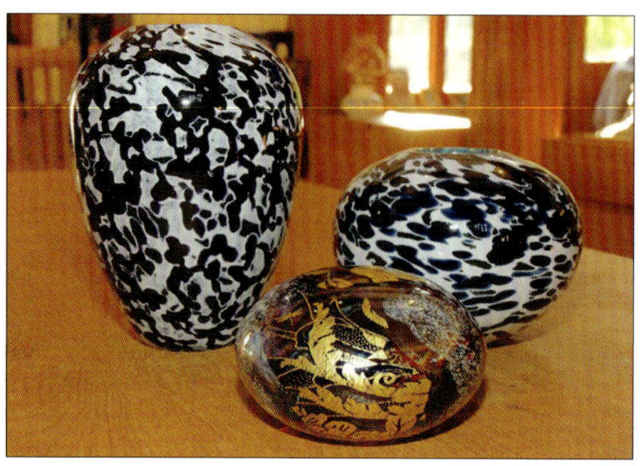

The trio that is FAVOURITE 6 (SIC)
Photo: Graham Fisher

flecking but which allows light to pass straight through so you can see ... no, I'm not making a very good job of this and it was only after a subsequent conversation with Allister that I could more fully appreciate what went into their creation.

They are made in the *Graal* technique (see below) and are noteworthy in that they represented at that time a departure from Lynn's more usual mode of expression. Prior to the event she had taken a layer of white onto which she introduced three layers of coloured chips, or frit, to create a multi-layered cup that was then annealed by controlled cooling. This removes all the stress from the glass that might otherwise spontaneously shatter if it cooled in an uncontrolled manner. Once cool, Lynn then carved various sections before then slowly re-heating the pieces ready for the demonstration. In view of their weight, which I gather was just about at the limit of Lynn's strength so no chances taken, they were picked up by Allister under Lynn's directions using a blob of gather on the end of an iron. He then cased them with clear glass and finished the rims. Spellbinding stuff. I watched it all happen on the night and still can't fully grasp how they did it.

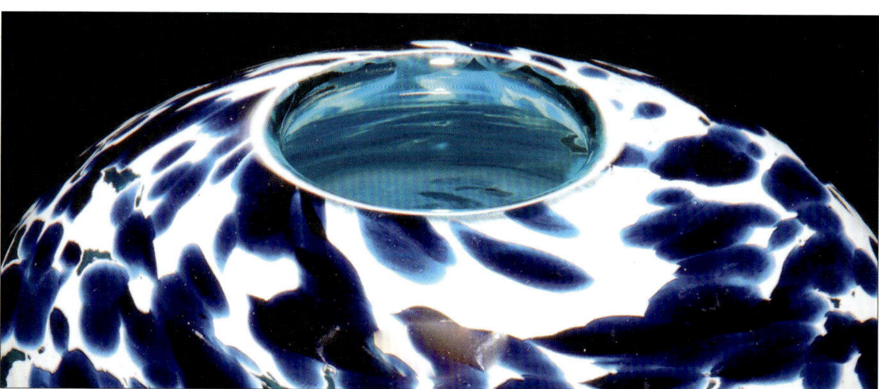

Detail of the smaller vase
Photo: Simon Bruntnell

GRAAL

'A type of decorative glass developed by Orrefors of Sweden in 1916. The design is carved, engraved, or etched on a parison of colored glass, which is then reheated and cased in a thick layer of transparent glass of a different color, and inflated.'

... with acknowledgement to
http://www.cmog.org/glass-dictionary/graal

The red paperweight is somewhat more off the page - no pun intended - since it actually started life as a vase. Now that one definitely requires an explanation.

Prior to the event Allister had fashioned a vase that was then overlaid with several hundred pounds-worth of gold leaf, kindly provided courtesy of his sponsors Gold Leaf Supplies. The intention was to then bring in master craftsman Jonathan Harris, who

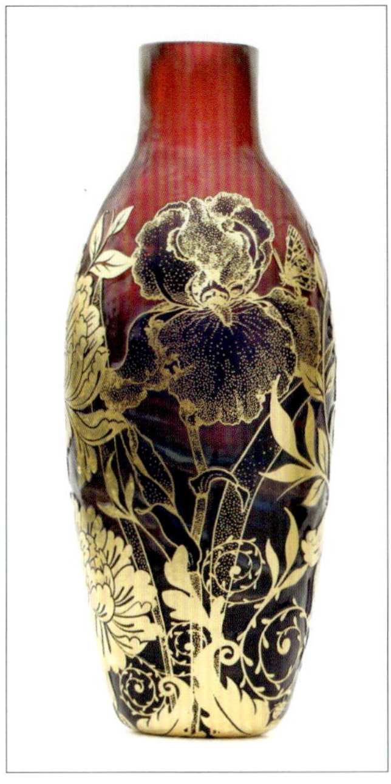

Left:
The carved red and gold vase before the fateful accident
Photo: Jonathan Harris

had by this stage carved the plain gold covering into a beautiful decoration, to further blow and encase the vase to completion during the demonstration. Ah, the best laid plans of mice and men - the heated vase broke away from the end of the iron and shattered on the floor.

Unperturbed and quick as lightning Jonathan and the team swept up the pieces for fashioning into three paperweights at a later date and then carried on with the task in hand. Not quite the original intention, but a rapid re-adjustment to the new circumstances that saved the day. Poignantly, for reasons that shortly will become apparent, who should be in the audience as the vase hit the floor but one David Whitehouse.

All the items from the demonstration were placed before Fieldings Auctioneers (Stourbridge) with proceeds to the British Glass Foundation. My dear ol' mom, a lover of auctions and gracious supporter of anything her little lad does, successfully bid for the three items shown here and in doing so not only acquired them for our home but also added to BGF coffers. Thanks, ma.

The denouement

Do bear with me because I just have to make a statement here: up to little more than five years ago I had never even heard of the International Festival of Glass (IFoG). What has transpired in the interim has been truly remarkable and has pointed my entire *raison d'être* along a different tack. Little wonder these bits of glass are of such significance.

For the 2010 IFoG, having entered the world of glass by dint of being appointed as an outreach for Broadfield House Glass Museum, I was invited to launch my book Jewels on the Cut and undertake tours and presentations. The book came about as a consequence of my role to promote the Stourbridge Glass industry; my palette was laid in front of me in the form of the Stourbridge Canal which passes right through the what once was - still

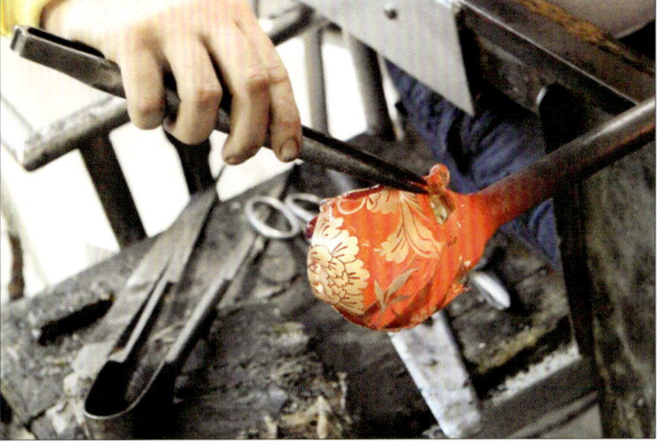

Fashioning a salvaged piece of the broken vase into a paperweight
Photo: Darren Weed

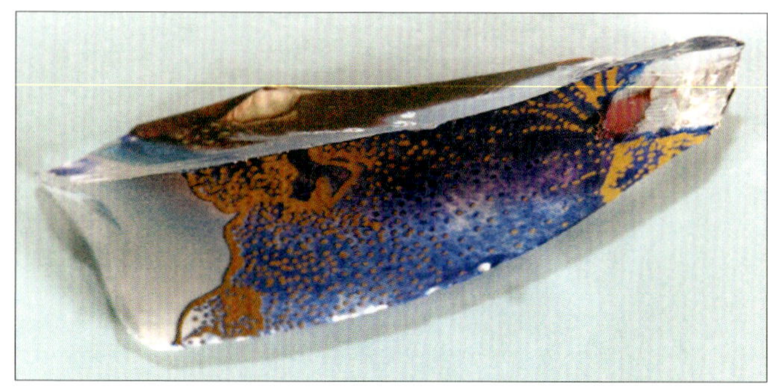

RIGHT:
7cm fragment from the shattered Jonathan Harris vase presented to the author by the maker. Little monetary value, sentimentally priceless.
Photo: Graham Fisher

is - its heart. As alluded to at FAVOURITE 1, by dint of my reference to the iconic Portland Vase, a Roman piece of cameo glass that was replicated twice in the 19th century alongside the Stourbridge Canal, the team who intended to recreate it for the 21st century - again alongside the Stourbridge Canal, only this time the Town Arm rather than the Main Line - invited me to be their biographer.

For the 2012 IFoG, by which time I had established sufficient credentials to have been appointed a Trustee of the British Glass Foundation, I was invited to launch my book THE 2012 PORTLAND VASE PROJECT: RECREATION OF A MASTERPIECE, to undertake tours and presentations and also act as MC for a unique live transatlantic link-up with the Corning Museum of Glass, Corning in New York state. Corning is the home for the two aforementioned 19th century Portland Vase recreations.

Now forgive me because I may just start getting a bit emotional here. We all meet countless people throughout our lives; most pass by fleetingly, some reverberate awhile, some become friends. Then there are those few who may have a profound influence and an impact that has no correlation with the longevity of the meeting. I can count such people on the fingers of one hand; Dr David Whitehouse is amongst them. It was he who joined me for the link-up. As David, at that time Senior Scholar at Corning, and I chatted across the airwaves - or, more accurately, the internet - with Corning's Resident Advisor William Gudenrath and compared notes on the Portland Vase in its various guises, little could I realize that the man by my side who had quickly become such a pal would be shortly to leave us.

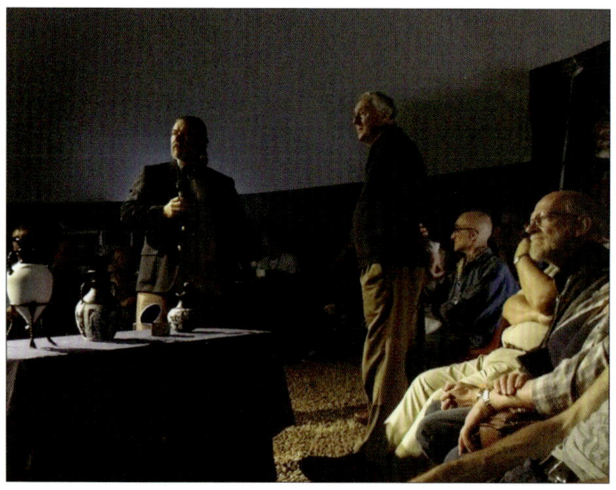

The author with David Whitehouse (right) awaiting the live link-up with Corning Museum of Glass
Photo: Mary Spence

David Whitehouse was a local lad, originally from Wildmoor near Bromsgrove, who emigrated to the States many years previously but who still maintained his ties to the Old Country. In early 2012 I had never heard of him; by mid 2012 he had written the forward to my book and by

August 2012 I was spending the weekend in his scintillating company. I was in his presence for a total of less than 96 hours yet I felt like I had known him all of my life and I was utterly devastated to hear that in February 2013 following a post-IFoG jaunt around Europe he returned home feeling unwell whereupon he died. Early in 2014 I met his wife Elizabeth and three members of her immediate family who were on a visit to England to lay David to rest and at which time I was able to personally convey my very sincere condolences. In the company of Ian Dury, 2012 Portland Vase Project Coordinator, and studio glass *artiste* Jaqueline Cooley we met at the Talbot Hotel in Stourbridge, a fitting location that is key in the history of Stourbridge Glass as a focal point for the Glass Barons of their day. I found a measure of comfort in the closure in being able to directly tell David's kith and kin just what a wonderful man he was.

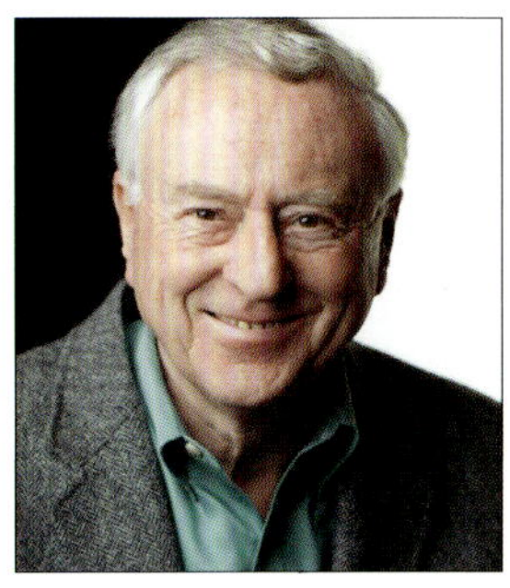

Dr David Whitehouse (1941-2013)
Photo: Corning Museum of Glass, Corning NY

The International Festival of Glass and the Biennale, by definition every two years, has for logistical reasons this time around skipped a year and the one following 2012 is scheduled for May 2015. If I pull my finger out and things go to plan then my mission to have a book launched at three consecutive IFoGs will have been accomplished herewith. I am also honoured beyond my station to have sat on the jury panel for the 2015 Biennale.

I therefore cannot but glance at these three items without thinking of the unimaginably affirmative change in direction of my own life over the past few years brought about by my involvement with this stuff called glass. The International Festival of Glass and all that entails, the delightful David Whitehouse, the friendships, camaraderie, passion, the sheer *joi de vivre* of being surrounded by beautiful people creating equally beautiful works; it really doesn't get much better than this. If only my much-missed father, himself taken away far too young, were here now I'm sure he would say: *'You ain't done too bad, son.'* That thought alone amply justifies why two vases and a paperweight are amongst my favourite things.

References and Further Information

Allister Malcolm
www.allistermalcolm.com

Gold Leaf Supplies
https://www.goldleafsupplies.co.uk

Jonathan Harris
www.jhstudioglass.com

Jacqueline Cooley
www.jaquelinecooley.com

Lynn Baker
www.artonthemap.org.uk/artists/the-wolds-and-coast/lynn-baker

International Festival of Glass and Biennale
www.ifg.org.uk and **www.biennale.org.uk**

Fieldings Auctioneers
http://fieldingsauctioneers.co.uk

Corning Museum of Glass, Corning NY
www.cmog.org

David Whitehouse, obituary
http://www.cmog.org/press-release/corning-museum-glass-mourns-loss-former-director-david-whitehouse

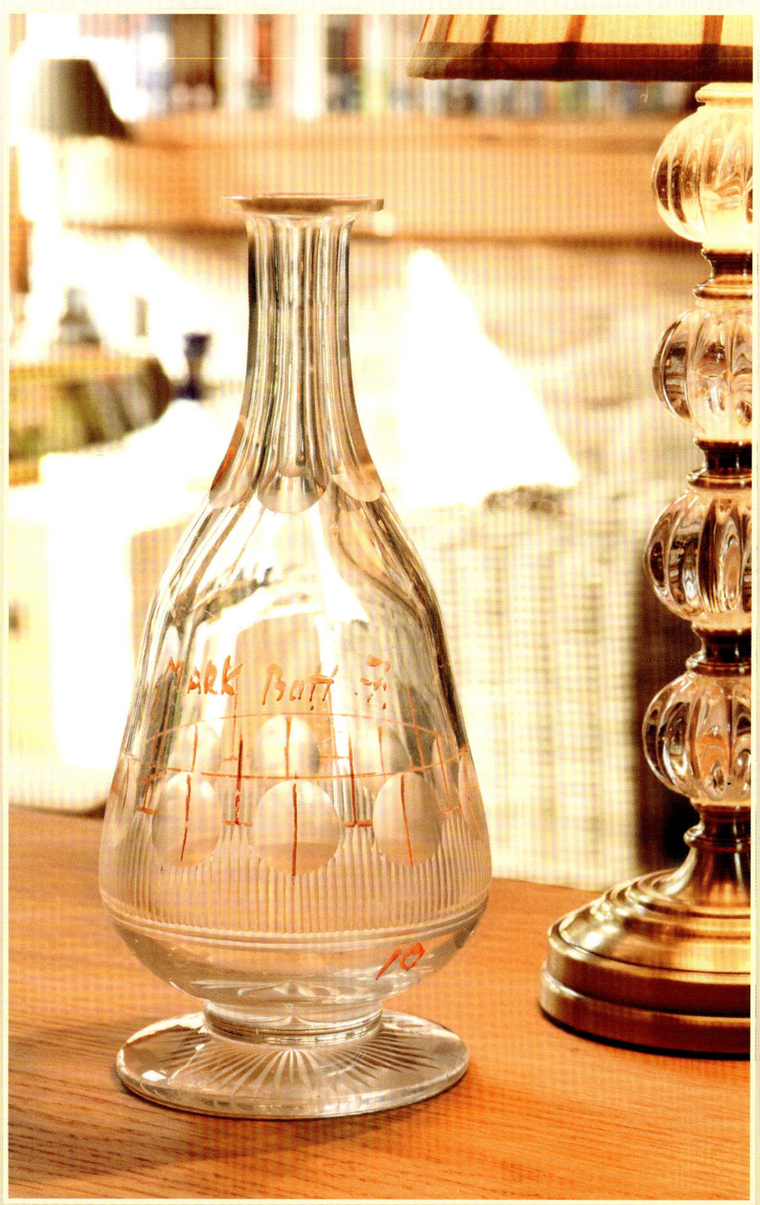

Favourite 7 : Wine Decanter

Favourite 7 : Wine Decanter

Description and aspects

WINE DECANTER in clear (unspecified lead) crystal 28cm tall with base of 11cm and main body of 12cm tapering to lipped neck of 3cm. Incomplete, stopper absent. Base, body and neck partially cut in patterns of indents and lines and with marking indicating areas to be cut.

Personal significance

There is this man I know whom I would describe as one of life's nice guys. He is unassuming, polite, pleasantly self-effacing and, as I discovered when I was sourcing a drawn image for one of my books, a talented artist. I will say no more that could help identify him because to do so may cause him an embarrassment that I would not wish to impose. Let me just conclude that he is yet another of the delightful characters I have met through my association with the glass world and with whom I enjoy a mutual respect.

He has also been singularly supportive in my work, no more so than when he waylaid me one day around six years ago in the foyer of a local glass facility where they had been having a bit of a clear out. Destined for the skip but saved only by the intervention of his grasp is this delightful partially completed decanter. I gather it is around 1940s vintage and was probably made by Thomas Webb but I have as yet been unable to verify that and if anyone else can add to my knowledge it would be much appreciated.

Opposite:
Wine Decanter
Photo: Graham Dale

Below:
Thomas Webb
Photo: Broadfield House Glass Museum

Thomas Webb

Thomas Webb entered the glass industry in 1829 and formed Thomas Webb & Sons in 1836. The first glass factory was established at The Platts, Amblecote, in 1840. By 1855, the firm had moved to nearby Dennis Glassworks; Thomas Webb and family lived at Dennis Hall. Thomas Webb died in 1865 and the company passed to his son, Thomas Wilkes Webb.

In 1897 Thomas Ernest Webb, the eldest son of Thomas Wilkes Webb, left the family firm of Thomas Webb & Sons to start a new firm with George Harry Corbett at the White House Glassworks. The trademark 'Webb-Corbett' was registered the same year.

On 31st March 1914 a disastrous fire broke out at the White House which resulted in the firm moving to Coalbournhill Glassworks. The firm gradually began to grow in stature and in 1952 was renamed Webb Corbett Ltd.

In 1969 Webb Corbett Ltd became part of the Royal Doulton group.

The works finally closed in April 2000 and part of the site is now home to the Webb Corbett Visitor Centre.

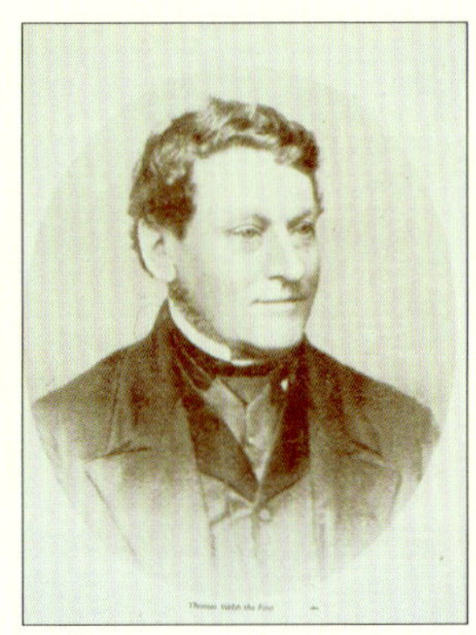

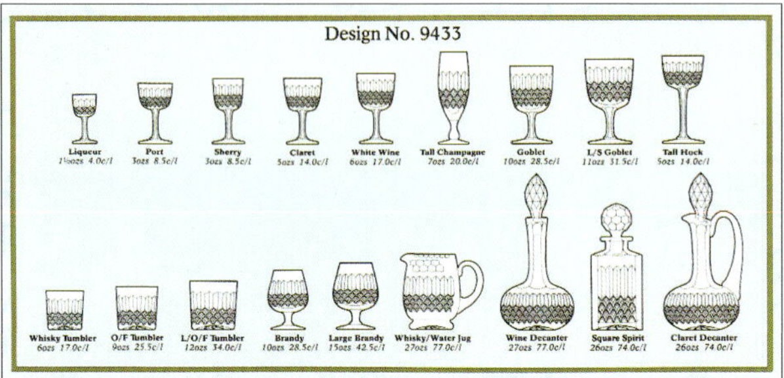

The 'Normandy' pattern was first introduced in 1873 and given the pattern number 9433. It is one of the most popular of all the Webb designs.

Having thus saved it from the unwelcoming maw of the rubbish dump, my colleague presented it to me in the expectation that it may be useful as a visual aid in my presentations. It certainly is, and has since been with me on numerous excursions where I have used it to highlight the process of 'marking out' and the early stages of decoration. This is significant in the tale of glassmaking since it highlights a demarcation between the sexes and even the roles they undertook, differences that are rapidly becoming relics of a very different time past.

Thus not only is this decanter a worthy piece of work even in its uncompleted state, it provides a lesson in the social order of its day.

The denouement

Glassmaking ran on its well-defined rails and, with the exception of characters such as the renowned designer Irene Stevens of Webb Corbett, it was a world very much dominated by males. Yet though women may have been shielded from the intensity and inherent dangers of hot work their lot in the cold department was little less hazardous and many of the chemicals they were exposed too, such as lead based powers and strong acids, were either highly toxic or simply downright noxious.

Each time I study this piece I become fascinated in considering the various hands it has already passed through in order to reach even this stage of completion. First there would be the team at the furnace who made and fashioned it. Inevitably men. After annealing it would be passed to the marking out team comprising 'ringing round' and 'lining down'. Inevitably women - ne'er should the twain meet - who would accurately mark out the patterning, sometimes with the aid of a machine, by the hundreds each day.

Irene Stevens, glass designer at Webb Corbett from 1946 to 1957
Photo: Broadfield House Glass Museum

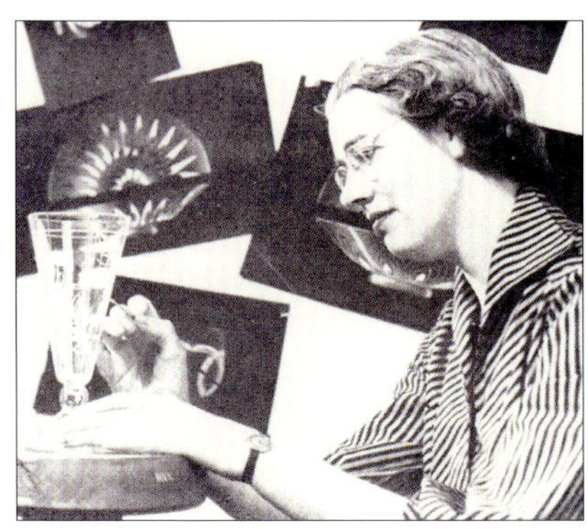

The first stage of then creating the pattern, or 'decorating' went to the 'rougher' who, as the name suggests, used a harsh carborundum wheel to initiate the cut. After perhaps further marking out it would then pass to a 'smoother'. Cutters worked in teams of three; one rougher and two smoothers. Patterns could be light, medium of heavy in cut and any blemishes that could not be hidden or removed rendered the piece as cullet for re-melting or destined for the 'seconds' shop, depending on the extent of the blemish. Cullet is the term given to waste glass that could be melted down and used again. Contamination being an issue - the entire melt could be ruined by just a small amount of stray - this was usually restricted to waste emanating from processes within the factory.

Each element of the process was undertaken by a specialist in that field, be it man or woman. There were at least four different stages of inspection. So, just how many hands of both sexes did this piece ultimately pass through to reach this stage? I can only speculate in this instance, though I would hazard a guess at least ten including the 'hot' team, process shop workers, markers, decorators, acid polishers and inspectors. My friend and colleague Ian Dury, now Heritage Officer at the Webb Corbett Visitor Centre, spent '22 years man and boy' as he puts it, with Stuart Crystal. He informs me that it was a proud boast of the company that each and every item passed through a minimum of 24 pairs of hands. And they were turning out items of quality by the tens of thousands. Whatever the perceived merits of this proud claim at the time, in hindsight the amount of hands involved could surely have done little to help minimize costs and must have played its role as just one of the numerous factors that slowly but inexorably contributed to the industry's decline.

I am grateful to Ian for furnishing me with information that further enhances my growing appreciation of this piece and which is reproduced overleaf.

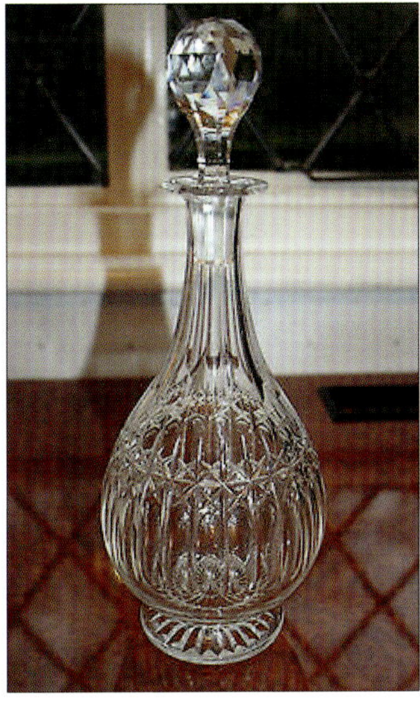

1935-49 footed wine decanter by Thomas Webb

Compare and contrast that with the contemporary Studio Glass movement in which a single artist or small collective uses glass as the medium for expressing skills to produce individual pieces of a usually decorative but sometimes functional nature. There were, of course, highly skilled artisans producing individualistic pieces in the heyday of Stourbridge Glass but the thrust was by and large mass production. How different the modern Studio Glass movement is in this regard, and Stourbridge has become something of a mecca for its practitioners. The most notable distinction between the two is the breaking down of the old barriers and it is not unusual for one person to undertake all aspects of creating the piece from working the 'hot metal' (molten glass) through to decorating or otherwise adorning the piece and finally using marketing skills to sell it. Even more remarkable - speak it softly - the artist accomplishing all this is now very often a *woman*. Within the space of just a generation or so, females have stepped out of the shadows embodied by my decanter and into a very brave new world indeed. It is reported that the glass facility at Wolverhampton University currently attracts over 50% female intake. I cannot realistically envisage anyone seriously doubting this trend to be anything other than in the highest interests of glassmaking.

'Glitz' contemporary wine decanter by Dartington Crystal

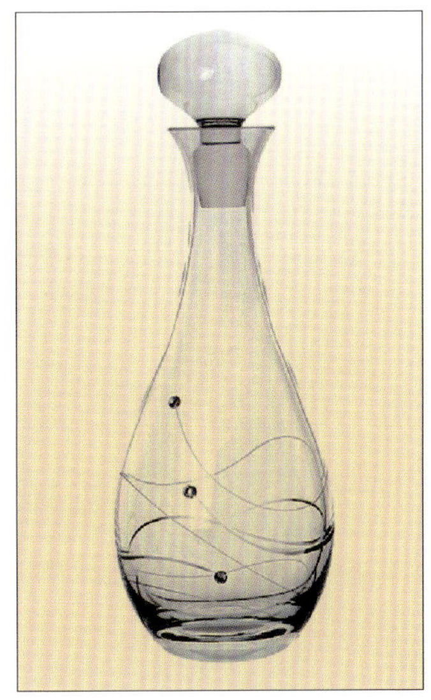

I suggest that this piece, even in its unfinished state, is crammed with so much social history it almost can be squeezed out. It is also indicative of strong family associations within the trade and could have been made by father, marked by mother and cut by son. I am delighted it did not end up in a tip and I feel a curious resonance with the workers of old whenever I handle it, hence it earns its rightful place amongst my favourite things.

Ian Dury comments . . .

One area of any glass works that seems to get very little attention is that at the start of the process and the mixing room where raw white silica was riddled, washed and dried.

It was then mixed with the 'red lead' (lead oxide, PbO). The workers toiled through the night washing and riddling the cullet, filling the pots and adding the famous family secret ingredient, which every company had. The mix was riddled to remove any foreign material; a single ½ inch bolt, for example, would be enough to turn an entire pot of glass green.

It makes me smile in an age where we are so health and safety conscious that these people, usually retired production workers, looked like they just came out of a slaughter house at the end of their shift, with their white overalls covered in noxious red lead.

Let us also remember the 'teaser' who was responsible for maintaining the quality and temperature of the 'metal' (molten glass) for the glassmakers to work on when they arrived at the start of a shift. The teaser's role was critical since a fluctuation of just a few degrees in temperature either way could render the mix either too runny or too stiff to work with. A good teaser knew his furnaces and could tell the temperature by the colour around the outside and inside of the pot; it was only in latter years that saw the introduction of instrumentation.

Left, Below and Opposite:
Webb Corbett glass workers from the 1950s
Photos: Broadfield House Glass Museum

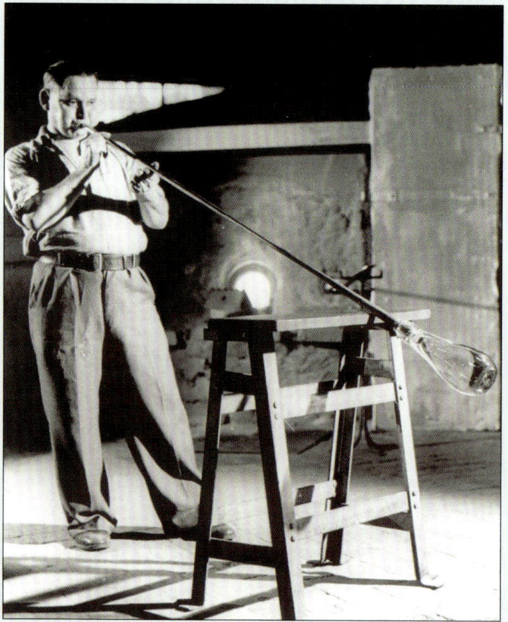

Ernie Franks, glass blower

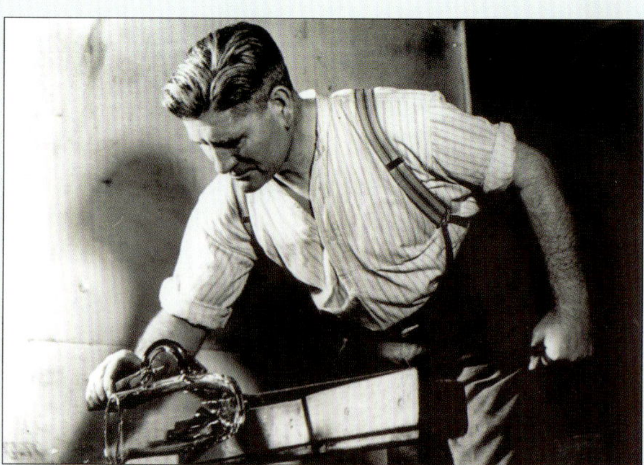

Frank Ostin, glass maker

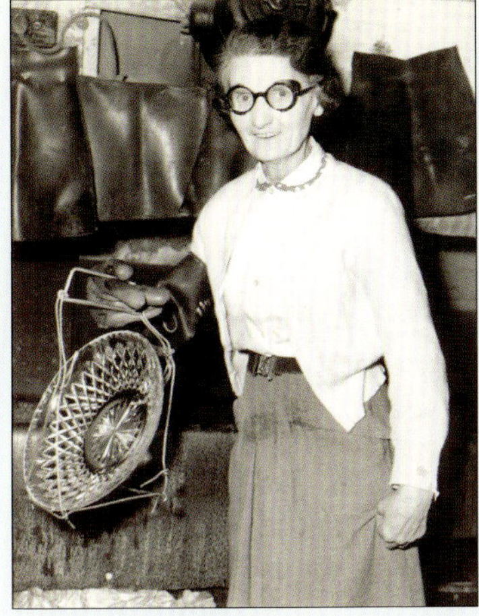
Edith Shutt, acid dipper

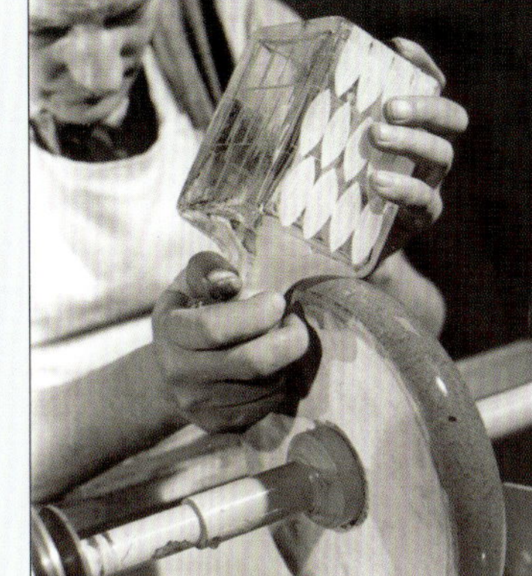
Glass cutter

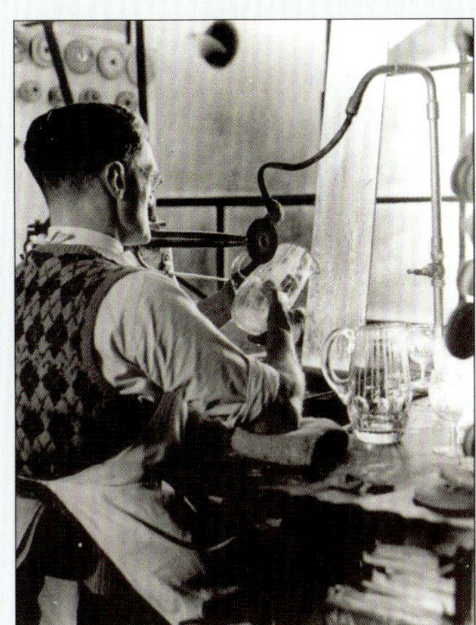
Billy Weaver, intaglio cutter

I find it interesting that if you put all the major manufacturers glass side by side you can see that each has its own distinct colour. Stuart's was described as a pinkish-blue hue and just 2oz of their decolouriser formula added to a 1-ton mix was enough to make a difference.

The decanter you have here is a pattern I am familiar with; I believe was a cutting shop pattern and would have been used by the markers to set their pen nibs to the correct height, the pattern would give the marker the information on the number of repeats to line down. It was also used by the cutters to be able to view and reference the overall pattern and, equally importantly, the strength of the cuts. This was essential to customers acquiring ranges of patterns and looking to match up elements of their collection.

The majority of the production was based on piecework, with the glassmakers and all of the decorating, stoppering and other departments working to a time. Each item would be timed and given a standard minute value (smv). Your decanter would have had a smv attached to it. For example, the figure for roughing and smoothing a Stuart Glengarry sherry glass was 2.49 smv.

There was always a team of work-study staff ('time and motion') walking around with clipboards and stopwatches. Great days!

References and Further Information

Irene Stevens
http://gorgeousglass.org.uk/webb-corbett/

Women in the Stourbridge Glass industry
Internet - various

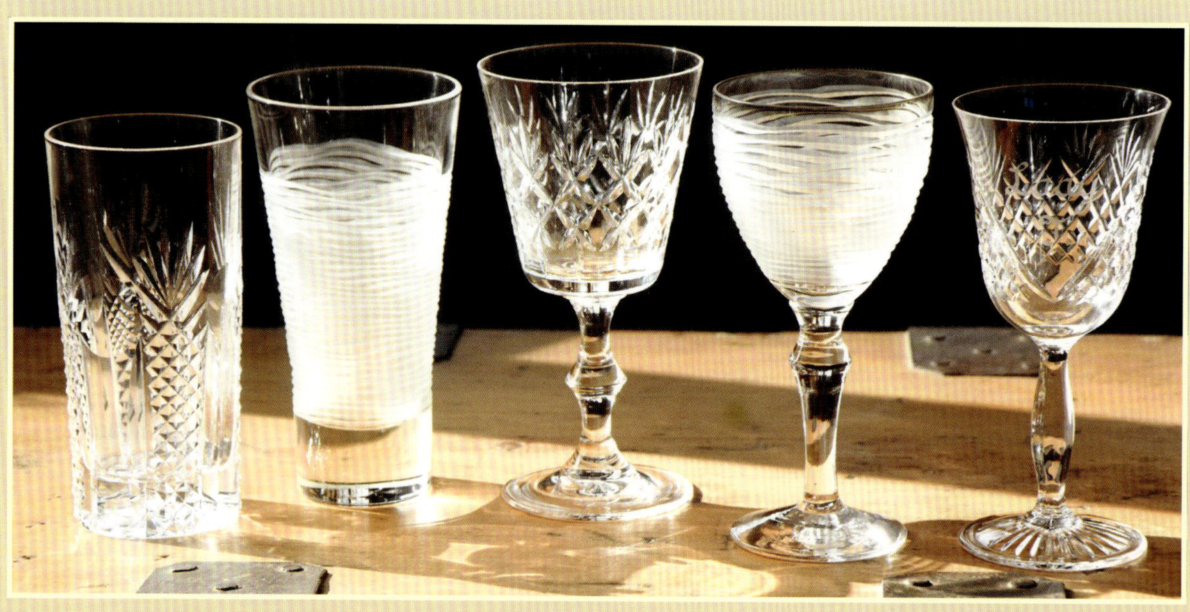

Favourite 8 : Cut Glasses

Favourite 8 : Cut Glasses

Description and aspects

In order of appearance (l to r):

TUMBLER (full lead?) crystal c1970s, origin uncertain. Straight sided, 16cm tall, 7cm circumference on heavy base. Decorated in 'classic' style of 'hobnails' with florets resembling a pineapple.

TUMBLER 24% lead crystal, semi-fluted, 5cm circumference on heavy base rising to 16cms height and 8cm rim, made c2012 abroad then decorated in Stourbridge by Kevin Barry Adams (trading as Kevin Barry Crystal) in deep cut diamond-wheel wavy pattern ('Riptide') around circumference extending from heavy base to 3cm from rim.

WINE GLASS believed c1990s. Semi-fluted with foot and stem at 8cm, overall height 17cm and opening from 6cm at base of main body above stem to 8cm at rim. Italian *Ascot* blank decorated in classic style of 2 single row diamonds with 3-cut fan.

WINE GLASS 24% lead crystal made c2012 abroad then decorated in Stourbridge by Kevin Barry in deep cut diamond-wheel wavy pattern ('Riptide'). Rounded semi-flute with foot and stem at 9cm, overall height 17cm, 8cm diameter at rim that is tinged with silver colouration induced during initial manufacturing process.

WINE GLASS c1998. Foot and stem to 8cm, overall height 17cm opening to 7cm circumference at rim. Italian *Orvieto* blank decorated in classic diamond and fan style with 24pt cut star, engraved *Lady J*.

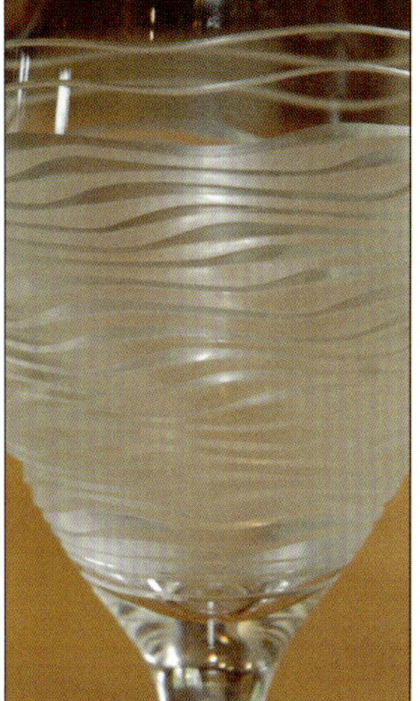

Detail of 'Riptide' pattern by Kevin Barry Crystal
Photo: Graham Fisher

Personal significance

For a family that, to the best of my knowledge, has no history of glassmaking - my father was an engineer - it may seem anomalous that our house is in fact crammed to the gunwales with the stuff. Apart from those items we have purchased ourselves, there are two principal reasons for this.

For starters, there is the lifelong family friend who has business associations in the glass world. Every Christmas and other celebrations for the past half-century or more, and still to this day, he has presented us with magnificent pieces of cut glass. Over the intervening years this has amounted to a considerable collection, every piece of which is cherished as a reminder of a rare depth of friendship that few are blessed with.

Second, some years after the premature death of my father my mother found happiness again with another man. Let me give a little background here in relating how my parents had no money so married in a Register Office in 1952. Their blissful-but-skint honeymoon was spent window-shopping in our local High Street with my father promising that one day he would give my mother all she

Opposite:
Cut Glasses;
tumblers and wine glasses from different eras
Photo: Graham Dale

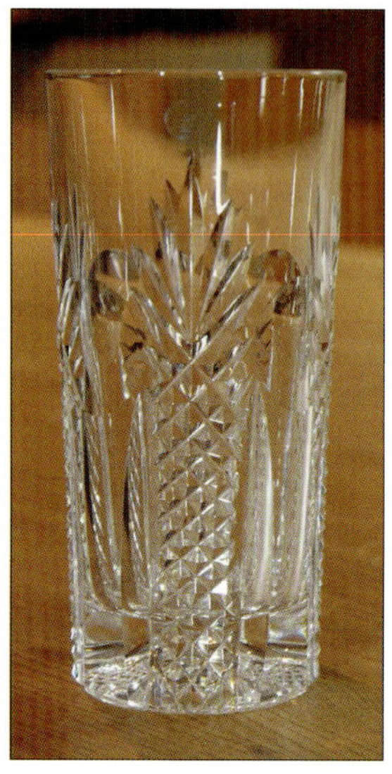

Detail of the 'classic' cut
Photo: Graham Fisher

desired. Gallantly he did, but having done so tragically died in 1989 before he could fully enjoy it with her. When some years later she met her future second husband, a bachelor, she was eligible for a church wedding. Having missed out first time around she went for it - big flowing cream dress, the works - and as Best Man I had the very great pleasure of giving my own mother away. Wonderful.

Although Mervyn - known affectionately by everyone as 'Our Merv' - was not a glassmaker himself his forebears were. Stuart, mostly. Which probably accounts for his sizeable collection, some of which dates back to the mid 19th century, emanating from that particular outlet. When he died in 2010 this all fell into our care.

I know the history of the majority of the items gifted from our friend and bequeathed by Our Merv; there are only a few that I cannot identify or know nothing about. There is thus good reason why I have placed this apparently random and equally modest selection together as one of my favourite things.

The 'classic' tumbler and wine glass shown here have been with us for years and, in light of the above, their significance is self evident; steeped in nostalgia they are part of the fabric of my home and are in daily use. The two Kevin Barry ones, being virtually brand new, may seem at odds with their older counterparts but they already assumed significance in being a particular favourite of my good lady, who has taken to collecting examples of each.

The final example in my arraignment, the *Lady J* glass, was given to me by a delightful man who spent his working life at Stuart Crystal up to its closure in

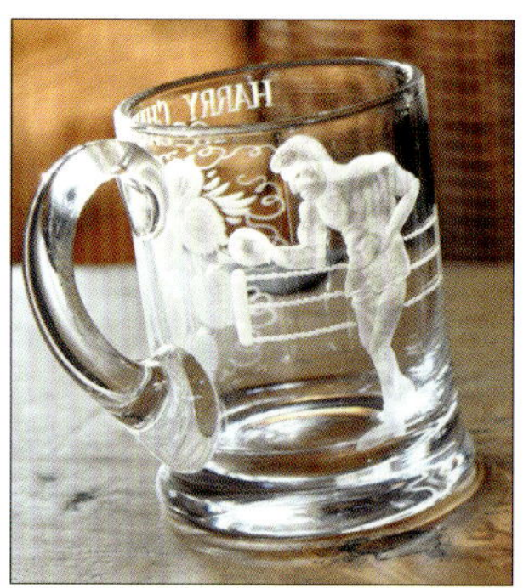

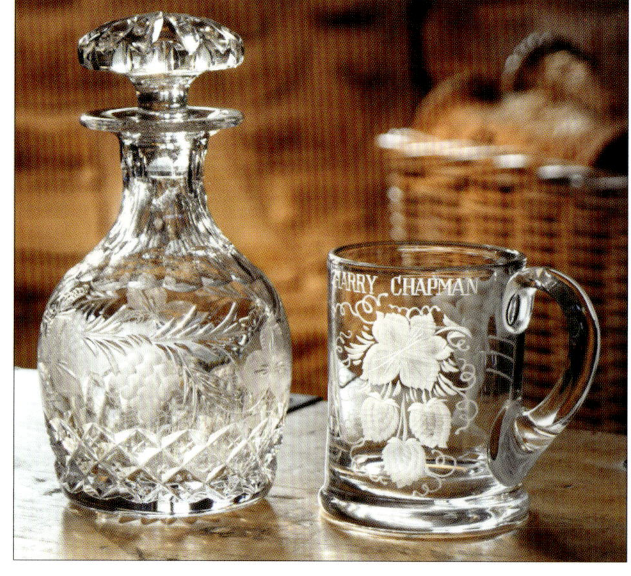

Items from 'Our Merv's' collection: Harry Chapman was his father and a professional boxer.
Tankard, with a pontil base that has been smoothed on a sandstone wheel and hand polished. Intaglio stone wheel hops decoration, copper wheel engraved boxer. Believed Stuart blank c1930s/40s (SIC)
(with thanks to Ian Dury for his opinion)
Photos: Graham Dale

2001. He subsequently moved home whereupon, to my chagrin, we lost touch and I have not seen him since, but he did leave me this rather special memento. *Lady J* was one of my narrowboats upon which friends were always welcome. On one such visit, around mid-1998 if I recall correctly, he accidentally knocked a wine glass to the floor. Mortified by the breakage and despite my protestations that it was of no consequence he very kindly presented me with this one in lieu and which he had decorated himself especially. As I said, a delightful man. *Lady J* is long gone, as is he. Happy memories are durable.

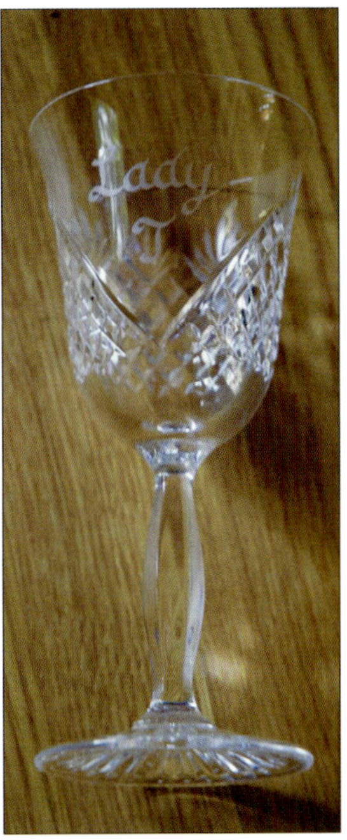

The *Lady J* wine glass
Photo: Graham Fisher

The denouement

Where to start?

At the beginning of this book (A Few Clarifications) I referred to Stourbridge Glass; then and now. Quite apart from my personal attachment to these glasses, if I were asked to pick any small group of items that so succinctly describes *then and now* it would have to be these. To me, they are screaming it out loud.

The 'classic' glasses are exactly that; classic. They are lovely and represent an elegance of days past. They are high quality, beautifully made, indicative of supreme skills, decorative and functional. Alas, they are also dated, old-fashioned and hark back to an era that no-one below a certain age would even recall, let alone aspire to.

I have already referred to the myriad factors that conspired to bring down the Stourbridge Glass industry. All played their part to varying degrees but here is one writ large; it is just so old hat. Restrictive practices, changes in legislation, outmoded and inefficient working practices, outdated business modeling, lack of investment, foreign competition, globalization, escalating costs, market forces, the list goes on. But even if all of these factors, every last single one of them, were countered and addressed there would still be the ball and chain of indifference and apathy, perhaps even smugness, around the industry's leg that stopped it dragging itself out of its own comfort zone. Maybe there is also an element of contemporary style and the perception that the classic décor of the past is overly fussy and no longer *de rigeur.* Give the customer what they want; some of the best selling commercial glass of the modern era, made largely by the likes of Denby Glassware and Dartington Crystal, has no decoration whatsoever and is deemed attractive by dint of its plainness, a sort of 'less is more'.

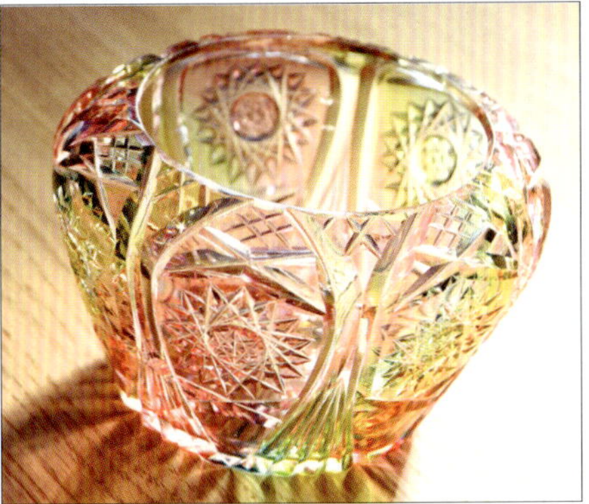

Multi-coloured bowl with decoration. Acquired at auction early 21st century, origin uncertain; just a lovely example of 'cut glass' that is a joy to own (SIC)
Photo: Graham Dale

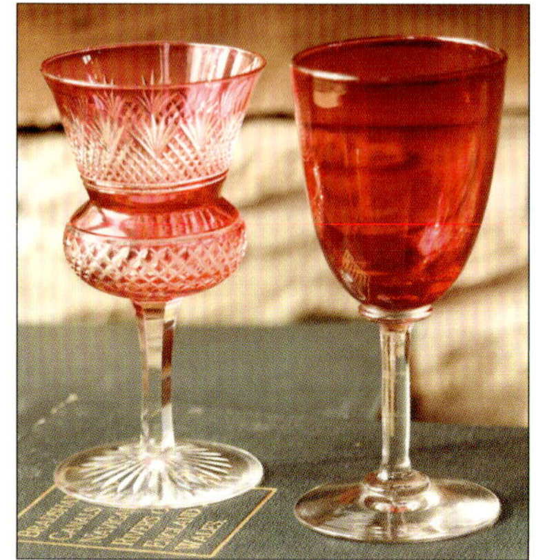

Ruby sherry glasses:
(Left) ruby cased with diamond decoration and hand polished by brush. Fluted leg cut on natural sandstone. 24-point star to foot. Believed pre-1930s, possibly by Thomas Webb in a design that was a precursor to the Edinburgh Crystal 'Thistle' range. (SIC)
(Right) ruby cased on clear leg, believed Webb Corbett c1900, hand made and held in 'gadget' at foot to facilitate hand shearing to rim (SIC)
(with thanks to Ian Dury for his opinions)
Photo: Graham Dale

This must also be a key dynamic in why, with rare exceptions notably at the higher end, prices at auction for 'traditional' glass are presently at such an undeserving low.

In stark contrast the Kevin Barry glasses offer a beacon of sanguinity with their contemporary simplicity yet unflinchingly bold statement that captures the *zeitgeist* for stylish functional elegance, simultaneously nodding to the old and melding it with the new. But what would I know? *Res ipsa loquitur*; I gather they sell like hot cakes. The sad thing is that Kevin has to buy his blanks in from abroad; no one in the UK now makes them in bulk any more.

The *Lady J* glass is an *Orvieto* wine blank favoured by many independent cutters between around 1980 and 2000. Rather like the oil lamp described in the next section, after being given to me around 1998 it spent the next fifteen years travelling with me around the inland waterways before being gracefully retired to my landlubber cocktail cabinet. It has become something akin to a venerated companion and has aided my enjoyment of many a glass of *Châteauneuf*. But quite apart from its happy connotations it is, for me, a litmus for the death-throes of the Stourbridge Glass industry as we knew it at the turn of the millennium. How sad yet ultimately how suggestive that a man with the talent to fashion this backed by a lifetime's experience should, for the last six months of his service, be found painting shelves and driving a van. A crushing indictment of a once-mighty enterprise, if ever there was.

'Classic' fruit bowls: origins uncertain but believed to be local, displaying yet more testament to the skills of the glass cutter. (SIC)
Photo: Graham Dale

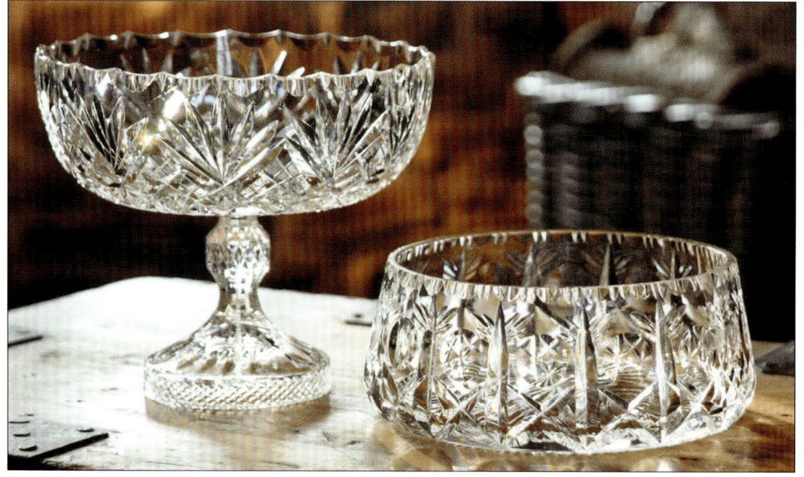

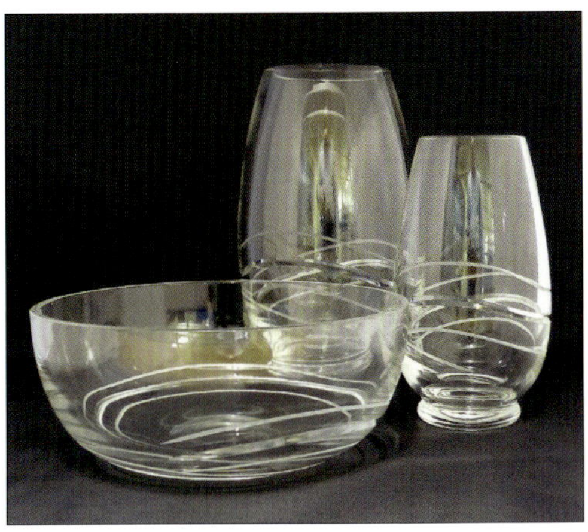

Left:
'Meteor' vases and bowl by Tudor Crystal; part of their new, contemporary range
Photo: Tudor Crystal

There is one final overarching element of these glasses that give them their sense of purpose. Take a close look at the *Lady J* glass and it has been subject somewhere along the line, since I started writing this book in fact, to a chip and crack. Similarly the Kevin Barry tumbler has, since this image was taken, been broken. It has been replaced with one identical; the *Lady J* glass may not be quite so easy. But it doesn't matter. Chipped or not, and sad as it is that it is flawed, no-one can take away what it represents and I continue to treasure it. For me, the damage represents a patina of use that is indicative of how it has served me well.

And this is the point; surely glass is to be used not shoved in a cupboard or hidden in a loft. Unavoidably, every now and then it will get broken. So go and buy another; at very least you are helping keep a glassmaker in a job.

The future? I believe it is bright. The millions of such items that were made, and continue to be made, means there will be a plentiful supply for years to come so the outdated nature of the 'classic' example is yet to be surpassed by any intrinsic value of rarity - stalemate. But there is one aspect on the horizon, unimaginable a century ago, which may offer an avenue of redemption and rebirth. In an age where oil and other fossil fuel reserves, once taken for granted, are now the focus of serious debate as they decline, attention is turning to renewables. Unlike many plastics and other throw-aways, most glass is recyclable. I am willing to stick my neck on the block here in predicting this may prove to be part of its salvation and renaissance.

'Drama' tumbler by Denby: 11cm tall. Stylish, elegant, functional and devoid of any decoration; a contemporary example of the 'less is more' school
Photo: Graham Dale

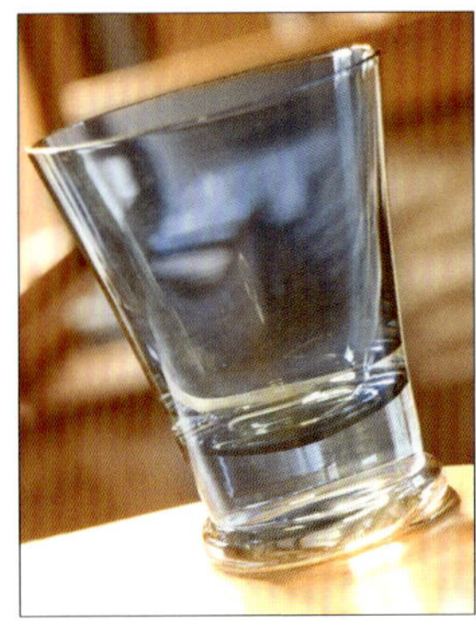

References and Further Information

Kevin Barry Crystal
http://www.kevinbarrycrystal.co.uk

Stuart Crystal
A succinct history of Stuart Crystal, together with suggested further lines of research, can be found in the author's work Jewels on the Cut (Sparrow Publishing 2012, ISBN 978-0-9548781-2-2)

The British Glass Foundation is, at the time of writing, seeking to develop a world-class glass facility on the iconic former Stuart's site in Wordsley.
www.britishglassfoundation.org.uk

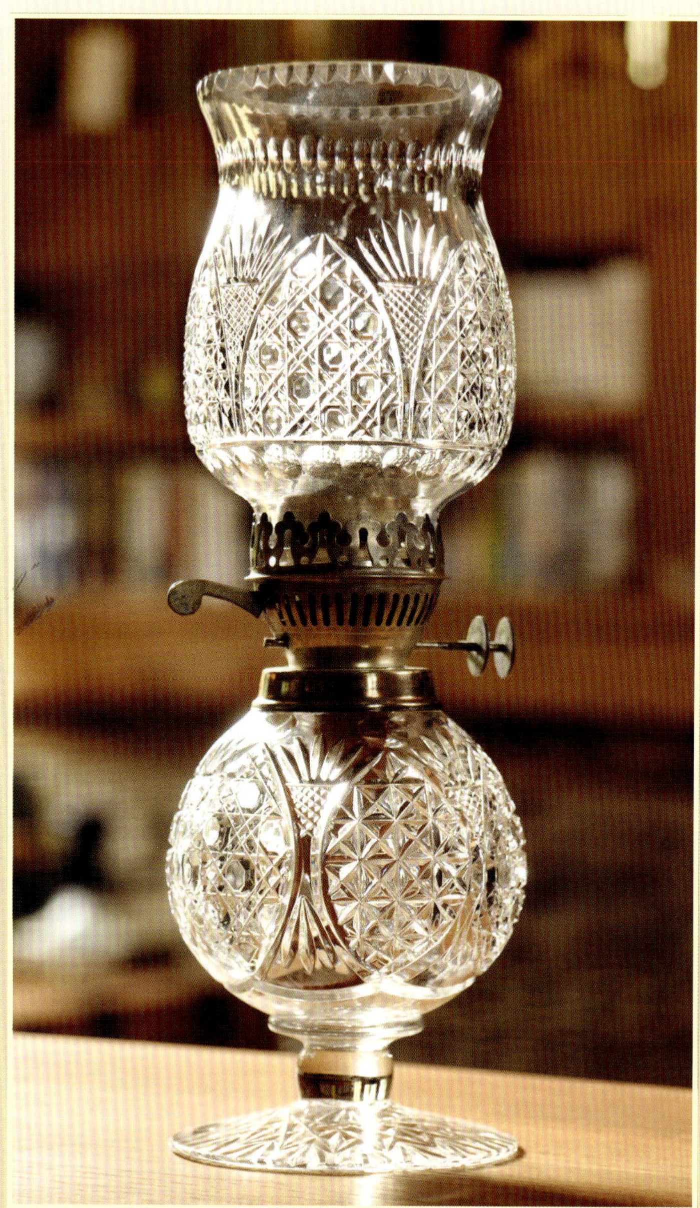

Favourite 9 : Oil Lamp

Favourite 9 : Oil Lamp

Description and aspects

OIL LAMP full lead crystal in 2 sections, font and globe, to a total height of 35cm on base of 12cm diameter, linked in middle by silver-coloured twin wick burner with side mounted extinguisher.

Personal significance

I don't know why but oil lamps have always captivated me. Perhaps it is their connotations with narrowboats and old houses; having been associated with the former for most of my adult life and nowadays living in a 17th century example of the latter the answer probably lies in there somewhere.

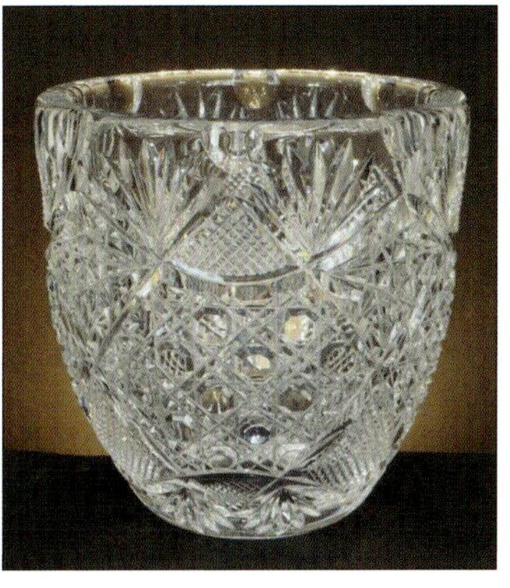

A bowl cut in the same 'Church Window' pattern as the oil lamp
Photo: Dawn Crystal

Whatever, I delight in oil lamps and have numerous examples; there was even a door in my old office that had the image of one sandblasted in the glass and which saddened me greatly when it could not undertake the move. So, in a variation on a certain radio programme, if I was cast on my desert island and I had to pick only one of my favourite things to take with me I reckon this would be up there. It is simultaneously all things sentimental, functional, delightful to look at, perhaps even valuable; this one piece has got the lot and I am deeply smitten.

But most of all it is for its provenance that I treasure it, having travelled extensively with me on various boats around the inland waterways for over a quarter of a century. What further elevates it to the ranks of the singular is that it was a gift from my dear mother, who had it cut especially for me shortly after my equally dear father died back in the 1980s. And, in squaring the circle of its huge personal significance, in consequence of my work on behalf of the British Glass Foundation I recently had the very great pleasure of renewing my acquaintance with the man who actually cut it before then seeing on-line the man who blew it.

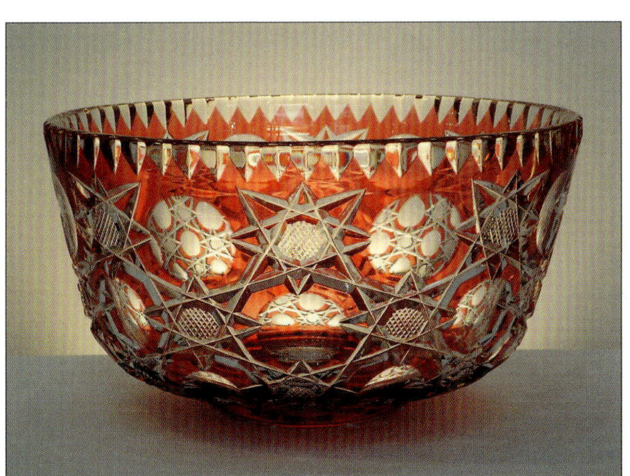

Opposite:
Oil Lamp
Photo: Graham Dale

Left:
Ruby cased bowl cut in the 'Constellation' pattern
Photo: Dawn Crystal

The denouement

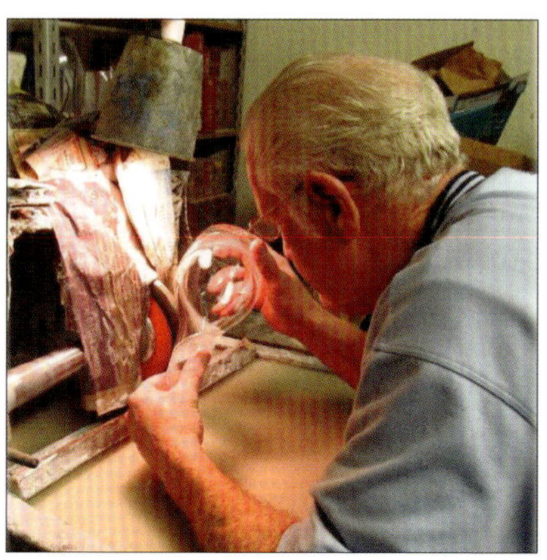

RIGHT:
Reg Everton cutting
Photos: Dawn Crystal

My enquiries have proved most fruitful and I am grateful to father and son team Reg and John Everton of Dawn Crystal, Wordsley, for their help. I am advised that the font and globe are by Pete Walters, ex-Webb Corbett then Harlequin Crystal, now closed. In January 2015 John Everton kindly furnished me with a 9-minute *YouTube* clip, filmed by father Reg, that he had uncovered showing Mr Walters making oil lamps; see the link below. The *frisson* this gives to further appreciating my own lamp is considerable when, after all this time, one can see them actually being made.

We can say with some certainty that Reg Everton decorated mine; he remembers doing it. The cut is in a style that he still uses today. Known as 'Church Window' it is an old Stuart pattern and remains one of his favourites.

The cutting is beautifully undertaken and evidently done with great skill that can only come from a combination of natural talent and years of practice. Yet how easy the trained craftsman makes it look, as the *YouTube* link below will indicate. At little over a minute in duration the clip is still long enough to show the inordinate skills that once graced this part of the world. It was kindly drawn to my attention by John in late 2014, and shows the apparent ease with which father Reg fashions a ruby cased glass bowl; it is quite entrancing to watch.

Not so very long ago such talent was far more commonplace than now. There have been no apprentices taken on in the Stourbridge glass trade for over 30

Blue cased crystal basket:
from rough cut to finish
Photos: Dawn Crystal

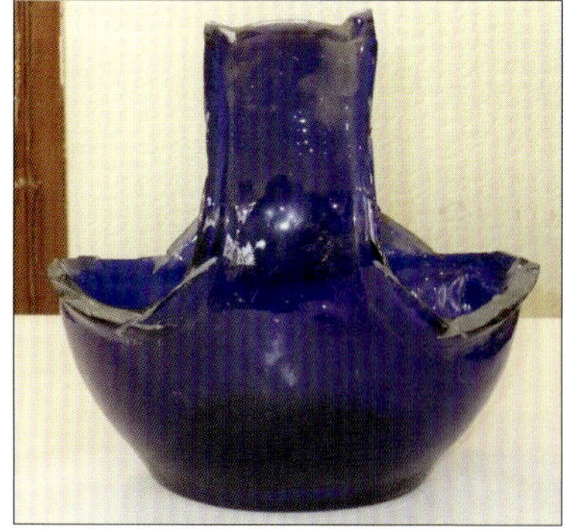

Rough cut out

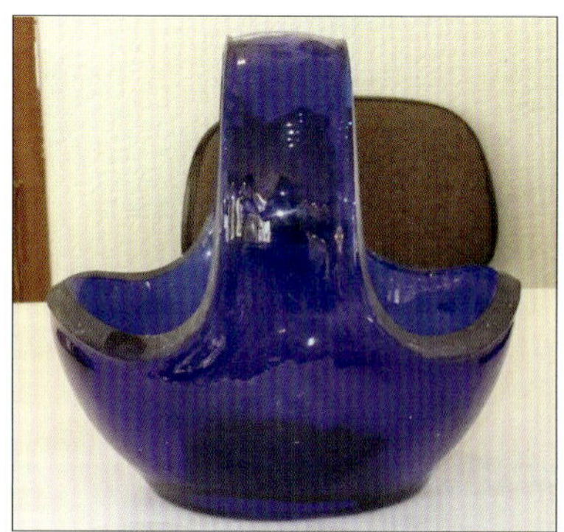

Shaped, ready for cutting

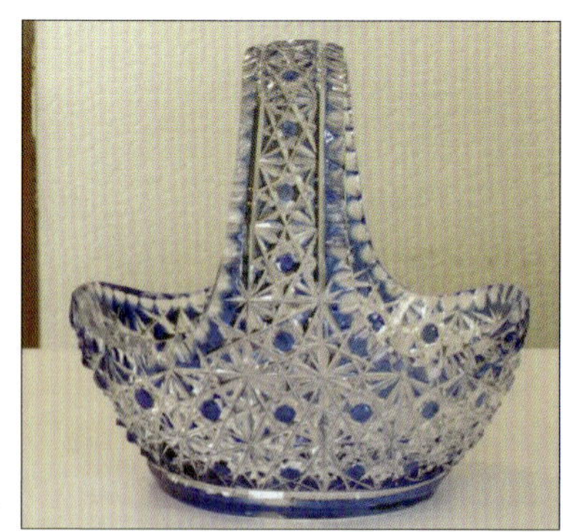

'Cobweb' pattern by Reg Everton

years. Fortunately, through the likes of Reg, John and various other practitioners, the art of cutting still survives. It is incumbent upon all of us that these skills are revered as part of our heritage but also studied, nurtured and passed on for future generations.

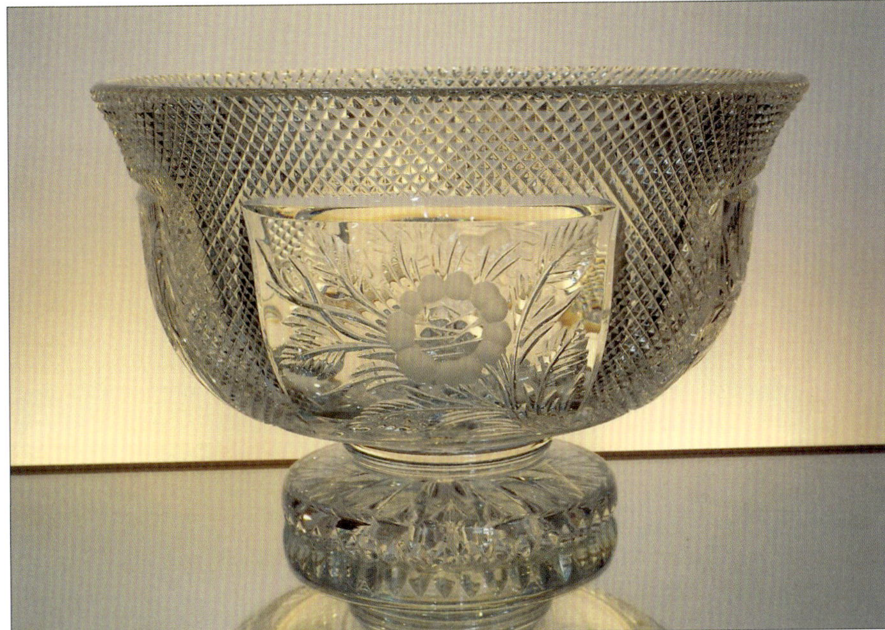

Large bowl with rose engraving
Photo: Dawn Crystal

References and Further Information

Dawn Crystal
Father and son team Reg and John Everton of Dawn Crystal are cited here in light of them supplying the oil lamp. There are, of course, others; glass engravers, Stourbridge in an internet browser will reveal more.
www.dawncrystal.co.uk

Pete Walters at work
https://www.youtube.com/watch?v=gBoyXjSxOLc

Reg Everton at work
http://www.youtube.com/watch?v=JqC5PRo5_6I

British Glass Foundation
GlassCuts is the informal *ad hoc* bulletin of BGF and routinely featured the work of Dawn Crystal, amongst others, as part of its support for the industry. Back issues are lodged on the website; subscribers can register and material submitted free of charge *via* the links indicated.
www.britishglassfoundation.org.uk

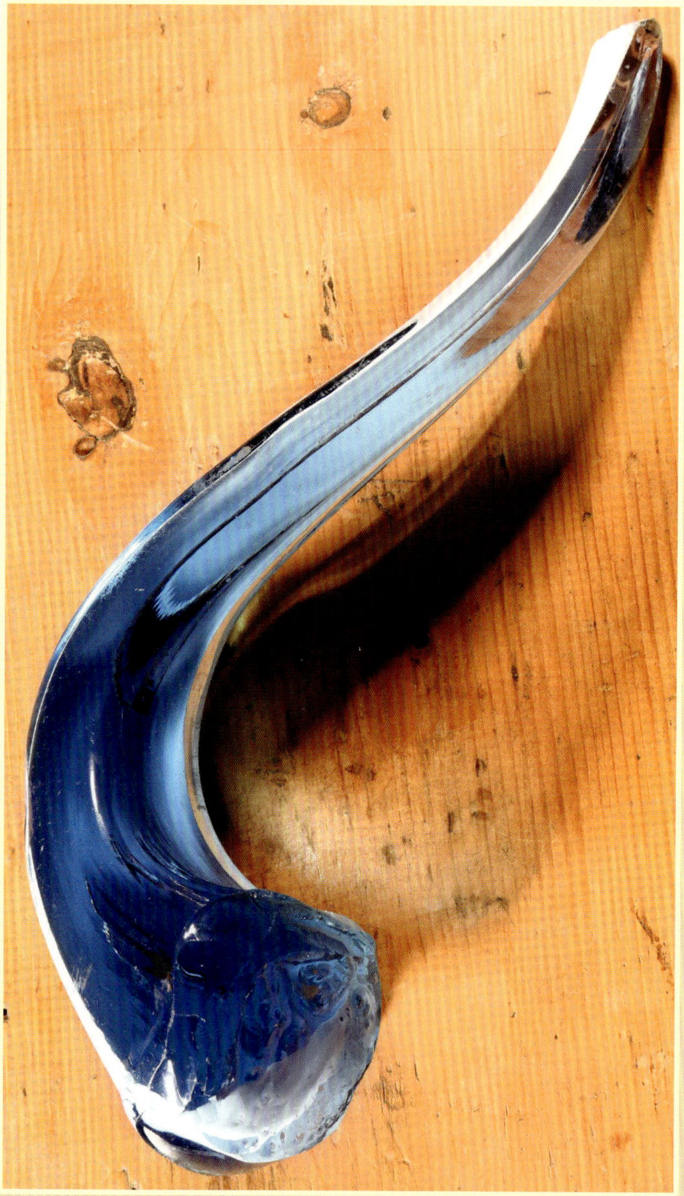

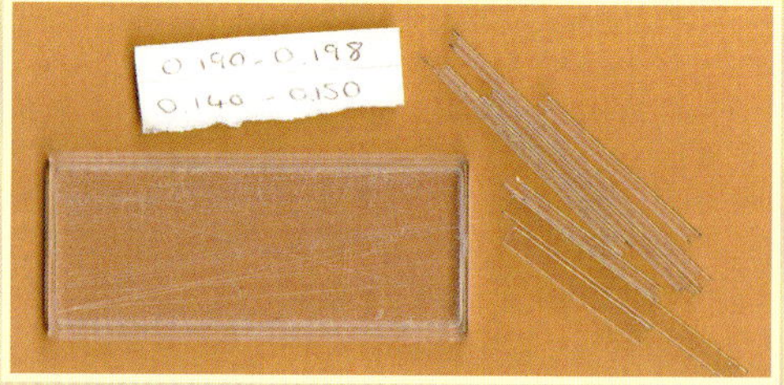

Favourite 10 : Pipe and Tubes

Favourite 10 : Pipe and Tubes

Description and aspects

Glass item in the shape of a smoker's **PIPE**, translucent dark blue body with opaque lighter blue insert, overall length 30cm broadening from 1.5cm at 'mouth' to 7.5cm at 'bowl'.

Quantity of fine hollow glass **TUBES**, each approximately 6cm in length, in acetate box with paper above showing internal and external diameters. Also sections of square-drawn tubing.

Personal significance

For my final gathering of objects I simply had to include these if only for their sheer idiosyncrasy and the story of how I came about them. They are also a touching reminder of the unforgiving transiency of life and of old friends no longer with us; the donor of the glass pipe died in 2012.

The tubes came into my possession around six years ago when as part of my induction into the world of glass I attended a guided tour of Plowden & Thompson (P&T) in Stourbridge. The proprietors at the time were Barbara and Richard Beadman. P&T is believed to be the only glassworks still extant where its cone, albeit in truncated form, is still used for its original purpose - making glass. Looks can be so deceptive and behind the abbreviated cone, replete with its birthstone dated 1788, the quaint olde-worlde charm of a distant era and all the remnants of yesteryear I noted that there was some serious modern high-tech stuff going on here.

Opposite:
Pipe (left)
Photo: Graham Dale
Tubes (right)
Photo: Graham Fisher

Below:
Detail of tubes
Photo: Graham Fisher

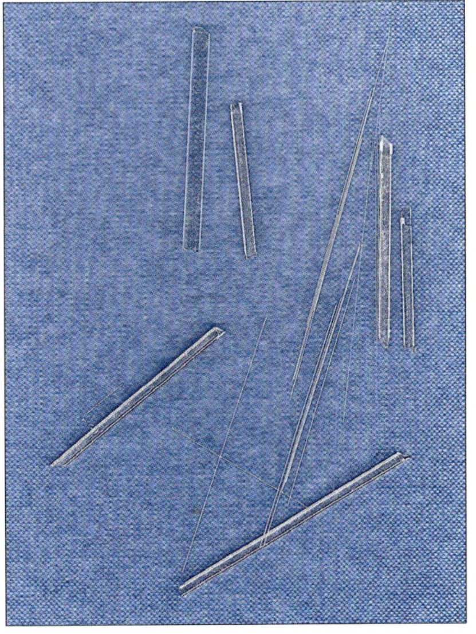

Listening to Barbara's commentary as she passed me a lens cover resembling what one would see on the tail end of a car but which was clearly something a bit more special, it suddenly became obvious that an airplane would need something a bit more special. I was fascinated by P&T and visited again several times thereafter. Barbara and Richard very kindly hosted the launch of one of my books, which also happens to feature their glassworks. P&T supplied coloured glass and all manner of specialist materials; the blue and opal mixes for the 2012 Portland Vase Project (see Favourite 2) came from here. Barbara also happens to be Chair of Friends of Broadfield House Glass Museum and it is through our serendipitous meeting that I have since had the very great pleasure of not only being welcomed as a member but also addressing several of their meetings. All as a result of a piece of glass. Splendid.

Seeing my enthusiasm for the industry Barbara gave me these tubes as a potential discussion point in my presentations. Be assured they have been well used ever since and never fail to intrigue an audience. These are only very short examples; the tubing is so fine it is flexible and can be

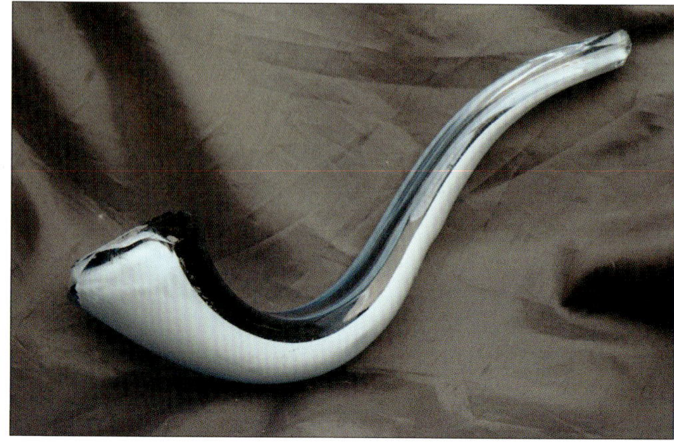

RIGHT:
It may look like a smoker's pipe, but it's actually upside down. The flared end is the result of a molten blob of glass with an air bubble inside it being cast onto a stump and then being drawn out rapidly to form a hollow tube with a different coloured backing.
Photo: Graham Fisher

rolled onto drums. I understand it is used in the delivery of tiny levels of coolant to drilling tips.

The blue pipe is a different kettle of fish and even baffled Barbara for a while. It has no function as it stands, no monetary value that I am aware of and other than in the eye of the beholder, has no artistic or aesthetic quality. It is, in fact, just a lump of scrap glass that was discarded. So, make me any offer. Double it. Double it again. Now put your cash back in your pocket. No chance. You may be interested as to why.

The denouement

I am inordinately proud of my Black Country roots and I just love all those stories that show what world-beaters we were, and still are.

First the tubes. There is a charming story, completely true, of an American engineering company who threw down the gauntlet to metal tube makers Accles & Pollock of Oldbury when they presented a sample of hollow tubing marked 'the smallest tube in the world.' A week later Accles & Pollock acknowledged the gesture by returning their 'smallest tube in the world' with another one *inside* theirs. As Corporal Jones noted: *They don't like it up 'em, Mr Mainwairing.* We are the Black Country; mess with us at your peril.

Stourbridge, formerly in North Worcestershire but whose identity was irreparably eroded when successive local government amalgamations reduced it to an outpost of the greater West Midlands, can boast a similarly proud lineage in glass. Look at these little hollow glass tubes upwards, downwards, sideward, backwards or from any angle. They are so tiny, so exquisite. They fire my imagination by just looking at them.

Their provenance to me was completed one night in February 2012 when I produced them at a meeting in Wordsley where I was extolling Stourbridge Glass. Showing my little tubes around and asking if anyone could hazard a guess as to what they were, a man in the audience confidently stood up and told me exactly. *'Gosh'* said I, *'How on earth did you know that?'* Beaming with pride he smiled as he replied: *'Because I made them!'*

There is an aside to this tale that I find deucedly puzzling and which, as alluded

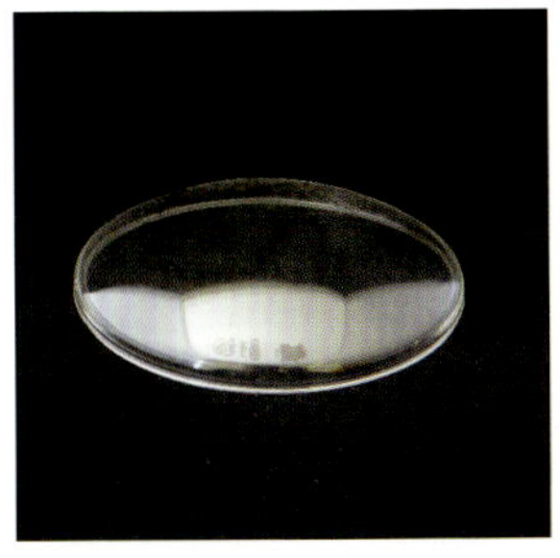

Concave discs

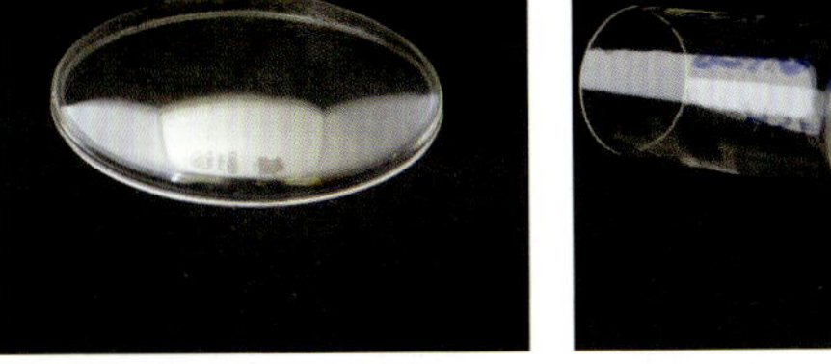

Glass bulb

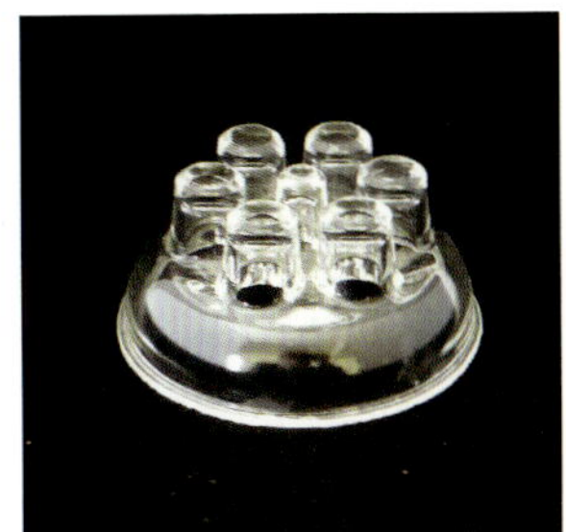

Glass distributor cap

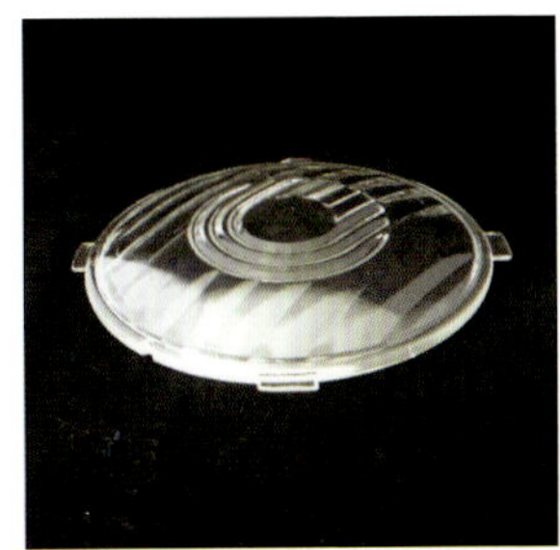

Headlight glass

Aircraft night vision glass

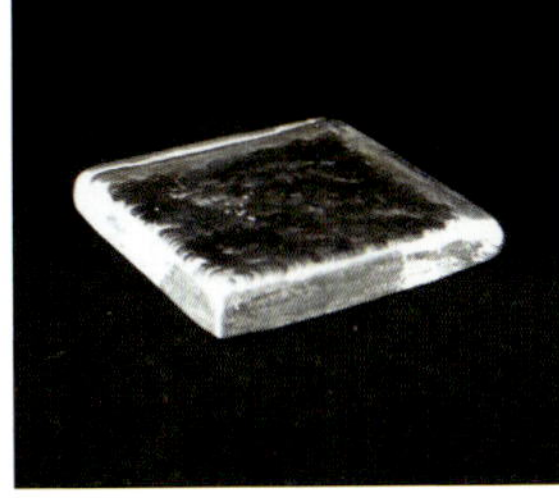

Radiation windows

Tube variations

Glass lock

Examples of technical glass for industrial use
Photos: Plowden & Thompson

to *passim*, may be just one of the factors in the demise of Stourbridge Glass as was. It is all so very parochial. To whit, the audience that night in Wordsley Community Centre comprised in excess of 160 people. This is smack in the heart of Stourbridge Glass territory so in answer to the opening question *'How many of you work, or have relatives that worked, in the Stourbridge Glass industry?'* it came as no surprise that virtually every single hand went up. A few days later the same question asked in The Lye, all of 5 miles away, resulted in well under half. And the same question posed less than 10 miles yonder on the outskirts of Birmingham raised so few hands that I resorted instead to asking: *'How many of you have even heard of the Stourbridge Glass industry?'* No prizes for guessing the response. Most curious. Most provincial.

Now the pipe. Plowden & Thompson, formerly known as the New Dial Glassworks and nowadays simply Dial Glassworks, directly abuts the Stourbridge Canal Town Arm. No surprise there; it was built by an enterprising John Pidcock who saw the writing on the wall in terms of double handling so took advantage of this exciting new transport medium

Borosilicate Glass

'Glass in which the flux is boric oxide instead of alkali. The first borosilicate glass was created by Otto Schott in 1882. It has a low coefficient of expansion and therefore withstands sudden changes of temperature.'

... with acknowledgement to
http://www.cmog.org/glass-dictionary/borosilicate-glass

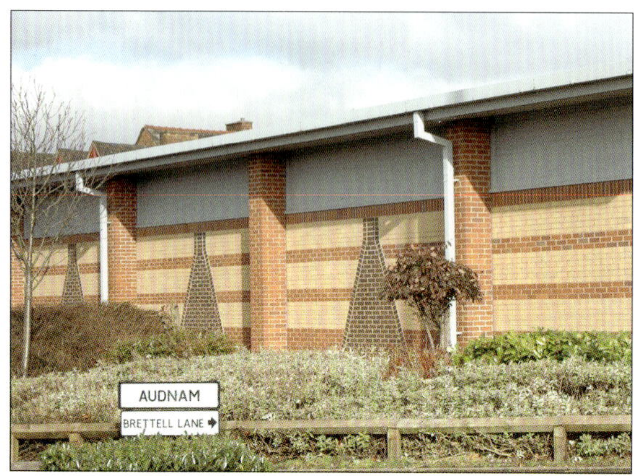

This modern superstore marks the approximate location of the Old Dial Glassworks; note the glass cones picked out in the darker bricks.
Photo: Graham Fisher

and relocated from his Old Dial Glassworks about 200 metres away on the old turnpike, the A491. The approximate area of the Old Dial site is denoted by a supermarket that, considerately, has an outer wall adjacent to the A491 in which darker brickwork picks out the shapes of glass cones.

There are all sorts of scurrilous suggestions as to how various bits and bobs would make their way from P&T *via* sacks on ropes into the canal during daytime, to be collected during the hours of darkness from the towpath on the other side, thereby enhancing the wages of the perpetrator. Perish the thought. This particular item enjoyed no such happy fate and was most likely chucked in the cut as rubbish. It was given to me at around the same time as Barbara gave me the tubes by a fellow boater who was big in the restoration movement of the 1960s onwards and which in turn saw the Stourbridge Canal rejuvenated. He told me how he had come across this in the canal bed right outside P&T, so it seems reasonable that's where it came from, and he had since kept in in his garage as a souvenir these past thirty-odd years. In view of my dalliance into the world of glass he felt it might be of some use to me so would I like to have it? Cost ... one beer, and he didn't even insist upon that. A lovely gesture, made the more so by his passing. But as for what it was, he had no idea. So I made the enquiry. The result was captivating.

At slack periods such as the start of the day the apprentice glassmakers would be allowed to practice and develop their skills and make practice pieces, or *friggers* with the leftovers in the melting pot. Initially I thought this was a *frigger* in the shape of a smoker's pipe. Until, that is, I examined the smaller end more closely; it is hollow down the length of the shaft. By this time I knew Barbara Beadman well enough to seek her observations. I queried whether it may have come out of the side window at P&T into the canal at some juncture, and asked her what it was. Her answer was of the stuff that could justify a book in itself.

Holding it like a smoker's pipe, I learned I was holding it upside down. The following explanation of what it is really does not imbue the skills involved with their true recognition and is akin to suggesting that the music of Beethoven consists of a series of notes strung together, but here's my best shot ...

The piece started off life as a blob of clear blue melt into which the lighter opaque blue was added. After introducing

Frigger

'English term for an object made by a glassworker on his own time. Most friggers were made from the molten glass that remained in the pot at the end of the day. Such glass was considered to be a worker's perquisite.'

... with acknowledgement to
http://www.cmog.org/glass-dictionary/frigger

an air bubble the molten blob was then slapped onto a block, hence the corrugations on the broader end, then drawn with pincers. The drawer would then run away at speed, taking the pincers with him and drawing the molten glass into an ever-finer tube replete with bubble along its centre. The result, when cooled, is a narrow tube with a clear view from the front onto an opaque background. Introduce mercury into the air line down the middle, mark off with graduations, *abracadabra* ... a thermometer.

The stump and shaft remnant left on the block was scrap. Out the window it went. Barbara was able to tell me, if I recall correctly, my remnant was made sometime between the 1920s and 1950s. This just gets better and better - she even took me to the long gallery on the ground floor, adjacent to the canal, where the man who made it would have ran along. So far so good. But, curiously, the P&T records show no trace of them ever using these colours in thermometers. Enquiries continue into that one; in the meantime I have here a piece of waste glass that has everything from incredible skillsets to mystery, intrigue, history and the memory of a departed associate.

Barbara and Richard Beadman have since retired but the business continues (see 'Reports of my death have been greatly exaggerated' below).

As part of checking permissions and clarifying details, in January 2015 I contacted the aforementioned Barbara Beadman, ex-Plowden & Thompson, who very kindly furnished me with the following information she compiled with husband Richard. I reproduce it here verbatim with due acknowledgement. I am indebted for this contribution since it succinctly describes the processes involved whilst simultaneously offering a delightfully reverential insight into the quite extraordinary skills of the specialist glassmaker.

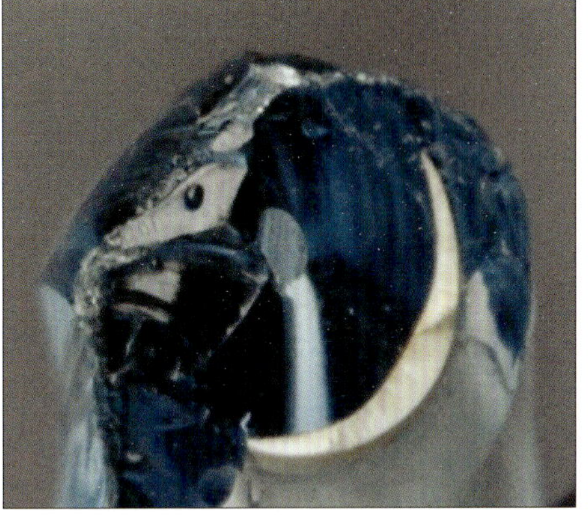

A view of the drawn end of pipe showing the lighter backing colour and the hollow in the middle running throughout its length.
Photo: Graham Fisher

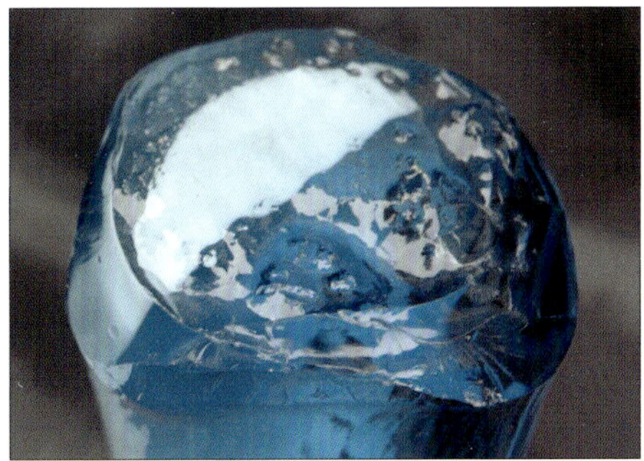

Markings at flared end of 'pipe' showing roughness where the molten blob has been cast onto the stump ready for drawing off.
Photo: Graham Fisher

References and Further Information

World's smallest tube
A mighty small feat of Oldbury engineering skill
http://www.blackcountrybugle.co.uk/mighty-small-feat-Black-Country-engineering-skill/story-21746304-detail/story.html

Plowden & Thompson
http://www.plowden-thompson.co.uk

Tudor Crystal
http://www.tudorcrystal.com

Barbara Beadman comments . . .

The blue pipe came from a hand blowing process of creating blue line opal backed thermometer tubing.

The skill required to do this was immense. Two pots of glass were needed - clear and white opal. The blue line was made by cutting strips of blue glass from pre-made blue glass tubes. It is said that the name of the 'monkey pot' is derived from the placing of a small pot of glass onto the shoulder of a main pot contained within the furnace, which was done for making this tubing.

Opal white is a very soft glass, difficult to control and creates a strange interface when a gather is gathered on top of the first one. A blowing iron is used to collect gathers of clear glass, blowing an elongated bubble, picking up a strip of blue, then half coating the back in opal white. Finally the whole is covered in a gather of clear glass. Meanwhile a 'post end' has been prepared - an iron with a flat front; the glass is attached and then the blowing and pulling process takes place to create a very long tube. It cannot be twisted or you would not have straight lines down the back of the glass. The long tube is measured with calipers as it is blown and a hand fan operated to indicate to the blower the speed at which he should be moving. The length is laid on to ladder racks to be cut into processable lengths, usually about a metre and a half. This was annealed in an oven before being weighed for packing. Gauging was an ongoing process as accuracy was paramount.

When the irons had been cracked off the tube, usually with a deft twist of the wrist, they were put into a metal tray. There was usually quite a lot of glass left on the iron that then deformed under its own weight and that of the iron. At the end of the day this glass was discarded since it could not be re-melted to be used in the same product. Result - a piece of art! *(as per the item here - GF)*

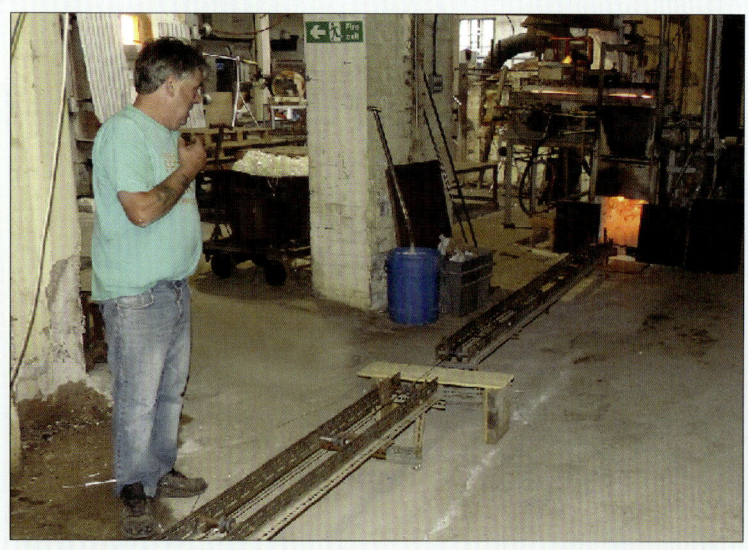

Other factories made thermometer tubing but by drawing the glass on the iron up to the top of a tower rather than across the 88 foot cone or down the drawing tunnel of the Dial. Methods of manufacture changed over the years, particularly as mercury became an unwelcome material.

The capillary tubes are usually made from borosilicate (temperature shock resistant glass similar to 'Pyrex') glass tube and then a process known as 're-drawing' is used to reduce the tube to the required size.

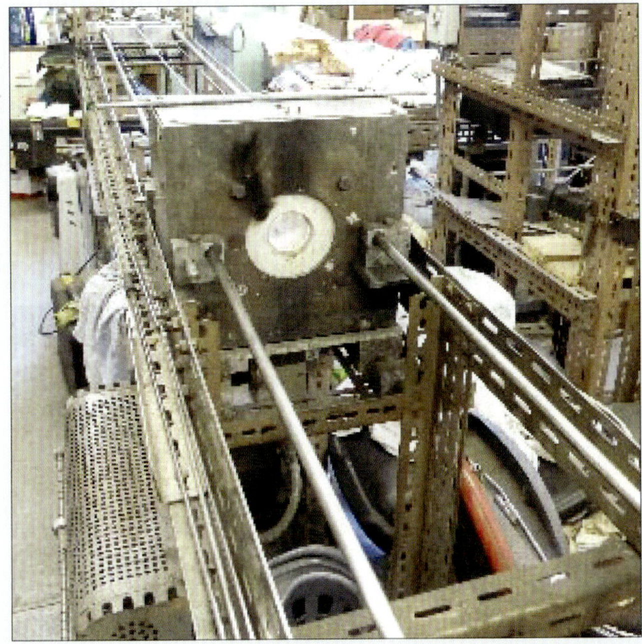

The actual machines my tiny tubes were made on, still going strong.
Opposite: Furnace tube making
Left: Redraw machinery
Photos: Plowden & Thompson

The glass tube is fed into a small electric furnace, heated and then pulled rapidly down, cooling as it descends. At the same time an electronic measuring head measures the outside diameter to enable small changes to the settings to be made. There is a formula that dictates the ratio of the starting size to the finishing size; but as always glass is its own master and thus experience matters.

The glass tubing is drawn onto a large diameter wheel, approximately 30 inches diameter and up to half a mile in length. When cold it is cut into metre lengths and retained in a long glass tube for transportation to the lab. Once there, it is accurately gauged on the outside and spot checks on the internal diameter are made by mounting a small length of tube onto the table of a television microscope where the diameter is measured and the wall thickness to check for ovality. A common size on the outside diameter is 0.190 - 0.198 mm with a bore size of 0.14 - 0.15 mm.

The tubes are subdivided into sizes and then waxed onto small boards for accurate cutting to length and squareness of the end. These have to be cleaned by washing in a dilute acid and rinsed to clean the tube without leaving water marks.

The tubes are then measured for diameter internally and externally, counted and packed into small purpose made boxes to be shipped to the next company for further processing.

Here they are mounted into drilling heads, up to 49 at a time, for electro-mechanical drilling of titanium turbine blades. The blade is effectively cooled with the tiny holes enabling the blade to operate at a higher temperature than the normal metal-deforming temperature.

The blades are in military aircraft engines and it is important to have the right size hole for the part of the world the plane is operating in, as sand grain size varies and can affect the operation when the air is drawn over desert areas.

Another note: the land on the other side of the canal, where the houses are now, was used as a 'tip' by P&T as they owned it at that time. There would have been plenty of opportunity for raiding!

'Reports of my death have been greatly exaggerated'

A common misquote of Mark Twain who, in May 1897 more accurately said: *'The report of my death was an exaggeration'* the sentiment implicit in either version is equally applicable to the Stourbridge Glass industry.

As noted elsewhere I grow increasingly weary of countering the nay-sayers who claim it has all gone and/or there is no future and, much as with climate-change scepticism, flat earth theory or conspiracies surrounding moon landings I am curious as to whence such nonsensical notions arise since the evidence to the contrary is both overt and compelling; the burgeoning Studio Glass movement, the International Festival of Glass, the thriving retail outlets and other specialists, the 2012 Portland Vase Project and a new home for the Stourbridge Glass collection, to name but a few. Then there is the sheer amount of monies spent on redevelopment of the former Webb-Corbett factory, now the Glasshouse College and Webb Corbett Visitor Centre in Amblecote. Such activity and largesse is simply at odds with any suggestion of a moribund industry; indeed it is clearly indicative of the contrary.

Which brings us neatly to goings-on at Audnam and an exciting pointer to the future of Stourbridge glassmaking that has its roots very much based on the manner of how it once was in Ye Goode Olde Days but which has been given a decidedly contemporary twist.

In 2012 Plowden & Thompson (P&T) and Tudor Crystal were purchased by E T Enterprises, a subsidiary of Ludlum Measurements in Texas, USA. The acquisition was as shrewd as it was practical; P&T are the manufacturers of componentry essential in the ETE production process so when the opportunity arose, and to safeguard their own long-term future, the end-user secured its own supplier. Tudor Crystal remains part of P&T and is the last major manufacturer in Stourbridge making 30% full lead crystal, using a traditional multi-furnace glassmaking cone.

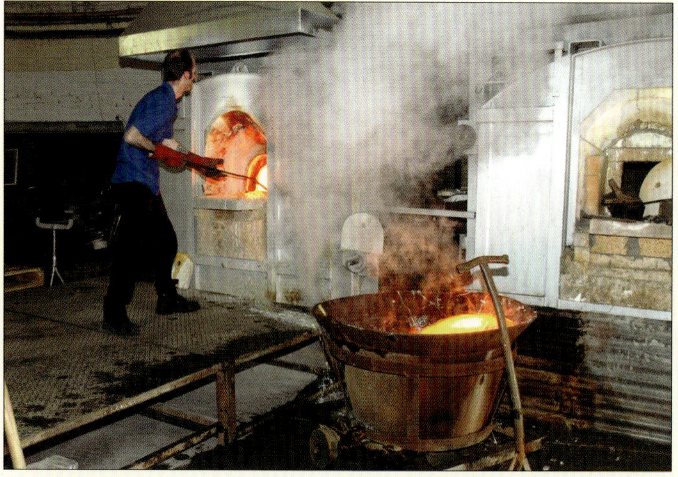

Emptying out a pot at the Plowden & Thompson glassworks.
This furnace is located in what is believed to be one of the last of the glass cones which, albeit in its truncated form, is still being used for its original purpose - making glass.
Molten 'metal' is being ladeled from the pot into a vat of cold water which intermittently results in the formation of glass bubbles as it cools. It doesn't come much more traditional than this.
Photo: Graham Fisher

Ian Dury - yes, that man again - brought my attention to, as he put it, 'exciting developments' at P&T that he felt may be of interest to me, particularly in my continuing desire to promote the re-emergence of the Stourbridge Glass industry from its years of decline. A quick exchange of emails to arrange a meeting led to me presenting myself on the morning of Monday 2nd March 2015 (immediately following my visit to Wessex Crystal - see A Sting in the Tale, later) where I was greeted enthusiastically by Sales Manager Keith Smith and introduced to some of his team. Which had a ring of familiarity, as I had known some of them here for years; they're a loyal lot.

Keith then gave me a comprehensive tour whilst simultaneously filling me in on the details. In essence, the restructuring of the business to meet the challenges it will face as the 21st century unfurls falls into two broad categories; a complete realignment of production techniques and procedures together with a root-and-branch review of the product range.

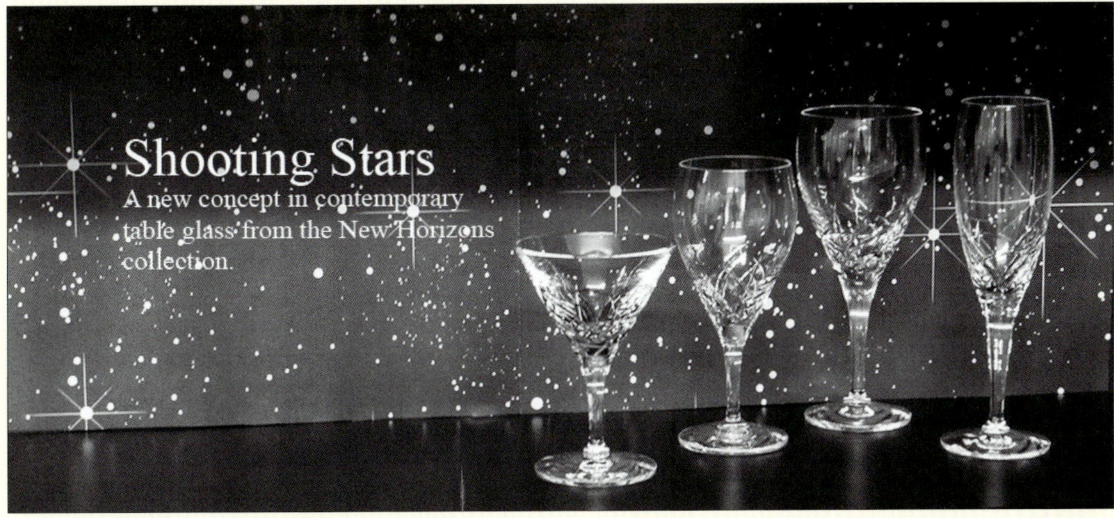

The distinction between the two arms is that P&T is very much the commercial side whereas Tudor focuses on the traditional hand-made lead crystal. Whilst both share common premises and production facilities - not least the furnaces in that rather special glass cone - there are of necessity two business models, although the ultimate aim of enhanced sustainability is of course common to both. On the production side, for example, there have been efficiency modifications to the furnaces, a reduction in stock - P&T have ceased supplying coloured powders and tubing to the industry, it is simply no longer economical - and, perhaps most crucial, a total streamlining of procedures which have now been brought in from their different corners and hidey-holes under the one inclusive section.

There is a delightful contrast between historic machinery *('It still works so we're happy to use it')*

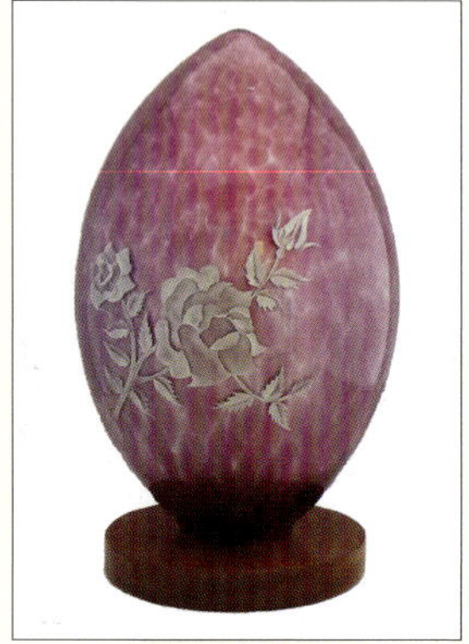

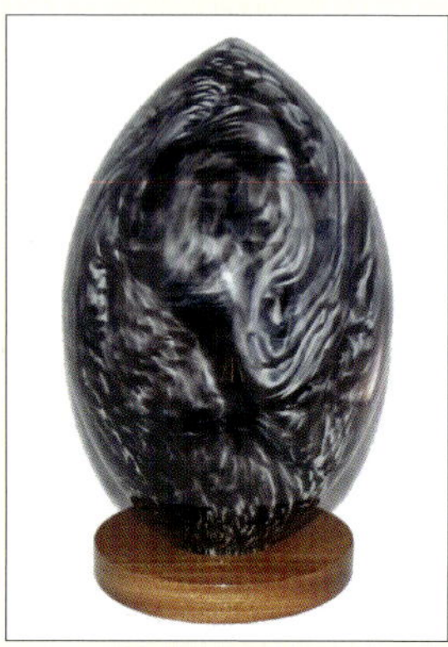

Prototype funeral urns, soon to be in production
Photo: Tudor Crystal

and the more modern equipment drafted in as part of a massive - and costly - reorganization with high capital investment. And blow me down with a feather if Keith didn't show me the actual machines my tiny tubes were made on, still going strong. There is some specialist stuff at work here and I had always felt there were some aspects of P&T's output that were a teeny bit hush-hush. My thoughts were confirmed by Keith who informed me there were some products that P&T were commissioned to make to confidential specifications and having an ultimate end use that not even he knew.

On the Tudor side of things I was shown a selection of beautiful multi-colored glass vase-type objects resembling an inverted teardrop, about a foot in height, on a base in the form of a stopper that also acted as a stand. Adjacent was a selection of identical but smaller vessels. *'They are in the development stage. Have a guess what they are'* teased Keith with a twinkle. I would never have managed in a million years - a new range of 'designer' funeral urns, with smaller versions for pets. Inspired.

A visit to the refurbished shop with its uprated lighting that glistened off every facet and cut of the sumptuous giftware that bulged the shelves, the room next door where I launched JEWELS ON THE CUT back in 2010, now being fitted with specialist machinery; then on to Keith's office and the most glorious array of utterly stunning glassware that is nigh-on impossible to fully absorb in one sitting. *'Take a look at our new range of sports trophies'* he said. *'We see that as a growing market, together with specialist commissions and glassware commemorating specific events.'*

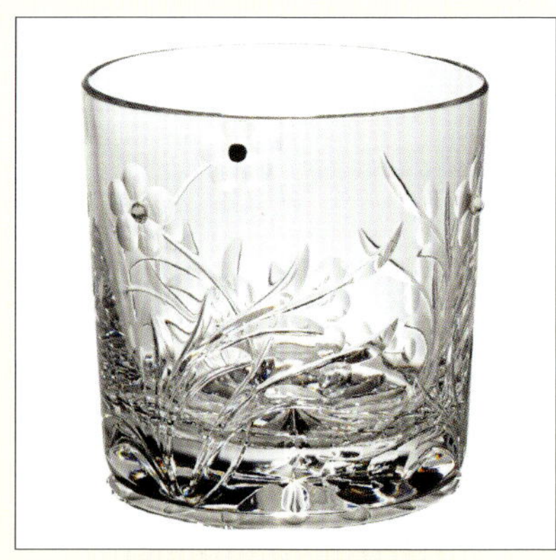

An example of their still-popular Connoisseur range: the XL Whisky in 'Catherine SW' pattern which incorporates Swarovski® crystal elements into each piece
Photo: Tudor Crystal

And here's where his years of accrued sales and marketing expertise came to the fore as he described how, amidst some opposition on occasions it must be said, certain elements in a range were boldly dropped and new ones introduced. The masterstroke is the retaining of the Tudor name and tradition combined with an *avant-garde* approach to every aspect from the business model to a bright, vibrant new range. The catalogue and website can do this far greater justice than I but by way of example take a look at the range of drinking vessels of various

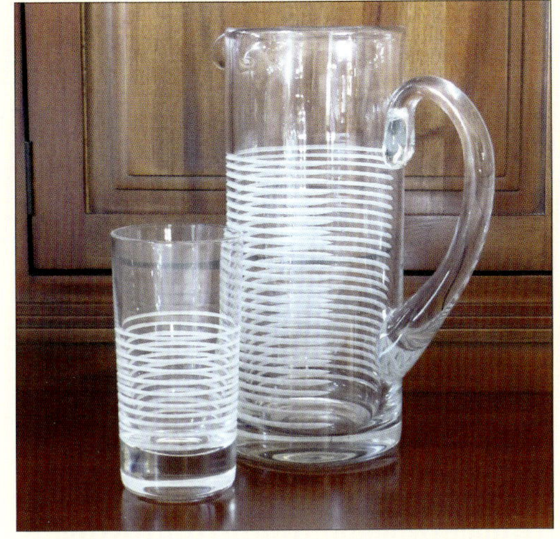

'Latitude' pattern, one of the new contemporary designs
Photo: Tudor Crystal

shapes and sizes that have minimalist cut. Changes to production techniques have resulted in a glass that does not require cutting to hide blemishes, allowing for a larger area of 'clear' glass on which the understated cut enhances the piece almost subliminally rather than being its focus. The result is a refreshingly vibrant piece of full-lead crystal that is clearly aimed at appealing to a youthful market. Conversely just a glance at a whisky tumbler in the classic traditional-looking *Connoisseur* range caused me some mental drooling as I imagined swilling a fine Islay malt around its base and whiffed its peaty aroma in anticipation of the joyous explosion on the taste buds about to come. At 11:00 in the morning.

The extensive product ranges of classic and contemporary glassware, together with a rejuvenated approach to the scientific and technical aspects, are reflective of a dynamic business that it is to be hoped will continue to fly the flag for Stourbridge Glass over many years to come.

Keith and I finished our meeting with him imploring me to mention how visitors are always welcome and whilst a modest charge may be levied for larger groups simply to cover the cost of brochures and material, small groups can be entertained free of charge. Website details are below or try 01384 392525.

If all of this sounds like an unashamed plug for P&T and Tudor Crystal then I rebound on my critics by saying: *'Why not?'* The English disease is that of constant self-denigration; may we just for once celebrate something that will be instrumental in not only keeping our proud industry on the map but actually helping to redefine it's future? 'Pon my soul, a thousand plagues be visited on the houses of anyone who isn't fully behind that.

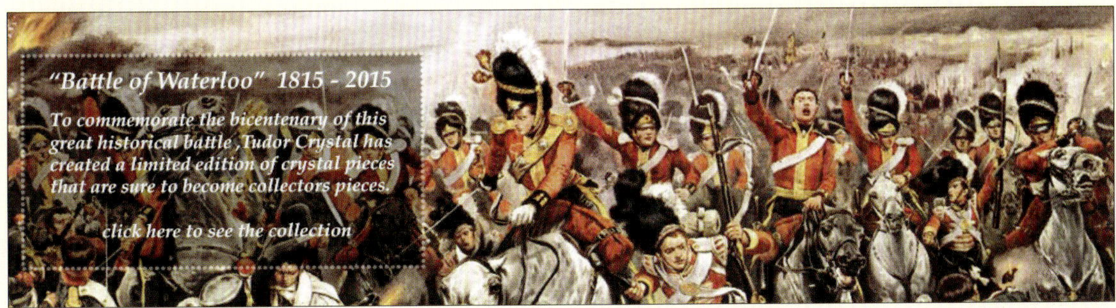

Round-up of Denouements

… the bit where it all comes together

WELL, THERE THEY ARE, a few of my favourite things and the reasons why they are so special to me. Collating and describing them was the easy part; threading them together by means of a central theme, such that their whole became more than the sum of the individual components, was a little more challenging. Help came through the most unlikely source when I was listening to a radio show playing 'golden oldies'.

In 1959 Wink Martindale, who last time I checked was still very much alive and well into his eighties, released a single that was touching, haunting, execrable, memorable or instantly forgettable according to your musical taste. Records don't show to what extent Wink was upset by any negative critique but we may at least surmise that he doubtless just carried on smiling all the way to the bank as his spoken rendition of *Deck of Cards* notched up one million sales and rocketed to No 7 on America's *Billboard Hot 100*. It also hit No 5 in the UK charts, which it revisited on a further three occasions on subsequent re-release.

If this all sounds like a distant land that time forgot, then let me give you the gist of *Deck of Cards* before then explaining how it suddenly came to me as the epitome of analogy that I was seeking here.

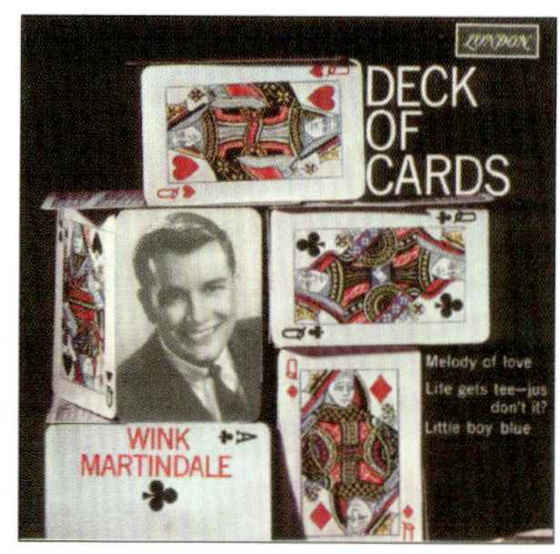

The setting is World War II where a group of American soldiers, weary from a long march through southern Italy, had camped in a small town. During a holy reading in the church a soldier pulls out a deck of cards and spreads them out in front of him. He is spotted by his sergeant who believes he is playing cards in church. The soldier is arrested and taken before a senior officer to be punished. Prior to handing down his deliberation, the officer demands an explanation. The soldier explains that he has no prayer book but instead uses his cards. He describes the significance of each card:

Ace: The one true God

Deuce: The Old and New Testaments

Three: The Holy Trinity

Four: Mathew, Mark, Luke, John

… I could go on but I reckon the point is made. The outcome is not directly stated but the inference is that the officer, suitably moved, imposes no punishment. The narrator states that the story is true and concludes with the memorably saccharine, oft-parodied line: *'I was that soldier'.*

Now, putting to one side the material discrepancies in the lyrics, some of which do not tie in accurately with the Bible, and the paradox of at least ten recording artists including Max Bygraves and others of diverse nationalities all claiming to have been 'that soldier', let me re-examine my favourite things from the perspective of them being my personal *Deck of Cards*.

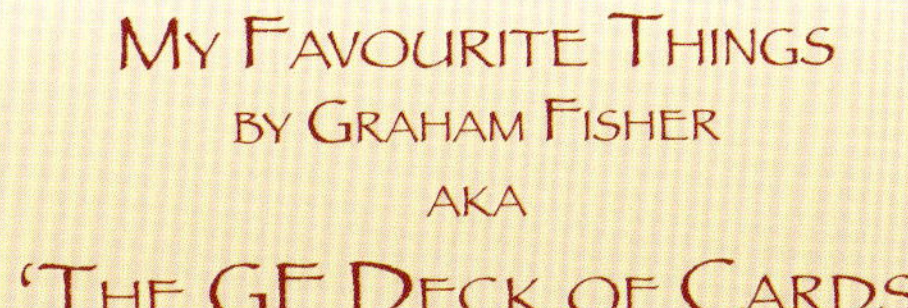

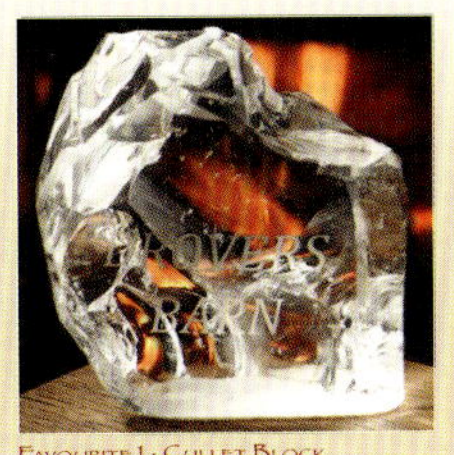
Favourite 1 : Cullet Block

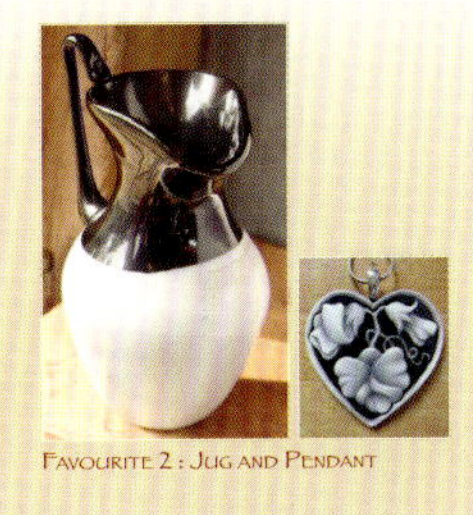
Favourite 2 : Jug and Pendant

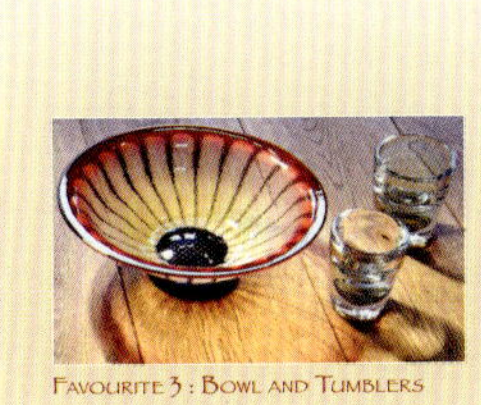
Favourite 3 : Bowl and Tumblers

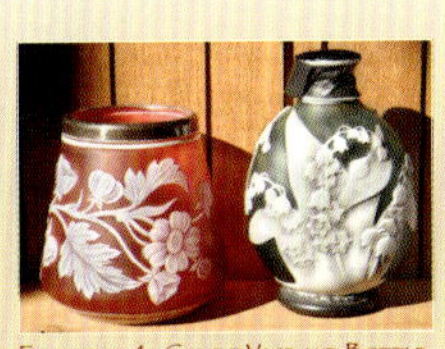
Favourite 4 : Cameo Vase and Bottle

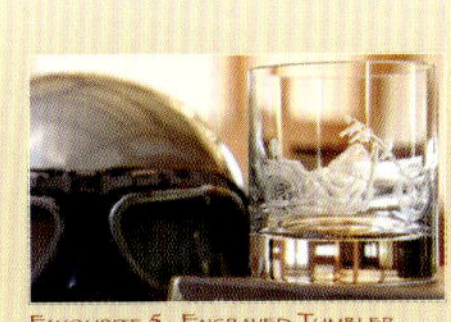
Favourite 5 : Engraved Tumbler

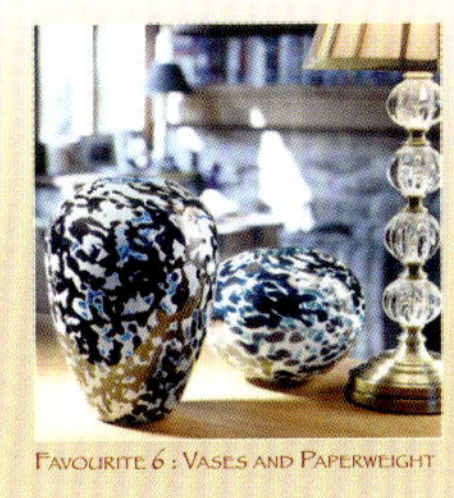
Favourite 6 : Vases and Paperweight

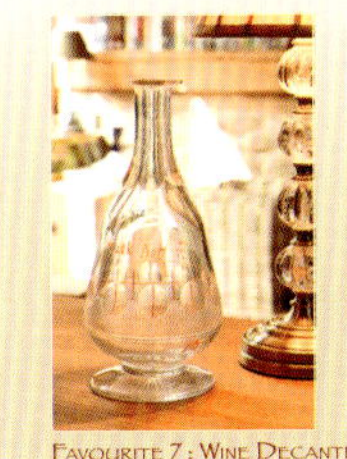
Favourite 7 : Wine Decanter

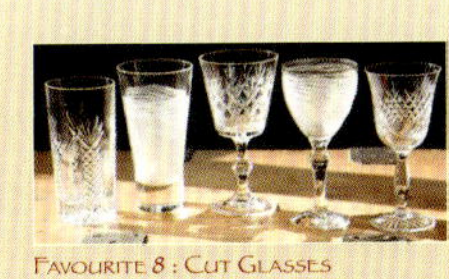
Favourite 8 : Cut Glasses

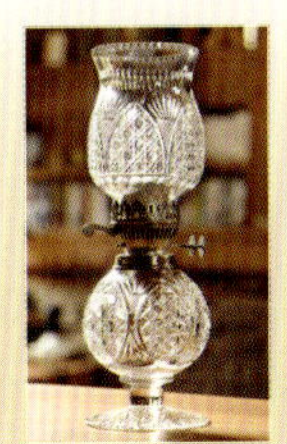
Favourite 9 : Oil Lamp

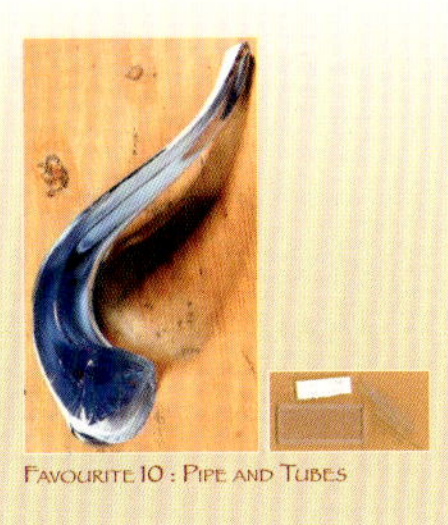
Favourite 10 : Pipe and Tubes

When I look at the Drovers Barn cullet block (Favourite 1) I think of Webb Corbett, once a mighty glassworks and now rejuvenated as part of an educational project that includes a visitor centre at which I am always made welcome. From a sad loss of a glass facility has emerged a bright future that is indicative of the resurgence of the industry in another guise. I take great pleasure in knowing one of the last pieces of waste cullet to be broken from the cold furnace is now a treasured item of simple elegance and basic function, recalling the friendship of the man who gave it to me and why he did so.

The jug and pendant (Favourite 2) will forever remind me of an memorably exciting period when I shadowed a unique project and came to know all of the delightful people associated with it; to achieve something I would never otherwise have done and to witness first-hand the creation of some truly unique artifacts from start to finish; to be afforded the honour of recording it all for posterity (The 2012 Portland Vase Project: Recreation of a Masterpiece, Sparrow Publishing 2012) and sharing in the sheer *kudos* of being part of a very special event that has already secured its place in history and which will be remembered for generations to come.

In representing some of the finest craftsmanship of the studio-movement age Allister Malcolm's bowl and tumblers (Favourite 3) are a testimony to the skills I have encountered, the relationships I would otherwise never have generated and my work with him and others as partners in the British Glass Foundation which could well form part of my own modest legacy. They are also a confirmation of Allister's magnanimity, a trait that I have found almost seems to be part of a glassmaker's birthright.

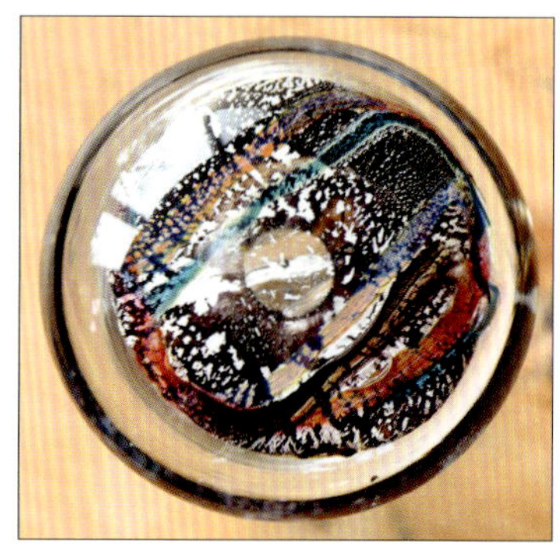

Paperweight by Allister Malcolm
Photo: Grahan Dale

The red cameo vase together with the green cameo bottle (Favourite 4) offer me a dichotomy between old and new; together they intrigue me by how similar they are whilst actually being completely different in many respects. The story behind the green one once more underscores the humility, dedication and bewildering yet understated skills that so typify the industry, whilst the red one brings bitter-sweet nostalgia for an item that probably represents the best part of a lifetime's acquired skill in its production yet which, sadly, is not nowadays represented as such in its market value. But this is of no interest to me since, more importantly; it actually belongs to my dear mother. At 83 years old she still enjoys the thrill of the auction; long may she be able to do so. It delights me greatly to see how, through my association with glass, her own newly discovered interest has brought her such pleasure.

Again, I could continue but I reckon the point is made. And here is where my *Deck of Cards* comes into play.

If I take a picture of all these items together then lay it on the table in front of me, in one glance I can interpret just about every aspect of the glass I have described set against the backdrop of an industry spanning back these past 400 years. I can see manufacturing techniques, personal skills and astonishing products. I can hear echoes from the past and I am minded toward the future. I can see acquaintances and alliances from parochial gatherings in a small room to celebrations across Stourbridge that attract people from across the globe. I am

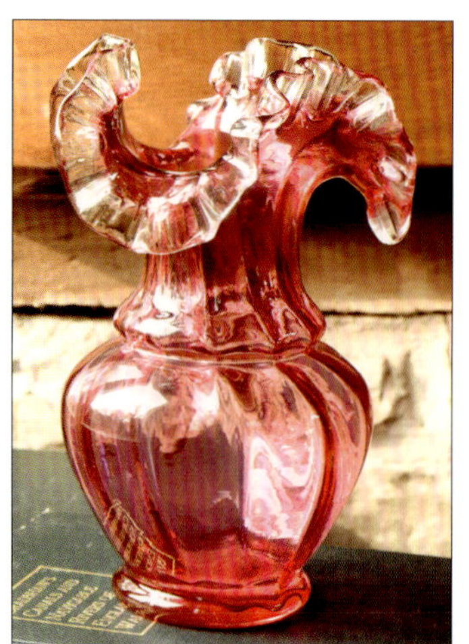

Vase, ruby cased, believed late 19th century, hand blown and dipped in optic mould with indications of foot being held in spring loaded 'gadget' to facilitate crimping and working of rim.
(with thanks to Ian Dury for his opinion) (SIC)
Photo: Graham Dale

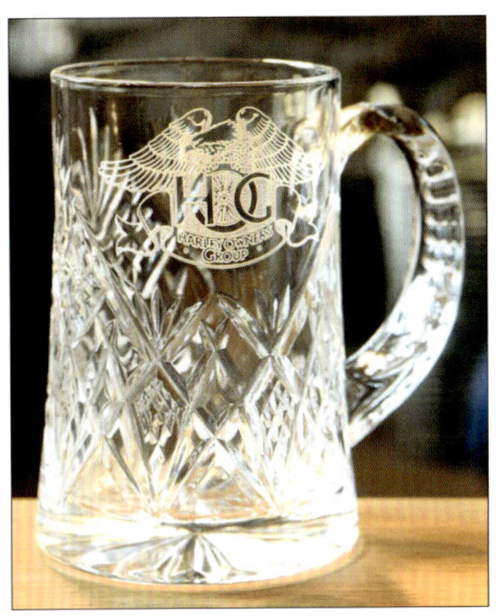

Tankard identified as *Amboise* 24% lead crystal blank with diamond wheel cuts and pressed star base, handle decorated with hollows. Almost certainly sand-engraved by the late Tony Prew of Crystal Craft Engraved Glass, noted for the depth of his engraving. (This ties in with the man who presented it to me in the early 1990s and whom I have since learnt used to take his engraving work to Tony Prew - Author). *'And I will put my wages on it that this was acid dipped by Wessex Crystal'* - Ian Dury. (see A Sting in the Tale for more on Wessex Crystal)
(with thanks to Ian Dury for his opinion)
Photo: Graham Dale

stirred through a range of emotions and bamboozled by the sheer scope and scale of that which is before me. Quite simply, there is enough about glass just here to stimulate me for several lifetimes. In 'glassy' terms, I was that soldier. Thanks, Wink.

But, and here's the punch line, which I will italicize for maximum impact; ***these are but a few examples of pieces that, right now, are all lying within about fifteen feet of where I am sitting***. There must be thousands of similar homes in the Stourbridge area alone, many of them crammed with far more than my modest accrual. And we have barely even touched upon lampworking, pressed glass, carnival glass *(John Northwood, he of Northwood-Pargeter Portland Vase fame in the 19th century, had a son Harry who went to the USA and was at the forefront of the development of what we know as carnival glass)*, bottles, jugs and other containers by the million, enameling, gilting, scientific glass, specialist applications and contemporary usage in everything from iPhones and tablets to deep space telescopes, paperweights, *mille feuille, pâte-de-verre* ... where to stop? For the enthusiast of the arcane or abstruse, glass eyes are made of ... you get my drift.

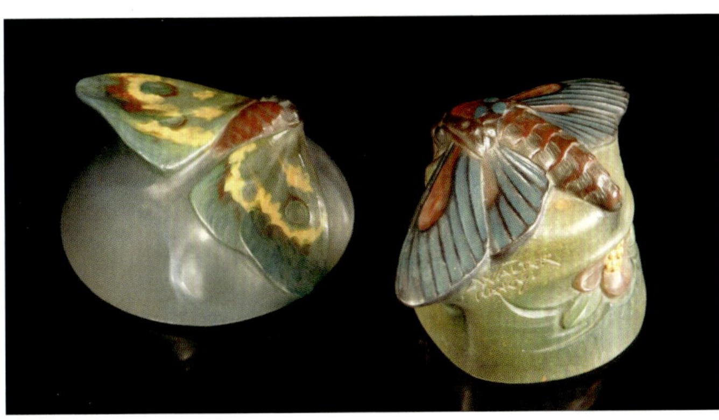

'Moths' in pâte-de-verre by Amalric Walter
Photo: Broadfield House Glass Museum

Then there are the numerous societies and clubs, many of them based in or with links to the area, each representing their own specialist interests: The Contemporary Glass Society, The Carnival Glass Society, The Glass Association, The Glass Circle, The Paperweight Collectors' Circle, The Bead Society, Friends of Broadfield House Glass

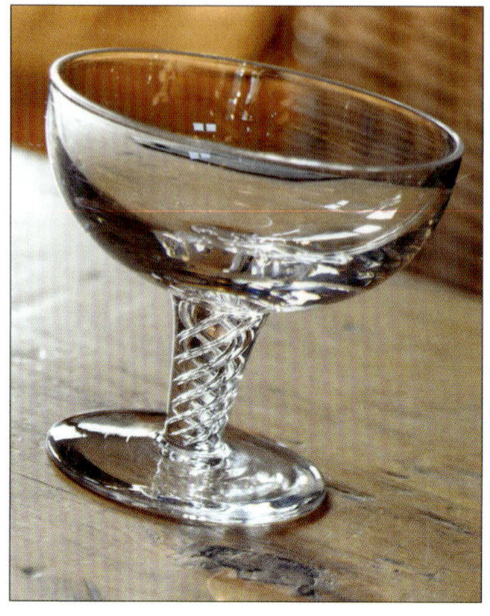

Ariel pattern No 29533 saucer champagne glass with air twist stem, 10cm in height and 10cm circumference at rim, as featured in the 1954 Stuart catalogue. (*'Interestingly there were no flute Champs available then, only saucer Champs'* - Ian Dury.) An item of beauty and grace that belies the sad loss of the final 'heavyweight' manufacturer of yesteryear. The quality of the glass for this range had to be flawless and the rejection rate was in consequence very high. Presented to S I Chapman in 2012 as part of a set by Ian Dury, formerly of Stuart (SIC)
(with thanks to Ian Dury for his opinion)
Photo: Graham Dale

Museum, British Glass Foundation and many more... with apologies to those not mentioned, just type your own glass interest into your browser and you will find something, and very likely with a connection to Stourbridge

So, what exactly is the fate of all of these items and why should we care?

Well, we should care because it matters, that's why. *QED* and notwithstanding those who possess items of great value, and hence most likely know it, I am also here referring to a swathe of anonymous examples that include innumerable trinkets, souvenirs, *bric-a-brac* and other ephemera that may by its very nature be unloved, unappreciated, perhaps even unrecognized in purpose or origin.

Each has over the years probably found its resting place covered in either blankets or thick dust in a dark cupboard, a loft, attic, garage or store-room. Yet, as my *Deck of Cards* shows, just a scratch beneath the surface can yield so much about its maker, provenance and history. It can relate tales, stir the imagination, rekindle memories. It can lead to entire new directions in our own lives; it can remind us of those we have lost, it can be re-affirming of those still amongst us. It can be a *memento* of things past yet it might also claim its place in the contemporary world; it could even offer a pointer to what is yet to come. Put in those terms, it is quite overwhelming, is it not? ***That's*** why it matters.

Yet a fundamental risk posed to such empowerment springs from a far more pragmatic source; how much is the piece worth in terms of hard cash? Whilst commercialism in glass is not an issue - it is, of course, the purpose of industry - it can be unhelpful if, as in this context, it is considered a prime driver. To explain, let me go back to my living room.

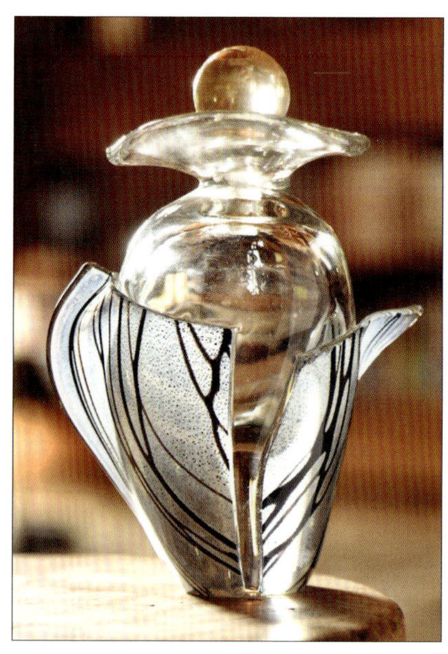

'Cloak' perfume bottle by Allister Malcolm
Photo: Graham Dale

Sitting on my bookshelf is a book. It happens to be *Bradshaw's Canals and Navigable Rivers of England and Wales* but that's neither here nor there. There are several of them. I collect them and over the years have saved quite a few. Note the use of that term 'saved quite a few'. For some curious reason I am fascinated by *Bradshaw's* and, if once more faced with the prospect of being cast on a desert island, this is most likely my one book I would take. Either that or the complete works of Sherlock Holmes, depending on how the coin landed.

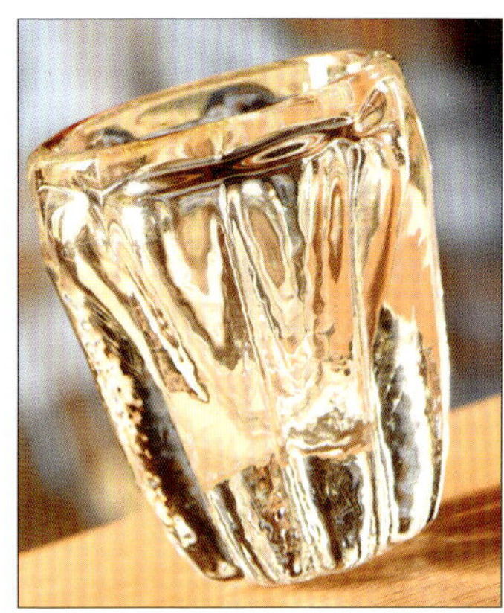

A personal triumph but no real threat to the professionals; hand-blown moulded whisky tumbler made by the author as part of an 'Allister Malcolm Glassmaking Appreciation Course.' As alluded to in The Glassworker: a Personal Tribute (see Leonardo and the Art of Glassmaking): *'I am not, nor would I ever claim to be, a glassmaker ... (but) I am able to relate to an audience how skilful it all is, based on the unimpeachable rationale that I have at least attempted it myself'.*
Photo: Graham Dale

My *Bradshaw's* would be better thumbed than the Bible or the works of that Stratford chappie. Published between 1904 and 1928 those that remain are mostly tatty round the edges, probably having spent years in libraries before being turfed out to the second-hand bookshops. They may also be missing the fold-out map in the back, which reduces their value considerably. Even so, poor map-less examples are still of some value.

Next to my *Bradshaw's* are a couple of similar-sized books, on waterways but again that's neither here nor there other than they look similar. Yet their provenance is immense by dint of who once owned them. They are of no notable monetary worth that I am aware of and it is more the sentimentality of their donation by a dear friend who has joined that increasingly disheartening list of those who are no longer with us.

Let us fast-forward to the time when I am no more and it is left to others to sort my effects. To the unquestioning eye that entire row of old books may represent very little, ether in terms of cash or sentiment, and one can thus imagine their fate. I do know their value and have willed them to a museum. They are saved.

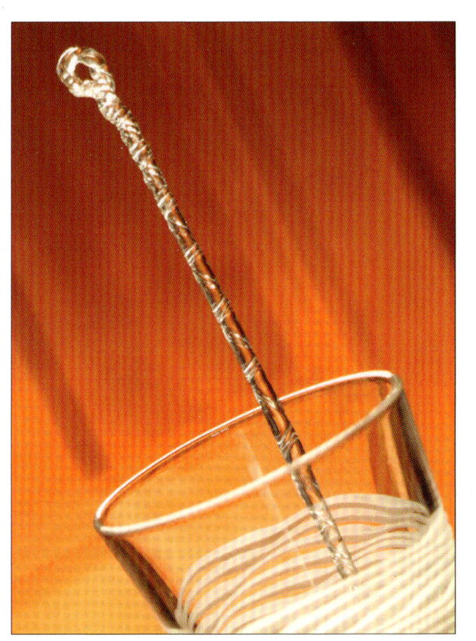

Twizzle stick made by author at the 'Allister Malcolm Glassmaking Appreciation Course.'
Photo: Graham Dale

With this in mind let me now return to my *Deck of Cards* and take a look at their monetary aspects from the standpoint of someone who, along with my books, may be clearing my other effects. Imagine the scene ...

'Lump of glass? Good doorstop. Shove that outside on the porch. Old blue pot with crooked handle? No use for anything, chuck it. Nice brooch, though. I might save that for the wife.

That bowl and the tumblers are OK, might get a few bob for them in the car boot sale. A shame that nice wine glass has got a chip and crack. Chuck it. The red pot's nice, it might hold a few flowers. That green thing's still got tape on it and isn't even finished. Neither is the decanter. Chuck them as well. Same with that blue pipe and the bits of glass, whatever they are.'

Hmmm ... I rest my case.

Model Harley Davidson 'Electra Glide', width 14cm, height 7cm
Mould-pressed glass, hand flattened at base to allow upright standing, late 20th century
(with thanks to Ian Dury for his opinion)
Photo: Graham Dale

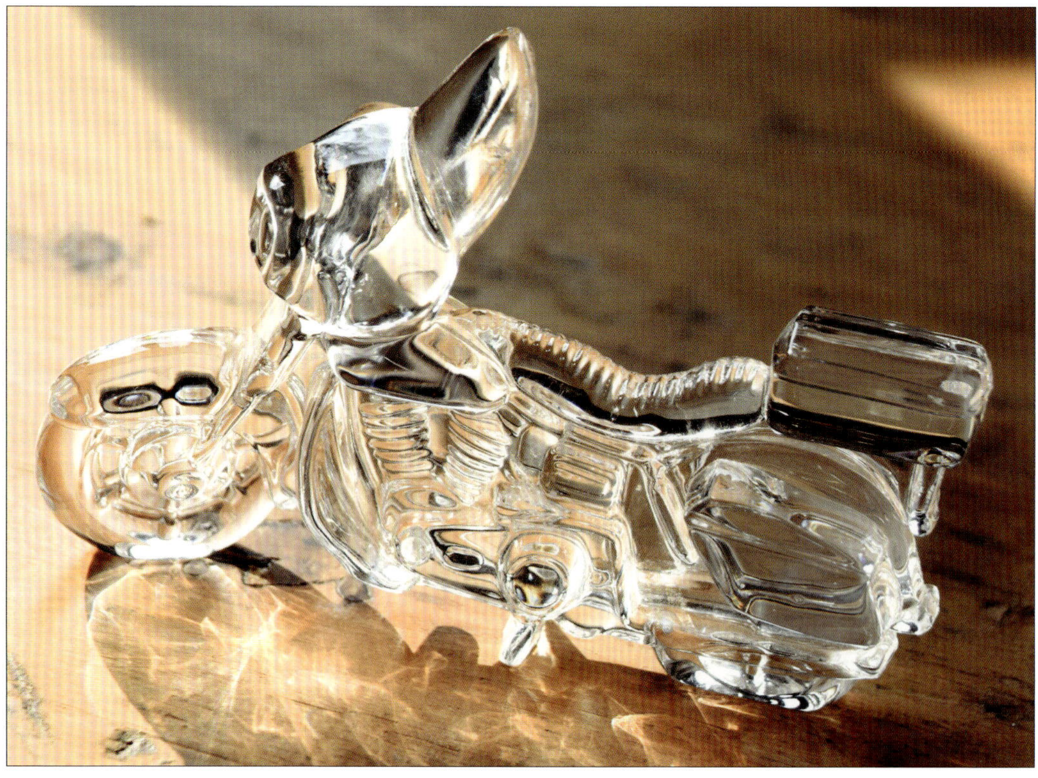

Throughout this book there has been very little reference to monetary considerations. That is the quintessence of my argument. *Every* piece of glass, no matter how humble, and irrespective of its cash value or even its appearance, has the capacity to tell a story. It should be encouraged to do so in its own way.

It's story should be listened to dispassionately, without bias and with an open heart. It should be savoured for what it represents, not that which is imposed upon it. It should be enjoyed with a *joie de vivre* of innocent pleasure that celebrates its very being. To hear its tale solely to derive an assessment of whether it will wash its own face financially is tantamount to Philistinism.

And Stourbridge Glass, indeed any glass, deserves better than that.

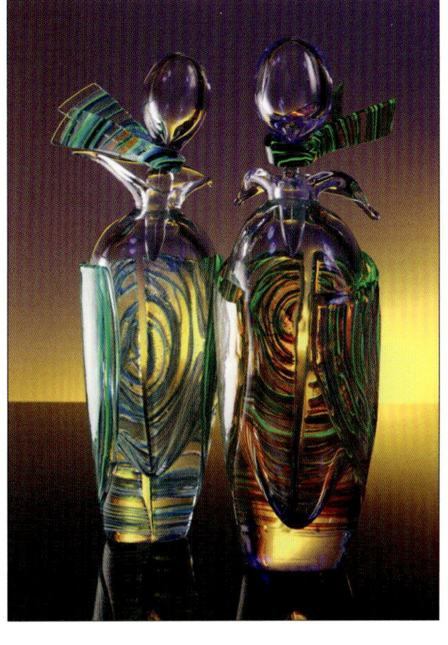

'Cloak' perfume bottles by Allister Malcolm. 35cm tall, coloured with a uranium content.
Photo: Simon Bruntnell
www.northlightphotography.co.uk

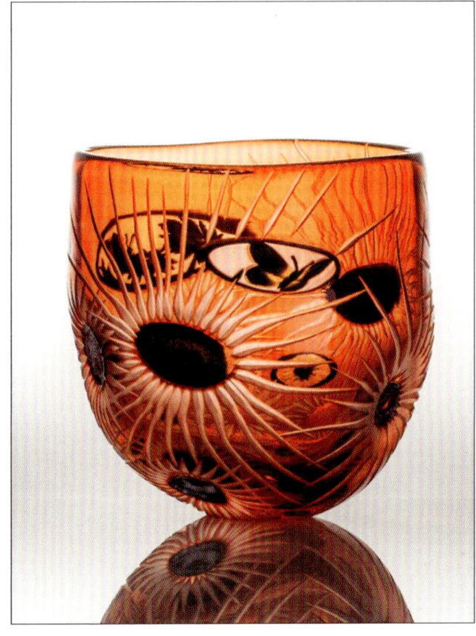

Vase, 25cm tall in innovative padded cameo ('Padeo') technique by Allister Malcolm and Helen Millard.
Photo: Lara Jane Thorpe
www.larajanethorpephotography.com

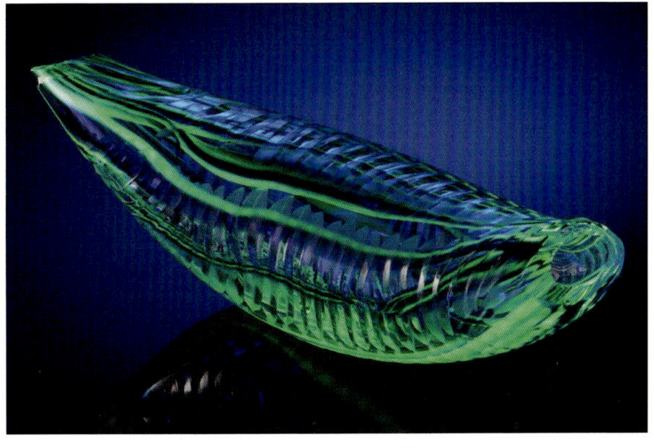

Cut crystal piece, 40cm across by Allister Malcolm who describes this as 'a contemporary approach'. Coloured with a uranium content.
Photo: Simon Bruntnell
www.northlightphotography.co.uk

Scratching the Surface

The Power of Glass - a case study

I HAVE RELATED, adequately I trust, the capacity for sheer excitement and the thrill of uncovering tales of the past that can be experienced in a piece of glass and by little more exertion than the simplest of enquiries or nugget of good fortune. Both are at play in this absolutely true scenario that not only proves my point but which has taken me down an absorbing route of personal discovery that continues to fascinate as I uncover more.

The image shows three items from the collection of SIC, ie Sheila Iris Chapman, my mother. They came into our home when she re-married in 1992 following the death of my father some years earlier. We know that her husband and former *matelot*, Mervyn John Chapman ('Our Merv') had forebears in the Stourbridge Glass trade and, probably as a consequence, he owned various items of glass. All of these passed to SIC on his death in 2010.

As part of my illustration, mentioned earlier in this section, of the numerous elements of glassmaking I have not even referred to, I brought together three items from the SIC collection. At least one - the red heart - I suspected was a *frigger* (see FAVOURITE 10 for definition). But the others? Hmmm ... what to do?

I knew just the man, and quickly dispatched an email and the image to Ian Dury. He promptly replied that, yes, the heart most likely would have been a *frigger* cut from a piece of cullet and made for a loved one - he has one similar in his own *frigger* case. The holder appeared a novelty item. However, it was Ian's tantalizing comments on the pen that exercised

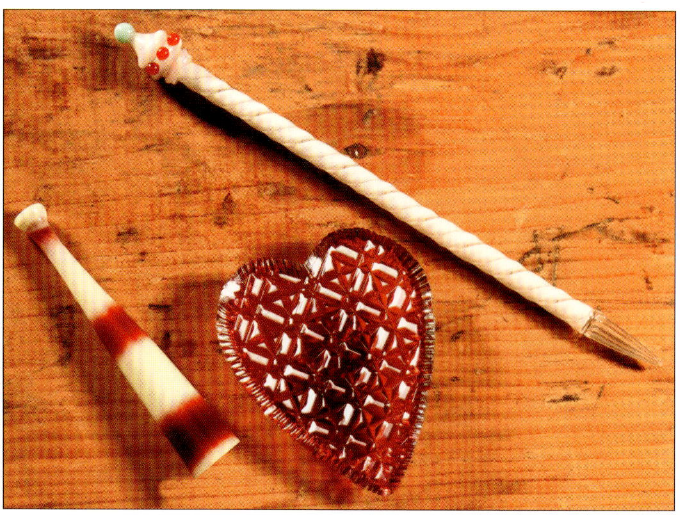

Left: novelty cigar holder, unlikely to be a production piece and almost certainly a *frigger*.
Centre: tri-colour cased heart in clear, ruby and opal overlay; the gently curved rear suggests the piece was salvaged from a previous item such as a bowl and re-worked. Most likely a *frigger* made for a loved one.
Right: white pen; Ah, therein lies a tale. (see opposite)
(with thanks to Ian Dury for his opinion and for his charming narrative that lead to my introduction to the Swingewood dynasty) (SIC)
Photo: Graham Dale

the little grey cells when I read: *'As for the glass pen I have seen something similar made by William Swingewood and which his grandson John and great grandson Paul now collect. I could give you details if required.'*

Details most certainly were required and a further exchange with Ian revealed a simply wonderful tale.

Ian Dury comments . . .

William Swingewood was working around the 1940s if memory serves me correct.

His wife gave birth to a son but sadly died a week afterwards. As there was no NHS the midwife was given items of his lamp work as a thank you.

When I held a glass valuation day last February with Will Farmer of Fieldings Auctioneers some early visitors were the current Swingewoods, father and son, who had brought in examples of their forebear's work for valuation.

Half an hour after they left a gent from Cannock came in with items that had been given as a thank you to his mum when she was a midwife. Will Farmer put two and two together and realised that this man's mother delivered the man that had just been in beforehand.

Unfortunately the first man had left and we had no contact numbers. We thought this would make a wonderful story. The Express & Star did a feature on it and asked for public help in tracking the Swingewoods. Eventually we tracked him down and arrange a meeting between the two men.'

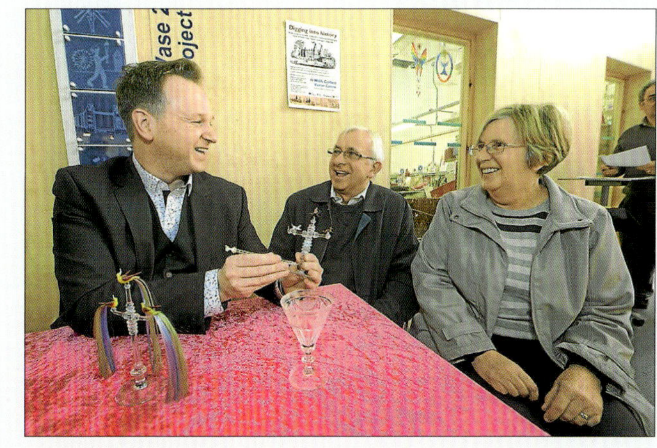

Will Farmer pictured with Graham and Pat Morris
Photo: Express & Star

Ian concluded his extraordinary narrative with a contact number for John. A short time later I was on the telephone to him, followed by a call to his son Paul, who confirmed that both his grandfather and great grandfather were named William Henry Swingewood and both made glass pens. The image I sent him needed some clarification - was it his great grandfather's hand, his grandfather's or even someone else altogether? I waited anxiously on that one as Paul promised to deliberate with his father John.

William Swingewood Jnr
Photo: Express & Star

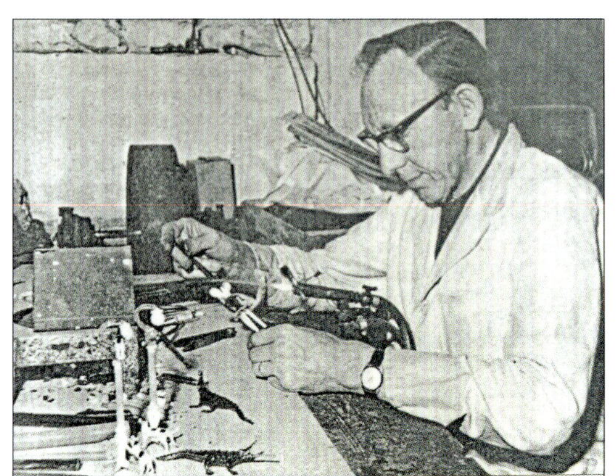

In the meantime they also kindly referred me to the articles in the Express & Star newspaper that give a fuller account. Go to **www.expressandstar.com** and type 'Swingewood glass' in the search field - it's all there, including a fine image of William Jnr at work with his flame.

A couple of days later, back come the response from Paul:

Paul Swingewood comments . . .

Hello Graham.

Good news. We've had a good look through the family glass and we're confident this is one of William Henry Junior's. (My grandad). He didn't make many and they don't have the same appearance and flair that my great-grandad's did.

I have attached a picture of one from my great-grandad. You can see the difference in style. This is the full pen holder and pen set. Grandad's were much plainer.

I hope that helps. If you need any Swingewood history just let me know. Also if it's possible I'd like to hear of any Swingewood glass that your readers might uncover; if you want to publish any of my contact details that would be great.

Good luck with the book

Best regards,

Paul

paul_swingewood@hotmail.com
0121 360 2881

OK, here is where you may need to get a hankie, because this is where the emotional bit really starts. On relating this incredible tale to my mother her reaction was typically big hearted; bless her. After a brief pause for thought she ventured: *'Hmmm ... it's been lying anonymously in my cabinet for decades, and probably in Our Merv's for decades before that. It has been a joy for me to own and a* memento *of happy times but now I know all of this I think it is time to complete the circle and return this to its rightful owner, don't you?'* Lo, did it come to pass.

And so by the time you learn of this, Dear Reader, the white pen that has 'lain anonymously' for these past years and which has given us all so much curious pleasure after a journey that has taken it who knows where, will have been returned to its spiritual home to once more delight the descendants of the man who actually made it.

So there we have it. For the researcher or enthusiast it doesn't come much better than this. A piece of glass of hitherto unknown origin that has lain in my mother's cabinet for a quarter of a century, and of which she doesn't know anything other than it is lovely to look at, suddenly assumes an entire *portmanteau* of provenance involving my family, a glassmaker with local connections, his family who are still extant and a succession of heartwarming meetings between diverse strangers from across the region and beyond, all brought together by an element of shared history of which they had no previous knowledge whatsoever. And all off the back of one small arcane piece of glass.

As oft am I wont to say; '*If that doesn't stir the soul then surely one has no soul to stir.*' The power of glass, indeed.

Now, see that little item on your mantelpiece? Go take a closer look ...

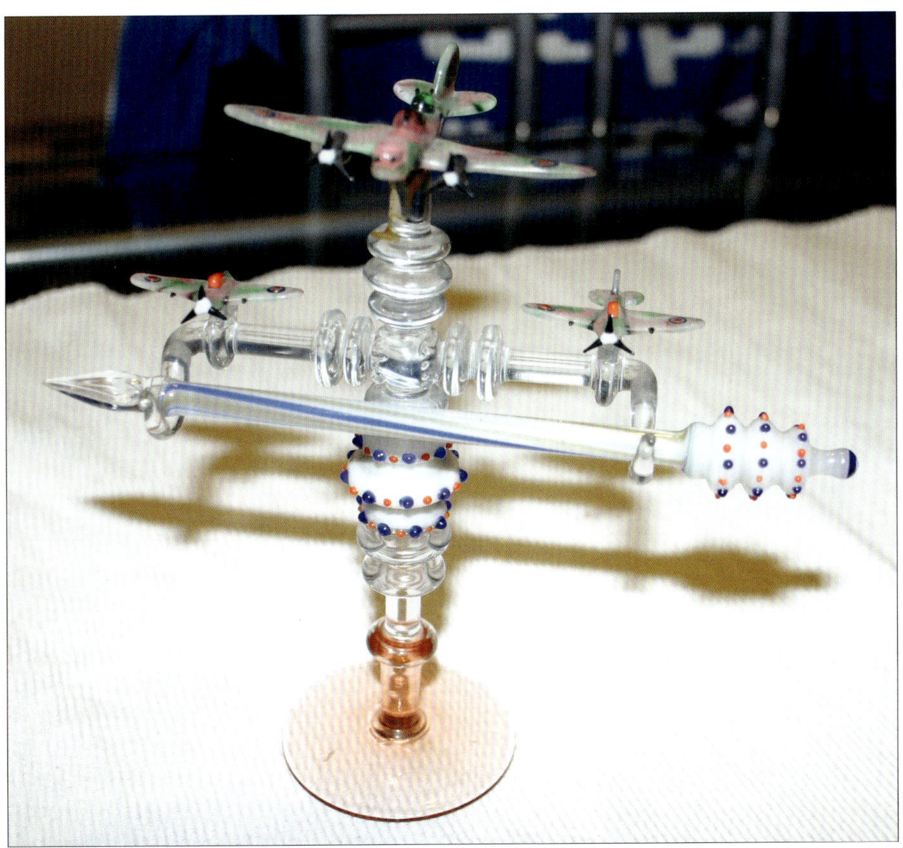

An elaborate penholder and pen made by William Swingewood Snr
Photo: Paul Swingewood

A Sting in the Tale *(sic)*

- the acid test

OUR EDITORIAL CONSULTANT Ian Dury has been in the glassmaking game long enough to know all the nooks and crannies of his arcane world, including some unsung heroes who, vital as their role may be within the Grand Scheme of things, he feels never seem to get the credit or recognition they deserve.

So it was he who suggested that for the sake of righting this wrong I might wish to pay a visit to a local company that many outside the business would never have even heard of yet who remain crucial in the production of high-calibre lead crystal for which the area is famous. He also tantalized me that he would reveal an intriguing fact after our sojourn.

Thus it was on a cool, bright morning in early March 2015 Ian and I found ourselves on an industrial estate in Silver End, Brierley Hill, at the premises of Wessex Crystal. This in itself took me aback a little since the unit at the end of the road once belonged to a friend of mine whom I had visited on numerous previous occasions without noticing this discreet, semi-anonymous low-roofed white building just a few yards away from its more cavernous neighbour.

Crossing the threshold into Wessex Crystal was like stepping into a parallel universe in which everything was in reality the same but paradoxically appeared somehow dissimilar; even the light outside shone differently from those errant beams that survived their transition through the cataracts of window panes. Within a sparse room not much bigger than most people's front parlour sat box upon box of glass ranging from domestic goblets and fancy-ware to bottles destined for a well-known whisky company, all vying for precious floor space as they awaited treatment in an array of rectangular tanks tucked along the far wall at the hands of men clad largely in curious rubber garb.

Directly opposite the entrance door a wooden staircase holding a patina that hinted it had already been there forever led to a secretive upper section with a measure of office space and comfort facilities but which was otherwise dominated by two cutting machines of 1960s vintage, old yet still capable of performing their duties faithfully for another several lifetimes, that were picked up for a song at auction when the big boys left town. Strewn slavishly in strategic positions around their masters were a huge variety of cutting discs and although I would never be competent to handle such equipment I took an innocent satisfaction in at least now knowing what they were as I noted the difference between the 'roughers' and the 'smoothers'. (see Favourite 7)

Acid Polishing

'The process of making a glossy, polished surface by dipping the object, usually of cut glass, into a mixture of hydrofluoric and sulfuric acids. This technique was developed in the late 19th century.'

... with acknowledgement to
http://www.cmog.org/glass-dictionary/acid-polishing

Proprietor Steven (Steve) Wright, who works here alongside his son Arron and brother-in-law Martin, is a time-served glass cutter; hence the machines up yonder. But between them the three men comprise one of the last remaining teams in the UK that specialises in the noble art of acid dipping. Let me tell you, happy enough as they seem in their work whatever these chaps earn it's not enough.

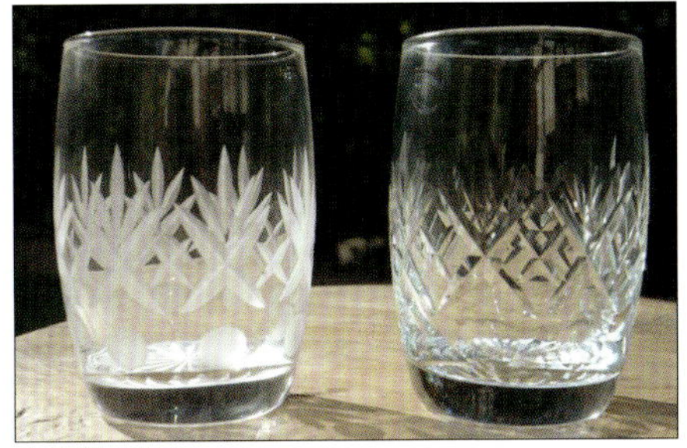

Before and after: diamond cut (left) and polished (right)
Photo: Graham Fisher

Acid dipping is a technique whereby crystal glass - the technique isn't really all that suitable for lead-free although it can be done - is immersed in decidedly corrosive acid to remove blemishes, smooth the cuts and give a sparkle of brilliance to the finished product. The length of dipping is largely down to the skill of the dipper and varies from piece to piece, being diversely influenced by factors such as glass composition, thickness and style of cut and the final sheen that is required.

Dipping is rarely for more than a few minutes since the longer the immersion the greater the erosion that in turn may render the cut too smooth or flat. At worst it can make a fine piece of hand-cut crystal look like a cheaper pressed piece, which is, of course, unsatisfactory. At the other end of the timescale Ian reminded me that his 2012 Portland Vase cameo objects, which were dipped here, needed but a few seconds - less than double figures - in the dip just to take off the chalkiness and emphasize the gleam; anything longer would have seen their entire outer engraved layer stripped away. Powerful stuff.

Three tanks are used. The first contains the acid in which the items are dipped before being rinsed and inspected in the second tank, which is full of water. Then it's back and forth between the two until the desired effect is achieved. The third tank is where the spent acid mixture is eventually diluted down for safe disposal. It's not cheap and Steve was more than a mite pained to tell me how prices for his raw acid constituents alone had tripled in the past

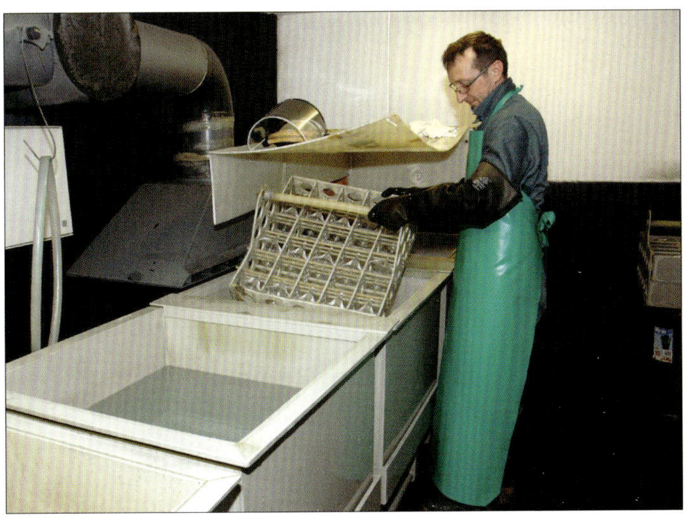

Martin dips the tray of glasses into the second tank
Photo: Graham Fisher

decade or so, with extra charges on top for handling and transfer brought about by ever more stringent Health and Safety requirements.

The dipping solution - don't try this at home, kids - is a mixture of hydrofluoric acid (HF) and sulphuric acid (H_2SO_4) producing a noxious potion that is perfectly capable of eating quickly through many things including, of course, lead-based supercooled amorphous silica. Glass, that is. The steel industry uses a similar brew in its pickling tanks. Mere human flesh and bones offers no resistance whatsoever so thick rubber gloves, aprons and other protective items are the order of the day together, naturally, with a good deal of common sense and working practices that afford due respect at all times to the venomous beast lurking in the corner.

Not so very long ago virtually every glassmaking facility would have had its own acid-dipping plant. But those days are gone. My visit to Wessex Crystal offered a fascinating insight into a diminishing world, a world that would wane even the quicker if the trend for lead-free glass took serious hold or if legislation simply proved too restrictive.

I can only wish Steve and his colleagues well on that score, for there is something indescribably sad in the very thought that one day all of this could be confined to the history books. Hence my thanks to Steve, Arron and Martin for the opportunity to experience it all before that may transpire.

Oh, and the intriguing fact Ian promised to reveal? Unknown to me until this point, there is a common thread to my favourite things that I would never have otherwise realized. Most of the manufacturers in the area use Wessex Crystal for their acid polishing. *Ergo*, virtually every one of my items most likely would have passed at some stage through these doors. My disparate collection of pieces, already treasured, suddenly becomes even the more intrinsically fascinating by dint of the connection. Now is that just uber-cool or what?

Wessex Crystal. 01384 481390. Tell them who sent you.

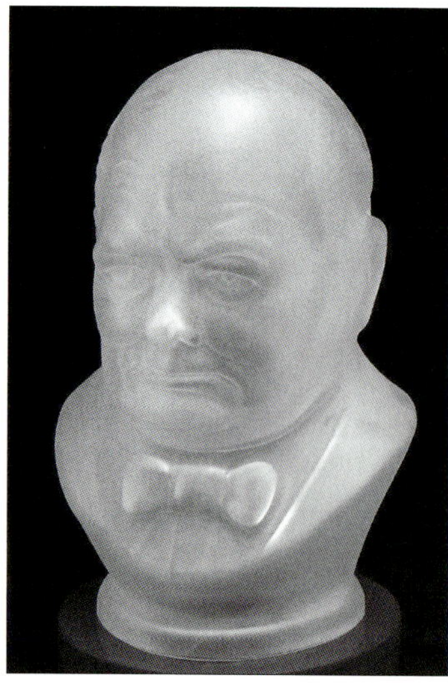

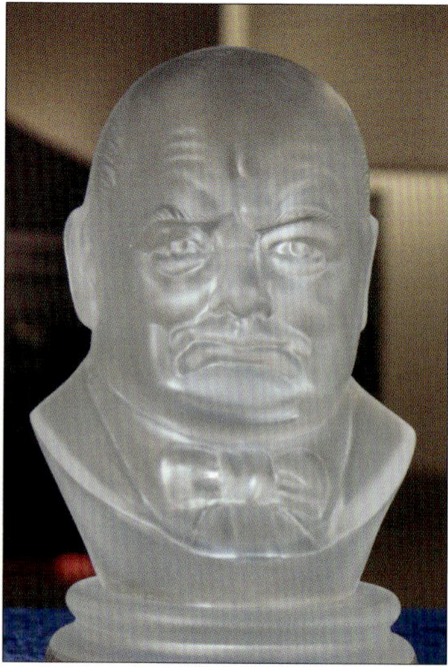

Before and after:
Bust of Sir Winston Churchill
Left: Sandblasted, ready for dipping
Photo: Tudor Crystal
Right: polished and complete
Photo: Webb Corbett Visitor Centre

Leonardo and the Art of Glassmaking

... formulaic skill or divine gift?

THE FOLLOWING IS MERELY an idea. I claim little intellectual rigour in its derivation but offer it as a catalyst for debate in the enduring quest to reconcile art and science. A theme that has exercised me since the halcyon days of my youth saw an article of mine titled *'How about artists and scientists getting together?'* finding its way into print way back in 1976. But it is my more recent induction into the world of glass, and my belief that the ostensibly polar opposites of art and science may in reality be far from mutually exclusive, that has revitalized my curiosity to re-examine the connection between high art and pure science from an alternate perspective; namely, the skills involved in glassmaking. For which, of course, Stourbridge is famous.

I will present the background to my conjecture before providing supportive observations upon which I will then offer my interpretation that, if ever validated, has the capacity to fundamentally modify our conceptualization of artistic ability and its expression. A bold claim, but we cannot soar with the eagles on the wings of a wren. Allow me to get airborne ...

First, the key player; a man whose name is now largely unknown outside the confines of his own arcane world. Which is *per se* a great dis-service since his discovery had astounding ramifications that still echo down the centuries.

Everywhere numbers are constantly at work and it was Bertrand Russell who suggested that *'numbers hold sway above the flux of life'.* Thus was it ever so and our hero of the moment is the Italian mathematician Leonardo of Pisa (c1170 - c1250) who, like Russell, was one of the finest minds of his day. For the record he is also known as Leonardo Pisano, Leonardo Pisano Bogollo, Leonardo Bonacci and, significantly in this context, Leonardo Fibonacci ('son of Bonacci'). His book *Liber Abaci*, published in 1202, examined a system of Hindu-Arabic numbering and featured the astonishing arrangement that came to be known by his name. It is said that he initially used the sequence to estimate the fastest rate at which rabbits could copulate but it proved to have far wider corollaries. Here it is ...

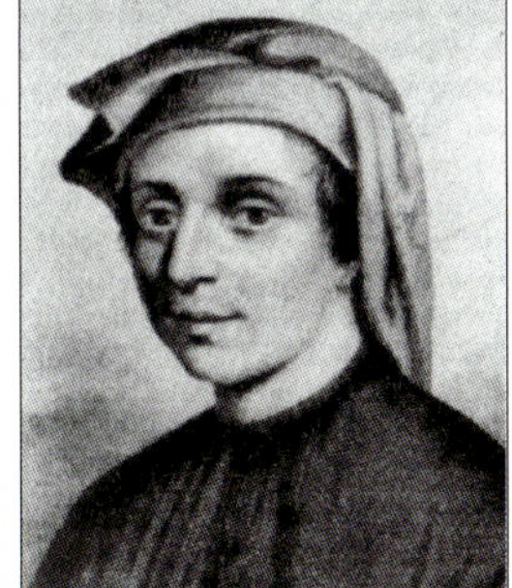
Leonardo Fibonacci

Fibonacci numbers comprise a progression beginning with 0 then 1 and followed by the addition of each succeeding number to its predecessor (sums shown in brackets) ie; 0, 1, 1 (0+1), 2 (1+1), 3 (2+1), 5 (3+2), 8 (5+3), 13 (8+5), 21 (13+8), 34 (21+13), 55 (34+21), 89 (55+34), 144 (89+55), 233 (144+89), 377 (233+144) and so forth *ad infinitum*.

Remove the sums for clarity and the sequence reads: 0, 1, 1, 2, 3, 5, 8, 13, 21, 34, 55, 89, 144, 233, 377 ...

Et voilà, here's the magic. In nature the number of petals on many flowers is a Fibonacci number. Some daisies, for example, have 34, 55 or 89 petals. There are numerous other instances of similar correlation to the extent that mathematician and philosopher Adolf Zeising (1810 - 1876) proposed it as a universal law of nature.

Fibonacci numbers in nature:

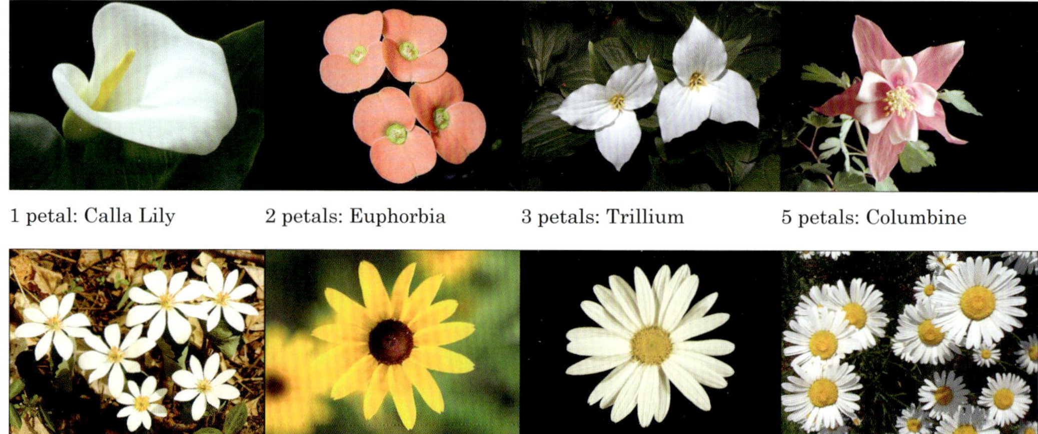

1 petal: Calla Lily | 2 petals: Euphorbia | 3 petals: Trillium | 5 petals: Columbine

8 petals: Bloodroot | 13 petals: Black-eyed Susan | 21 petals: Shasta daisy | 34 petals: Field daisies

But this is merely the beginning. If the larger number is divided by the one preceding it in the order then, ignoring the first few until everything settles, the ratio steadies out at 1.618 or thereabouts. This has become known as the Golden Ratio, Golden Mean or Divine Proportion and even has its own mathematical symbol, the Greek letter *phi* (Φ).

The ratio has been shown to be 'psychologically pleasing' in that it is a natural ratio that the eye coordinates to the brain. Thus, perchance, no surprise that its dimensions were deployed extensively throughout the Renaissance, albeit the artists may have had no more concrete reason to do so than its ease of assimilation as a format, perhaps even underpinning the expression of beauty being very much in the eye of the beholder.

Most books of the 16th century onwards conformed to these proportions until recent times and to this day artists and photographers still use a Fibonacci ratio as the most popular shape of canvas or image. Yet it would be interesting to hear how many would be willing to quantify why, other than 'it just looks right'.

And still the elegant beauty of the Fibonacci sequence unfurls. Take the lowest number and create a square of one unit, then place it adjacent to another of the same. Below these, place a 2-unit square then build up the squares. (Figure 1). The longer side of each square is the length of two successive Fibonaccis and each square has sides that are Fibonaccis. The *coup de grace*: describe a quarter circle in each of the squares (Figure 2) and behold; the shape of numerous *objets* that occur in nature, from nautilus shells to broccoli florets and even the human ear.

Figure 1

Figure 2

Fibonacci spirals in nature:

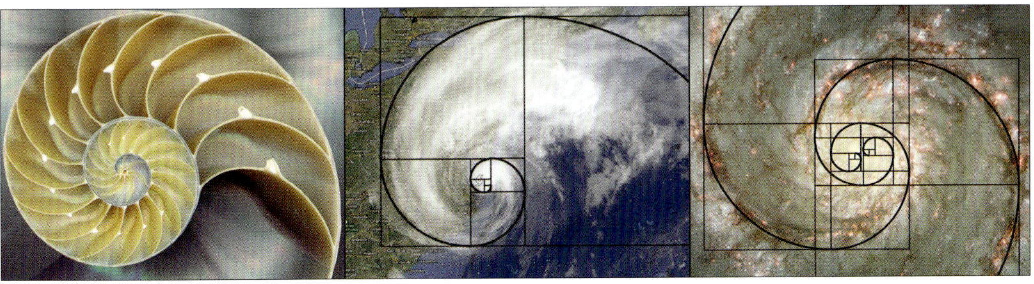

Nautilus shell — Hurricane spiral — Galaxy spiral

Let us hold this in abeyance for a while as I turn to the 2012 Portland Vase Project when Ian Dury, at the time the proprietor of Stourbridge Glass Engravers, brought together a team of artisans to recreate this iconic piece of Roman cameo glass for the 21st century.

I was official biographer for the venture and shadowed it throughout. Page 54 of the resulting book THE 2012 PORTLAND VASE PROJECT: RECREATION OF A MASTERPIECE (Sparrow Publishing 2012) records my modest attempt to capture the sheer brilliance of master glassmaker

Richard Golding as he started it all off by blowing the blanks on that historic day in September 2011. Mere words are almost inadequate to the task but I gave it my best shot when I wrote:

The Glassworker: A Personal Tribute

NOW I AM NOT, nor ever would I claim to be, a glassmaker. Even so, as part of my immersion in the industry as much as for my own edification, I have had a valiant stab at several of its processes, including making a draw from a furnace onto a blowing iron and forming it. Thus am I able to relate to an audience how skilful it all is, based on the unimpeachable rationale that I have at least attempted it myself. To watch a competent glass craftsman at work is mesmeric; to study an artisan such as Richard Golding is to find oneself in the presence of those who do not emanate from a world comprising ordinary mortals.

The effortless ease in which he teased just the right amount of molten glass onto his iron, as if it were of its own mind and eager to submit joyously unto his control; blowing it akin to a small balloon; dipping it into the white opal, draining off the excess, blowing again, constantly shaping, reheating, and shaping the nascent form with the focus and passion devoted to nurturing a tender child. His colleagues stood by, each with their role to fulfil at precisely the correct moment - a blob of melt for a handle, an opening of the glory hole door for a re-heat, the extending of an implement - each player responding to a gentle nod or subtle gesture by stepping into the Master's sphere before retiring to the fringes to watch earnestly lest they be summoned again.

Amongst a crowd, yet isolated in my thoughts, I was transfixed as, with an efficiency of movement and a deftness of touch that redefines sublime, he slowly, resolutely enticed that amorphous gobbet of semi-liquid into a masterpiece of exquisiteness that would feign serve the Gods themselves. This, dear reader, transcends mere talent; we were witnessing a gift that was nudging at the echelons of pure genius. And it was amazing; simply amazing.

Fast forward to May 2014 when I delivered a presentation on Stourbridge Glass to Pedmore Sporting Club. My host was Graham Knowles who, apart from being Chairman of the club at the time - and thus it being his role to source a speaker - is also Chairman of the British Glass Foundation of which I am a Trustee.

The BGF is seeking to create a world-class glass centre to house the equally world-famous Stourbridge Glass collection and I am optimistic that by the time this piece hits the shelves we are well on our way to achieving our aim on the old White House site (formerly Stuart Crystal) at Wordsley. Either that, or something hasn't gone quite to plan but let us not be negative. Anyway, back to the story in hand ...

Following my talk at Pedmore I was presented with a stunning glass bowl (Favourite 3) made by Allister Malcolm, a fellow BGF Trustee and at the time resident artist at Broadfield House Glass Musuem. It sits in pride of place at home, next to a couple of 'his and hers' glass tumblers that Allister presented to me on a previous occasion. These are little gems too, and in a delightful combination of artistic exuberance and sheer craftsmanship that for me typifies the

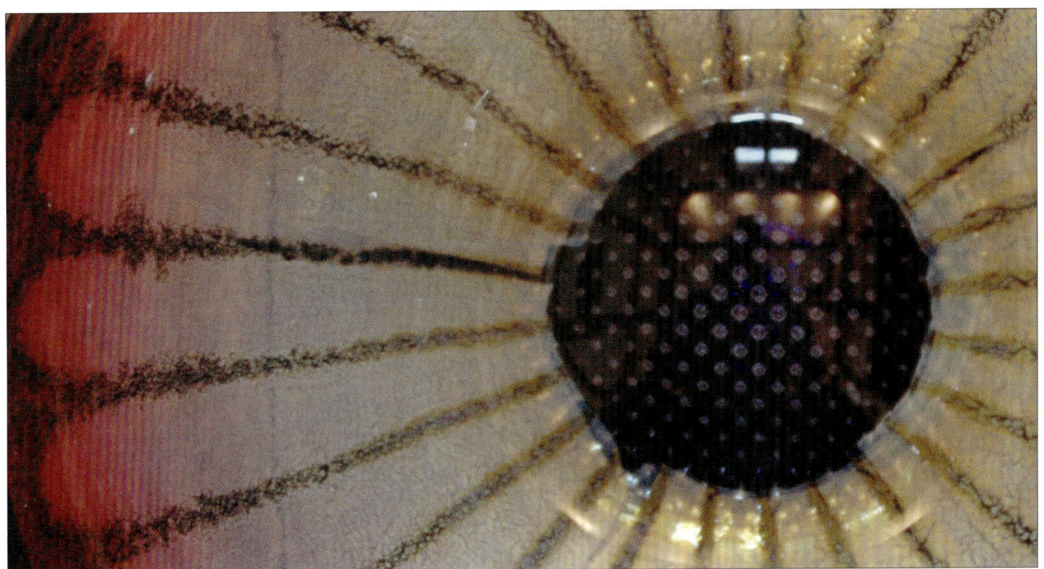

'Absolutely nothing. No correlation whatsoever … Until that is, I took another look at the glasses.'
Photo: Graham Fisher

man's output, their heavy bases, with a delightful whorl of coloured glass inside, are signed by Allister and inscribed: *'This one is to be used after a Bitch of a day'* (smaller) and *'This one is to be used after a Serious bitch of a day'* (larger).

I treasure these and frequently sit and contemplate them in the glow from the hearth on a dark evening or as the sun rises on them in the morning. And yet … and yet … I have no idea why, but one crisp dawn I was doing exactly that when I wondered if the amount of striations or patterns on Allister's bowl could be a Fibonacci number. For reasons unfathomable I was compelled to settle down with a magnifying glass to count every dot and marking in that bowl. The sun was high by the time I had finished. And my findings?

Absolutely nothing. No correlation whatsoever.

It was with considerable dejection that I placed the bowl back next to the glasses and rued my fool's errand. Until that is, I took another look at the glasses. The image of Sherlock Holmes admonishing his loyal chronicler *'You see, Watson, but you do not observe'* punctuated my thoughts as I made closer inspection of something I had looked at a thousand times but failed to observe; the whorls in their bases resembled nautilus shells. Not exact, I confess, but near enough to rekindle my excitement as I scrabbled to find the telephone to ring Allister. The burning question on my mind: 'Was this something he had done deliberately, consciously and knowingly or did it simply 'just look right?'

Allister is usually busy working with molten glass so he can't always get to the phone very quickly. As the tone burr-burred I passed the few seconds by making a wager; I bet myself a tenner

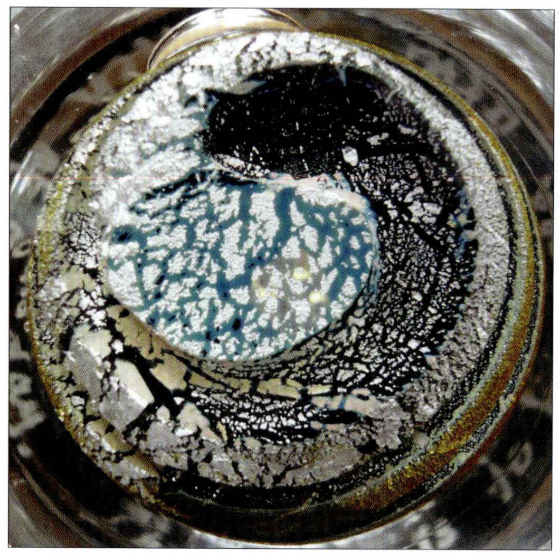

The whorl within the tumbler base
Photo: Mary Spence

that Allister would dismiss me, courteously, as some sort of crank.

I lost.

It transpired that Allister had learnt about Fibonacci in his undergraduate days and was familiar with the Golden Mean to the extent that he had on occasions discussed it during collaborations with a glassmaking colleague. It was not something he had particularly engaged with in his work but he had found it a useful bookmark when exchanging ideas that 'didn't quite look right' by dint of being outside of what he felt was 'pleasing proportions'. So, the acid question; was the shape in the base of his glasses deliberate or unplanned? *'I never gave it a thought'* *he told me. 'It's just how I made them ... but now you come to mention it ...'*

I allude once more to the Master Detective and *The Adventure of the Greek Interpreter*, when Holmes, describing how his own talents *'may have come with my grandmother, who was the sister of Vernet, the French artist'* remarks to Watson: *'Art in the blood is liable to take the strangest forms'*. The quote is particularly prescient here since art surely takes no stranger form than the ability to manipulate a blob of molten silica into a thing of exquisite beauty. But, in what amounts to a slant on the classic nature-nurture conundrum, how much of this is *'a gift ... nudging at the echelons of pure genius'* (above) or to what extent, however subliminally, are such talents the consequence of a pragmatic rationale that is yet to be quantified?

And this is the very quintessence of the discussion; if such talent is cogently quantifiable then it can be distilled to its fundamentals and expressed as a strand of logic, represented by a mathematical function. That being the case it can be learnt. *Ergo*, if it can be learnt, *it can be taught*. Thus, by extraction, its teaching is not constrained by geography or timescale.

The implications of communicating across divides by means of prescription - and to store in retrieval systems for future generations - that which we presently consider to be almost divine are truly awesome. Yet the broader principle is a valid one that is already employed routinely by those teaching cognitive skills. Consider driving a motor vehicle, for example:

The coordination required for someone unfamiliar with a car to learn to control it, as many a 17 year old will testify, is a formidable cognitive task. The task is made the more palatable by breaking down the action of, say, changing gear for the first time into a series of steps whereby each step is represented by a succession of the simplest elements to which the task can be reduced. Master each element in sequence - crucial, or the entire deck of cards collapses - then put them all together for the completed action.

Hey presto; a crossover between cognitive and psychomotor behaviour - the distillation of basic motion elements to a series of *therbligs*, thus named by Frank Bunker Gilbreth (1868 - 1924), a time-and-motion specialist who branded his brainchild by spelling his surname backwards.

Broadly analogous to *therbligs* in terms of function, algorithms were known in ancient times *(viz Euclid of Alexandria)* but have been elevated in our consciousness more recently with the massive expansion in computer technology and programming.

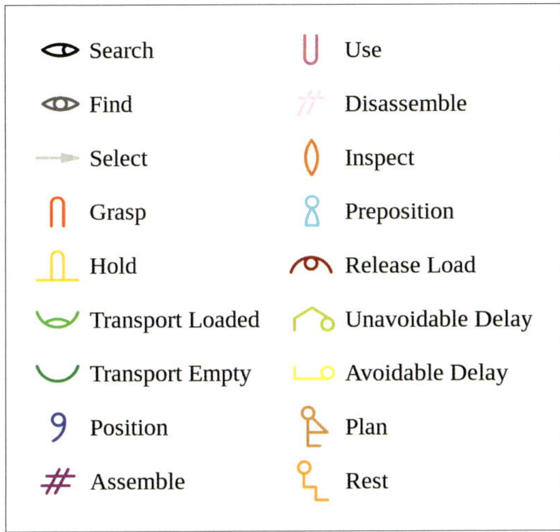

The basic motion elements or *therbligs*

Quite simply, an algorithm is a step-by-step procedure - *à la* therblig - for calculating, data processing and even the somewhat sinister-sounding *automated reasoning*. Commencing from an initial pre-determined state, which could be zero, the algorithm describes a computation that proceeds through a finite number of defined states until its objective is attained.

Unless one has somehow remained impossibly isolated from the contemporary world then we are all now exposed to algorithms routinely - and often without even realizing it - in our daily lives. Accessing a bank account, using a loyalty or credit card, virtually every on-line transaction; the list goes on - all are based on increasingly powerful algorithms that were the stuff of wild imaginings just a few years ago. *Moore's Law*, named after Gordon E Moore who founded the Intel ('Integrated Electronics') Corporation, suggests that computing power increases exponentially by doubling approximately every two years. Whilst this is more correctly an observation rather than demonstrable fact his 'law' has proved unerringly accurate and has been used as the basis for setting targets for research, development and sales. It is thus a plausible *sequitur* to postulate that it is merely a matter of time before psychomotor skills, including glassmaking, may similarly be decanted and represented by a formula as a function of automated reasoning.

I contend it is not a question of if, but when. The period that it may take to still be at a state of inconclusiveness should be viewed as an incentive more than a deterrent. The Higgs-Boson particle, now identified courtesy of the CERN Large Hadron Collider, was but a fantastical notion in the mind of David Higgs and his colleagues for over forty years. Similarly, not quite there but getting ever closer, the as-yet unexpressed 'theory of everything', which unifies discrepancies by coherently bringing together all known theories of the universe, has been pondered by Steven Hawking, his contemporaries and their predecessors for generations.

By these yardsticks the formulation of an encryption founded on the principle of Fibonacci that may be primal to glassmaking and other artistic skills would appear to be relatively small beer. Its discovery may ultimately prove to be by a fortunate individual who has the good providence to see further than others by standing on the shoulders of giants (© I. Newton) and simply inserting the final piece in a complicated jigsaw.

Should it then be possible to remotely interchange these skills is quite another matter. As is the question of whether we even consider this desirable, which raises issues of morality and ethics. Do we embrace such developments with the optimistic anticipation of Huxley's *Brave New World* or do we reject them in trepidation as a nightmarishly Orwellian analogy of *1984*? Ah, I see the cue to take my bow, for it will require far finer minds that mine to negotiate through that one.

In the meantime, casting science aside I shall continue to frequent the Glass Quarter and marvel at these *virtuosos*, for surely that is what they are, plying their mesmerizing art in time-honoured fashion. Do join me there; I guarantee you will be impressed.

The Golden Ratio can be seen in many disciplines . . .

. . . in architecture

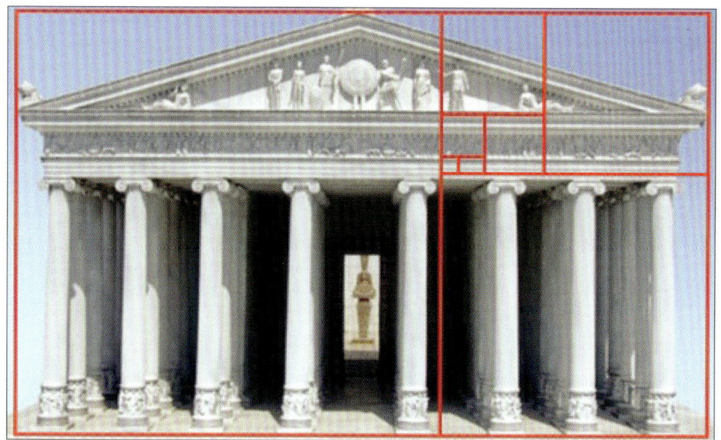

. . . in art

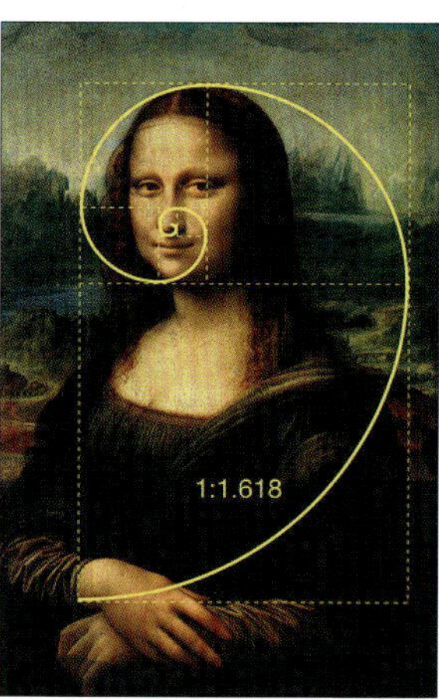

. . . in photography

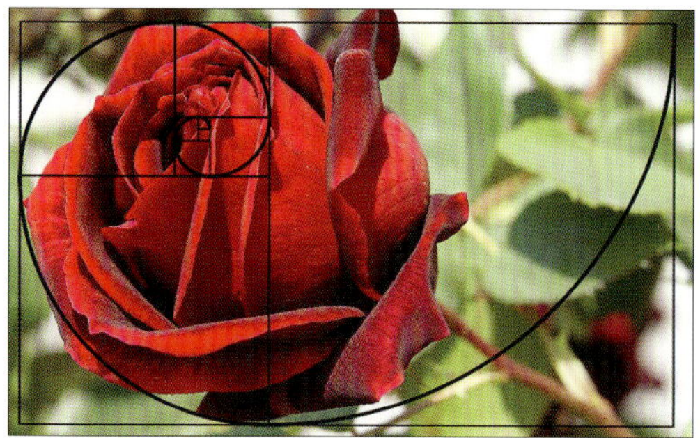

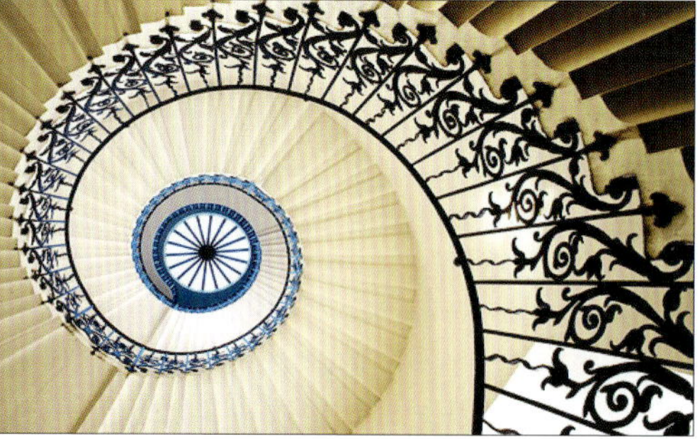

This chapter is based on an article which appeared in the *The Blackcountryman* in Spring 2015

It's the Last Word from Me ...

MY USUAL *MODUS OPERANDI* is to write a book or feature, gauge it's success then take it 'on the road'. This one was something of a first insomuch that I did things backwards - the talk before the book - and so such reckless deviancy surely merits an explanation. Here's how it came about ...

At FAVOURITE 3, the Allister Malcolm bowl and drinking glasses, I made reference to a talk I gave at the Pedmore Sporting Club in May 2014. The thrust of this particular chat was the significance of Stourbridge Glass and the area's importance both historically and for the future.

Following this talk I was asked by Barbara Beadman, Chair of Friends of Broadfield House Glass Museum (FOBH) if I would do similar for their Christmas party on 5th December that same year. Other than something to do with glass the choice of subject was left to me. OK, no problem. Quick thinks ... it being a Christmas bash this clearly had to be something that was as entertaining as it was informative, perhaps even more so.

The basis for the talk was described in A Writer Explains and, as noted in Acknowledgements, my original working title of *Raindrops on Roses* was ditched when my other half suggested the much snappier *Whiskers on Kittens*. Many thanks indeed to her for that. Hence the story of how this originally started out as a 'one-off' bespoke presentation for FOBH and, with the quirky title just crying out for a quirky exposition, thus came the idea of it being presented by felines with only intermittent assistance from me. This was developing nicely.

As the preparations for a PowerPoint progressed it became evident there was potential for something beyond this and I began to see an opportunity for simultaneously promoting the British Glass Foundation, the Stourbridge Glass industry, various exponents within it, some of its greatest achievements especially the magnificent 2012 Portland Vase Project and much, much more. To do so with any measure of perpetuity would require this to be recorded - a book. Therein lies a problem.

I can handle a camera with modest proficiency and my efforts are up to the task for an evening's PowerPoint. But a book - something of longevity that may be referred to in a distant land in a far away time - now that is a different level of expertise, especially when photographing glass. Step forward my good friend and broadcasting compatriot Graham Dale, who happens also to be an ace professional photographer of many years experience. On a glorious summer's day in 2014 he visited me to ascertain the job was viable; we parted with the agreement that if I were to proceed with the book he would undertake the requisite images. He got the gig.

The inaugural presentation of Whiskers was, as planned, delivered in the Cameo Room at Broadfield House Glass Museum on Friday 5th December 2014. I thoroughly enjoyed the evening but whether I was actually any good is not for me to say. Let me instead offer the following piece that was penned by Roger Noons of FOBH for submission to *Cameo*, their in-house magazine. My thanks to him for allowing me to reproduce it here *verbatim*.

Roger Noons writes . . .

The Friends of Broadfield House Glass Museum
Whiskers on Kittens

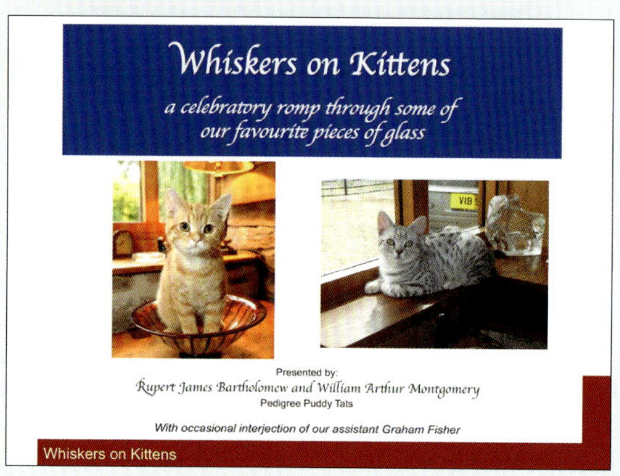

Whiskers on Kittens

He promised us a 'romp' and he delivered. No-one romps better that Graham Fisher MBE, who entertained Friends at their Christmas event. During his presentation, loosely based on the idea of Desert Island Discs, he didn't choose any records but on a couple of occasions, he did sing to us. His title came from the song, as many people knew; *These are a few of my favourite things*. He didn't however get too carried away, as his mum was there to keep an eye on him.

Graham, a waterways specialist with a passion for glass, has dedicated much of his life to the local canals alongside which many of the famous glass factories were or are situated. The two, inextricably linked, therefore fill him with joy and satisfaction. He stressed how he admired glass people, not only for their skills in making, blowing, carving or engraving, but for their humility and generosity.

Using projected images, Graham showed us ten favourites from his collection, many of which had little or unknown monetary value, but meant an enormous amount to him. Whilst not always in perfect condition, they were precious, often because they had been gifts, personally engraved, or acquiring them had related to special occasions in his life. The pieces included a wine glass, a chunk of cullet, unfinished and modified portions of blanks, a bowl, a decanter, tumblers, paperweights and what appeared to be a Sherlock Holmes chin-warming pipe, in solid glass.

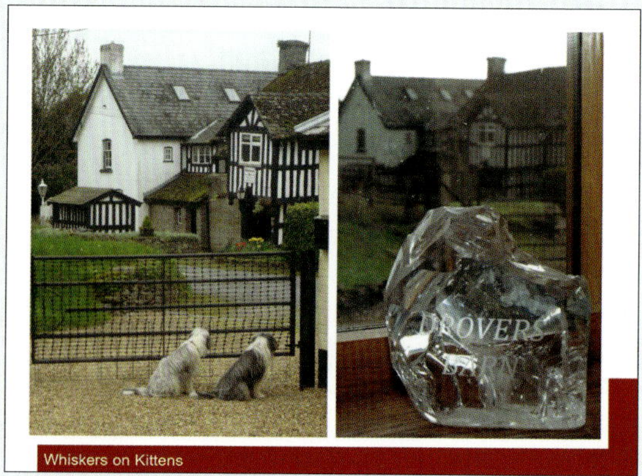

Whiskers on Kittens

At the end of his talk, he uncovered a number of the pieces about which he had spoken and Friends were able to examine and discuss them. The highlight of the evening however, came when he presented his mother with a repaired pendant which had been broken *(the Terri-Louise Colledge piece,* Favourite 2 *- Author)*. It was special to both of them as it featured a portion of one of the models for the Portland Vase Project, with which Graham had been involved.

In a dart back to the long running radio programme, Graham produced what, had Kirsty been interviewing him, would have been his choice of extra book, *Bradshaw's Canals and Navigable Rivers of England and Wales*. He is proud of his copy which it turned out had been bound upside down.

Before Friends retired to the café for festive food and drinks, Graham shared his philosophies. Don't hide your glass away, use it, enjoy looking at it. If it gets damaged, then you can always get some more. Buy glass for yourself and as gifts for others, share your pleasure of owning it.

Whiskers on Kittens

a celebratory romp through some of our favourite pieces of glass

Job Done. Time for a nap.

Thank you and bye bye.

With love from ...
Rupert and William.

'Dogs have masters, cats have staff'

Whiskers on Kittens

Rupert and William, his two pedigree cats, had they been present, would no doubt have been as pleased with his performance, as were the two legged creatures who made up the audience.

Thank you, Graham.
Roger Noons
Friends of Broadfield House
Glass Museum

A most generous tribute, for which I am much obliged. And, largely on the strength of which, the book you now hold in your hands went ahead.

I DO HOPE you have enjoyed this unashamedly celebratory romp through the wonderful world of Stourbridge Glass. Even more so, I would dearly love to think that it may encourage you to take a closer look at what is, for me, one of the greatest glass industries the world has ever seen and to share my very great pleasure in having come to know both it and its gifted practitioners.

Keep the faith. Keep it glass.

Thank you.
GF

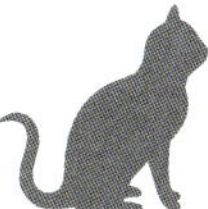

… and it's the Very Last Word from Him

I HAVE COLLABORATED with Ian Dury extensively over the last few years, not least when he granted me the priceless accolade of being the biographer for his eponymous 2012 Portland Vase Project, and I have consistently been impressed by his refreshing honesty and frankness when it comes to glass. Or anything else, for that matter.

In December 2013 Ian kindly invited me to draw his celebrated project to a close with the launch of my book IN OUR TIME whereby the creation of the vase and other artifacts was formally acknowledged as being completed before moving into the next phase of securing their provenance in history. In recording my indebtedness to him once more for his unstinting support in my work it is fitting that I now return the compliment in bringing this tome neatly to a close by my recounting of some characteristically scattergun remarks Ian threw my way one afternoon.

For me, his random yet prescient observations epitomize the contemporary attitude to glass, especially amongst the young, and offer evidence from a man working at the 'sharp end' as to where it all went awry but equally provide some indication as to where future manufacturing and marketing opportunities may lie.

Ian, dear friend, for this and everything else you have done to help me navigate my way through the wonderfully arcane world of amorphous supercooled silicate; many thanks. This bit is all yours.

Author.

IAN DURY WRITES . . .

I quote my daughter when she was setting up her first home:

'I want a plain glass to drink from when I have my Chinese take-away. I can put it in the dishwasher. If it gets broken it can easily be replaced and won't cost the earth'.

My reply was that she needed to go to Ikea. Which is exactly what she did.

The sad fact is that companies like Stuart did have plain glassware ranges but the economic reality was that melting glass in a one-ton pot was not a viable option as the pass-rate at inspection was so low. I seem to recall that at one stage only around 30% of output was deemed good enough to be classified as first quality. We were geared to a different market, a market that was seriously in decline.

Backstamping started in the early 20th century whereby company logos or trade marks were etched on a piece to signify it had passed all relevant inspections. Items not making the grade were sold as seconds at typically 33% less than High Street retail prices. Whilst this was a significant component in the company's finances it could never be a sound basis for long-term sustainability.

The 'continual manufacturers' invested in new technology, with tank furnaces operating around the clock to produce a continuous flow of good quality glass. This, together with automated gathering and blowing, meant that we simply could not compete either on price or quality.

Stuart and Royal Brierley, amongst others, did install tank furnaces in the late 1980s but by then it was too late. Together with the other factors you have alluded to here, this all led to the ultimate demise of a once-great industry as we interpreted it.

However, I am always fascinated when I see 'new' patterns being brought out today by famous designers such as Jasper Conran *et al*. In my honest opinion, they just seem to go through old pattern books of designs by the likes of our own Iris Stevens and John Luxton and reinvent them. There is nothing out there that has not been done before and your earlier comment of *plus ça change plus c'est la meme chose*. (The more it changes the more it's the same thing) rings very true to me.

Glass, made with the most basic of elements, fused by heat and crafted by hand has the capacity to last virtually forever and will certainly long outlive its creators. Museums around the world are testament to this fact; the original Roman Portland Vase in the British Museum is over 2000 years old.

Proof, if proof were needed, that when cherished and handled with care every piece of Stourbridge Glass, no matter how small its size or insignificant its market value, represents a piece of glassmaking heritage that was created by a team of glassworkers all of whom took an inordinate amount of pride in their work.

Amen to that Ian; much obliged.
GF

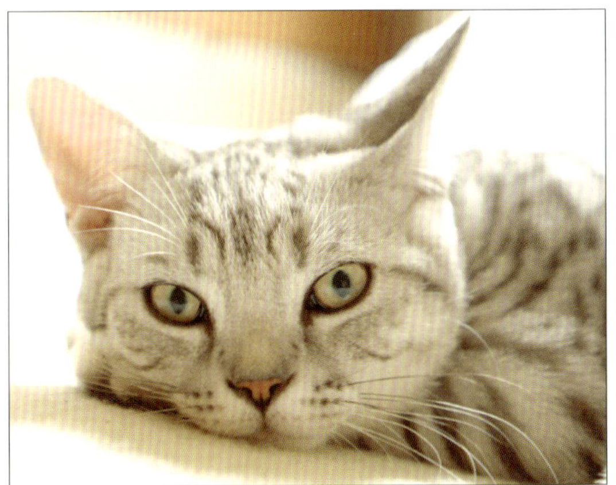

'Hear, hear!' says William
Photo: Graham Dale

Overleaf:
Rupert James Bartholomew in his favourite glass bowl with William Arthur Montgomery awaiting his turn
Photo: Graham Dale

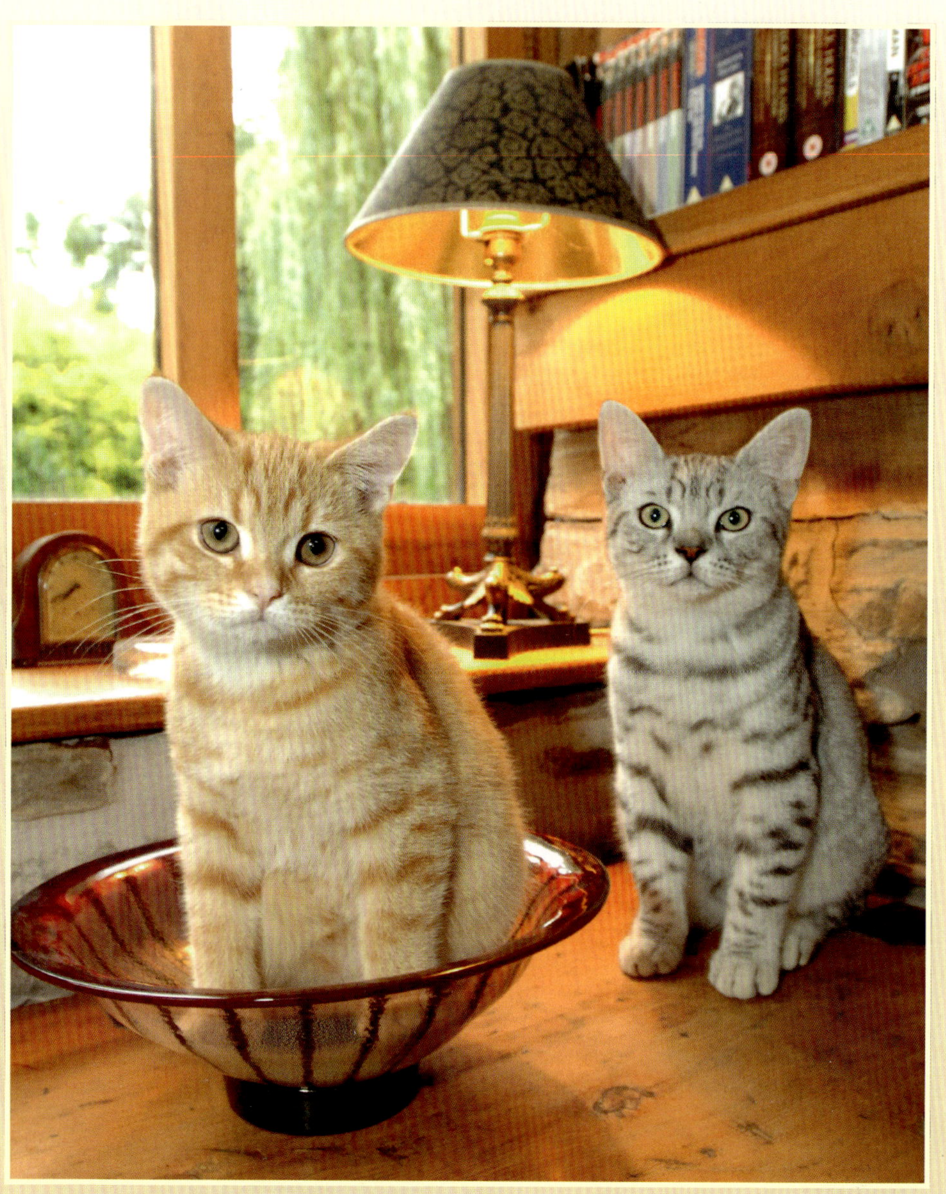

And it's 'Bye bye' from Us

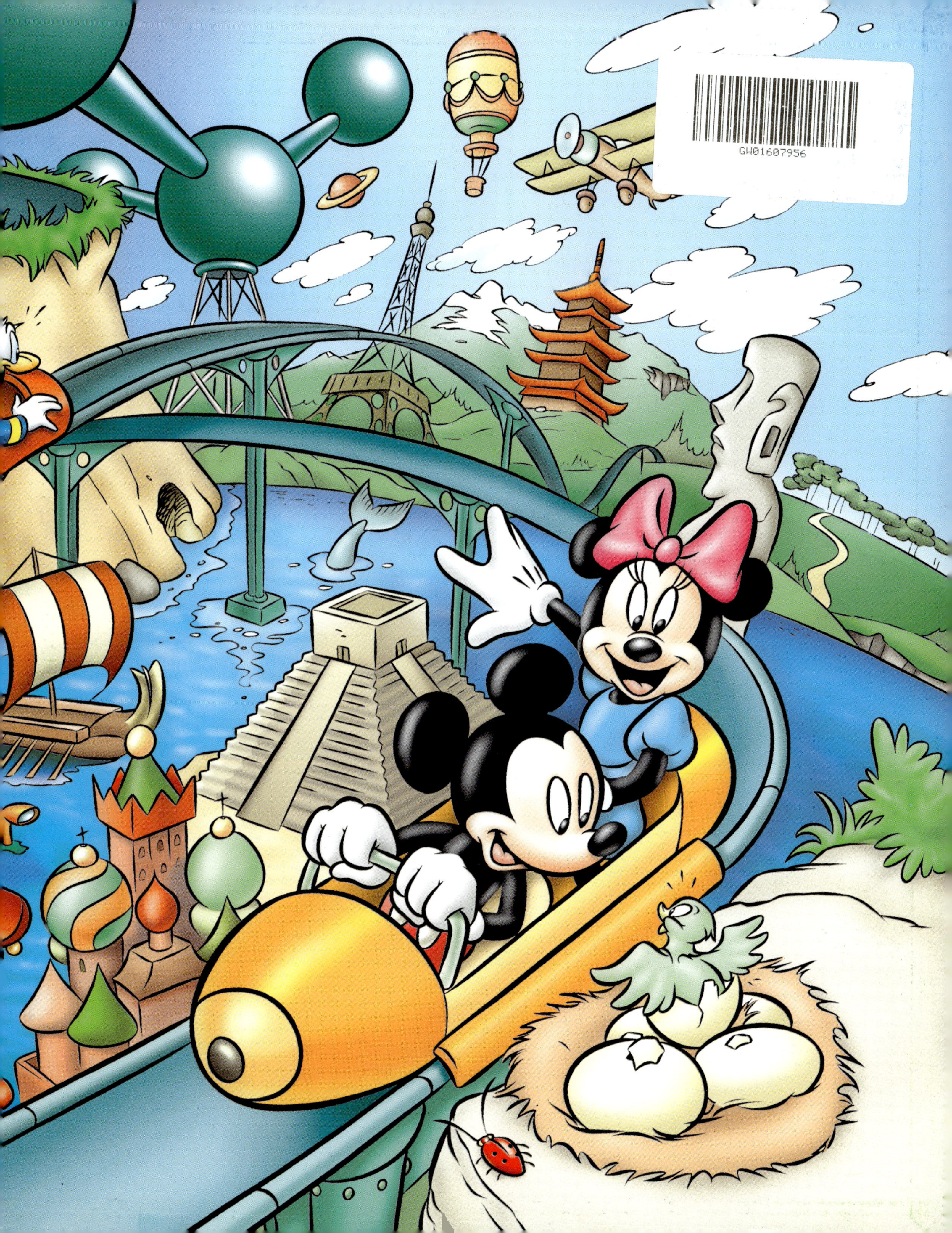
GW01607956

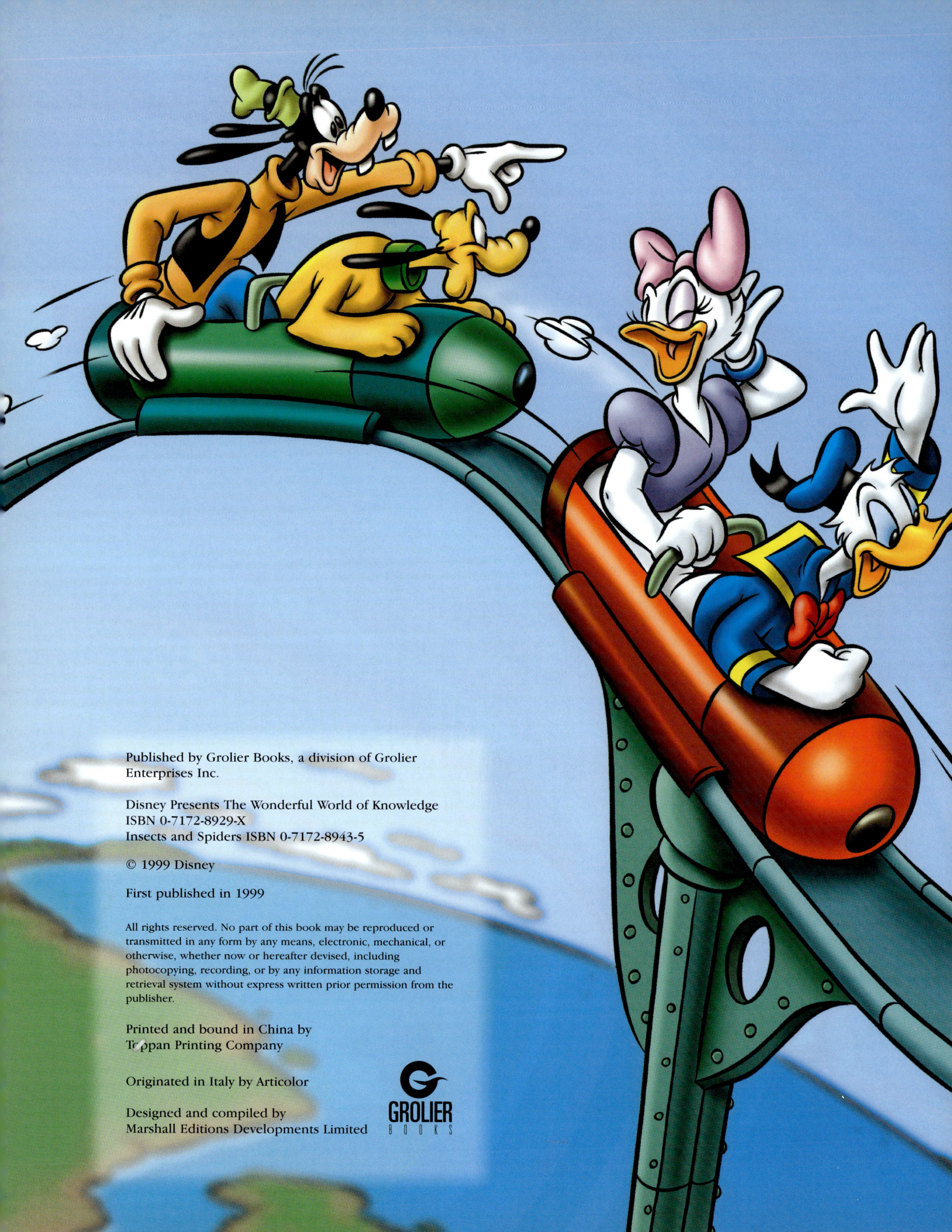

Published by Grolier Books, a division of Grolier Enterprises Inc.

Disney Presents The Wonderful World of Knowledge
ISBN 0-7172-8929-X
Insects and Spiders ISBN 0-7172-8943-5

First published in 1999

Printed and bound in China by
Toppan Printing Company

Originated in Italy by Articolor

Designed and compiled by
Marshall Editions Developments Limited

GROLIER
BOOKS

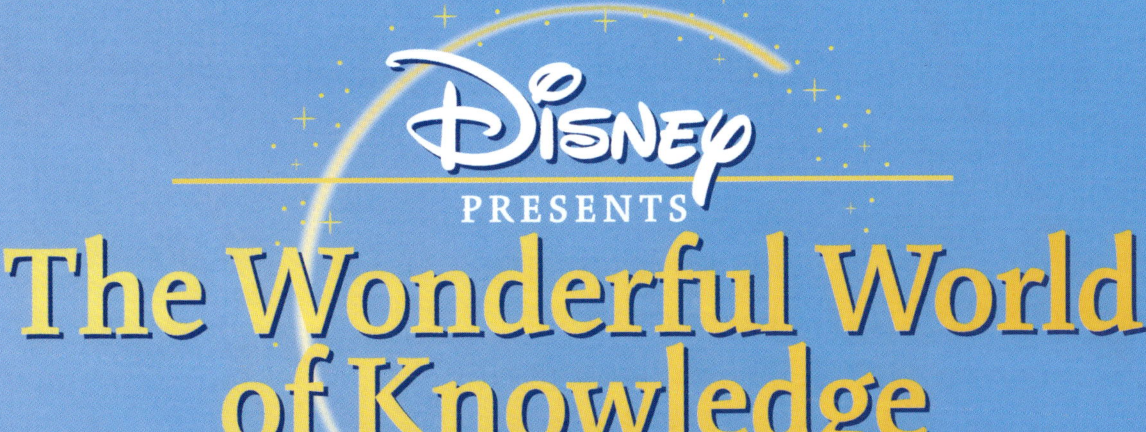

Insects and Spiders

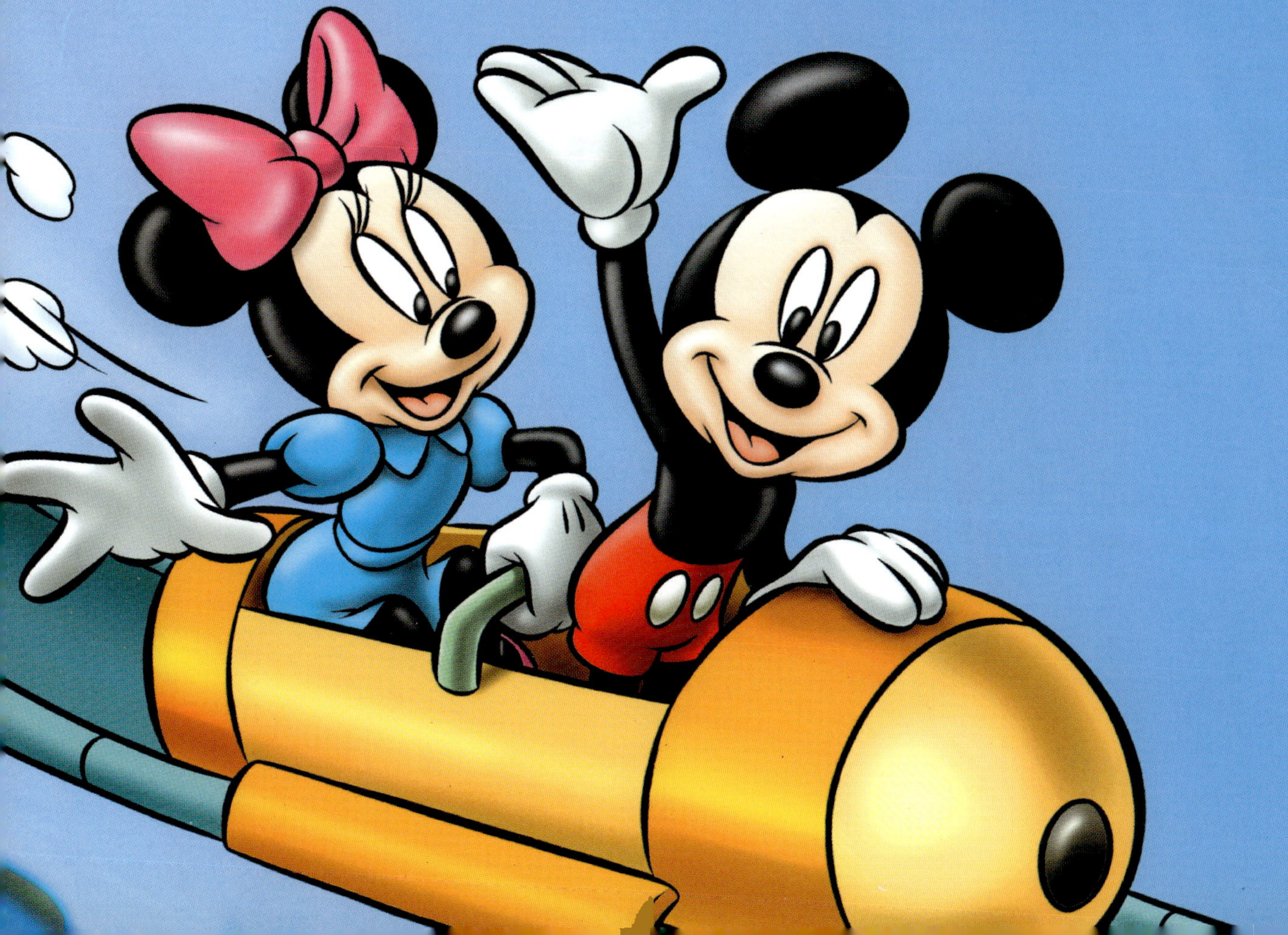

Using The Wonderful World of Knowledge

Mickey, Minnie, Donald, Daisy, Goofy, and Pluto are ready to take you on an adventure ride through the world of learning. Discover the secrets of science, nature, our world, the past, and much more. Climb aboard and enjoy the ride.

Look here for a general summary of the theme

Labels tell *you what's happening in the pictures*

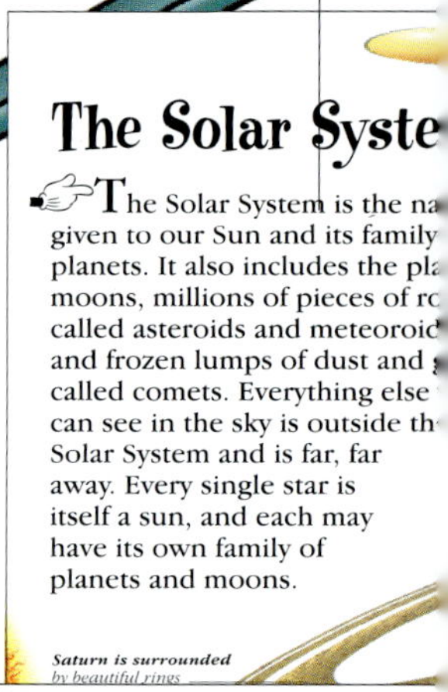

The pictures by *themselves can tell you a lot, even before you read a word*

Mickey's ears *lead you to one of the main topics*

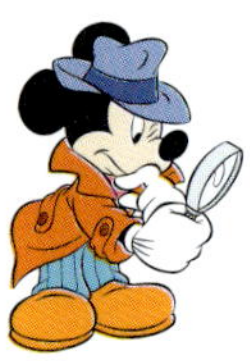

Watch out for special pages where Mickey takes a close look at some key ideas

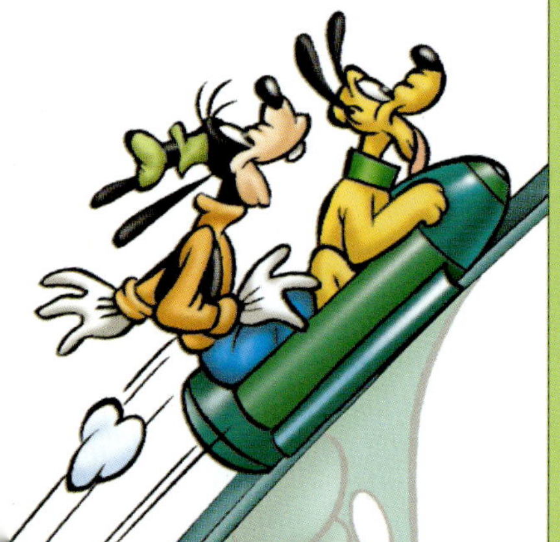

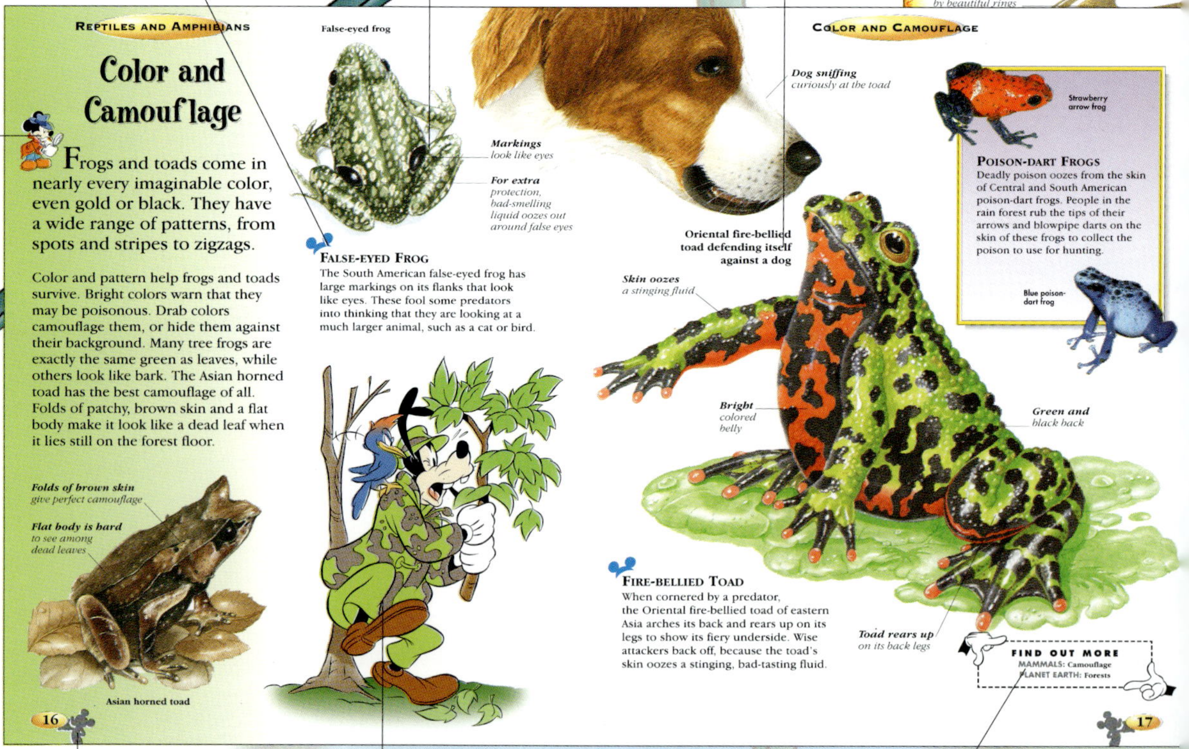

The Solar Syste

The Solar System is the na
given to our Sun and its family
planets. It also includes the pla
moons, millions of pieces of ro
called asteroids and meteoroid
and frozen lumps of dust and g
called comets. Everything else
can see in the sky is outside th
Solar System and is far, far
away. Every single star is
itself a sun, and each may
have its own family of
planets and moons.

Saturn is surrounded by beautiful rings

REPTILES AND AMPHIBIANS

Color and Camouflage

Frogs and toads come in nearly every imaginable color, even gold or black. They have a wide range of patterns, from spots and stripes to zigzags.

Color and pattern help frogs and toads survive. Bright colors warn that they may be poisonous. Drab colors camouflage them, or hide them against their background. Many tree frogs are exactly the same green as leaves, while others look like bark. The Asian horned toad has the best camouflage of all. Folds of patchy, brown skin and a flat body make it look like a dead leaf when it lies still on the forest floor.

Folds of brown skin *give perfect camouflage*

Flat body is hard *to see among dead leaves*

Asian horned toad

False-eyed frog

Markings *look like eyes*

For extra *protection, bad-smelling liquid oozes out around false eyes*

FALSE-EYED FROG
The South American false-eyed frog has large markings on its flanks that look like eyes. These fool some predators into thinking that they are looking at a much larger animal, such as a cat or bird.

COLOR AND CAMOUFLAGE

Dog sniffing *curiously at the toad*

Oriental fire-bellied toad defending itself against a dog

Skin oozes *a stinging fluid*

Bright *colored belly*

Green and *black back*

Strawberry arrow frog

POISON-DART FROGS
Deadly poison oozes from the skin of Central and South American poison-dart frogs. People in the rain forest rub the tips of their arrows and blowpipe darts on the skin of these frogs to collect the poison to use for hunting.

Blue poison-dart frog

FIRE-BELLIED TOAD
When cornered by a predator, the Oriental fire-bellied toad of eastern Asia arches its back and rears up on its legs to show its fiery underside. Wise attackers back off, because the toad's skin oozes a stinging, bad-tasting fluid.

Toad rears up *on its back legs*

FIND OUT MORE
MAMMALS: Camouflage
PLANET EARTH: Forests

16

17

Mickey's page *numbers help you look things up. Don't forget there's a glossary and index at the back of each book*

Goofy and his *friends know how to give you a chuckle on every topic*

Mickey points you to more information in other books in your *The Wonderful World of Knowledge*

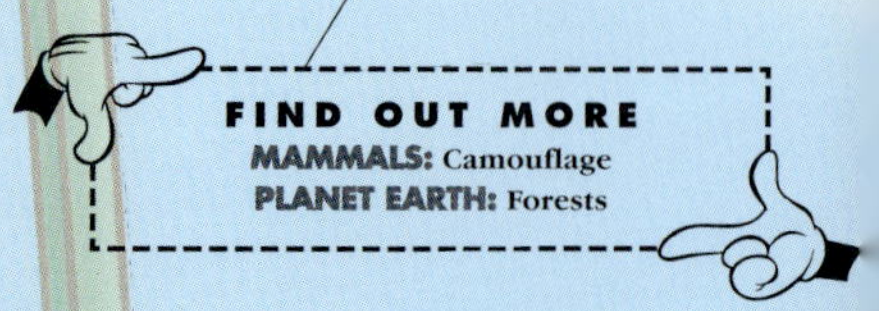

FIND OUT MORE
MAMMALS: Camouflage
PLANET EARTH: Forests

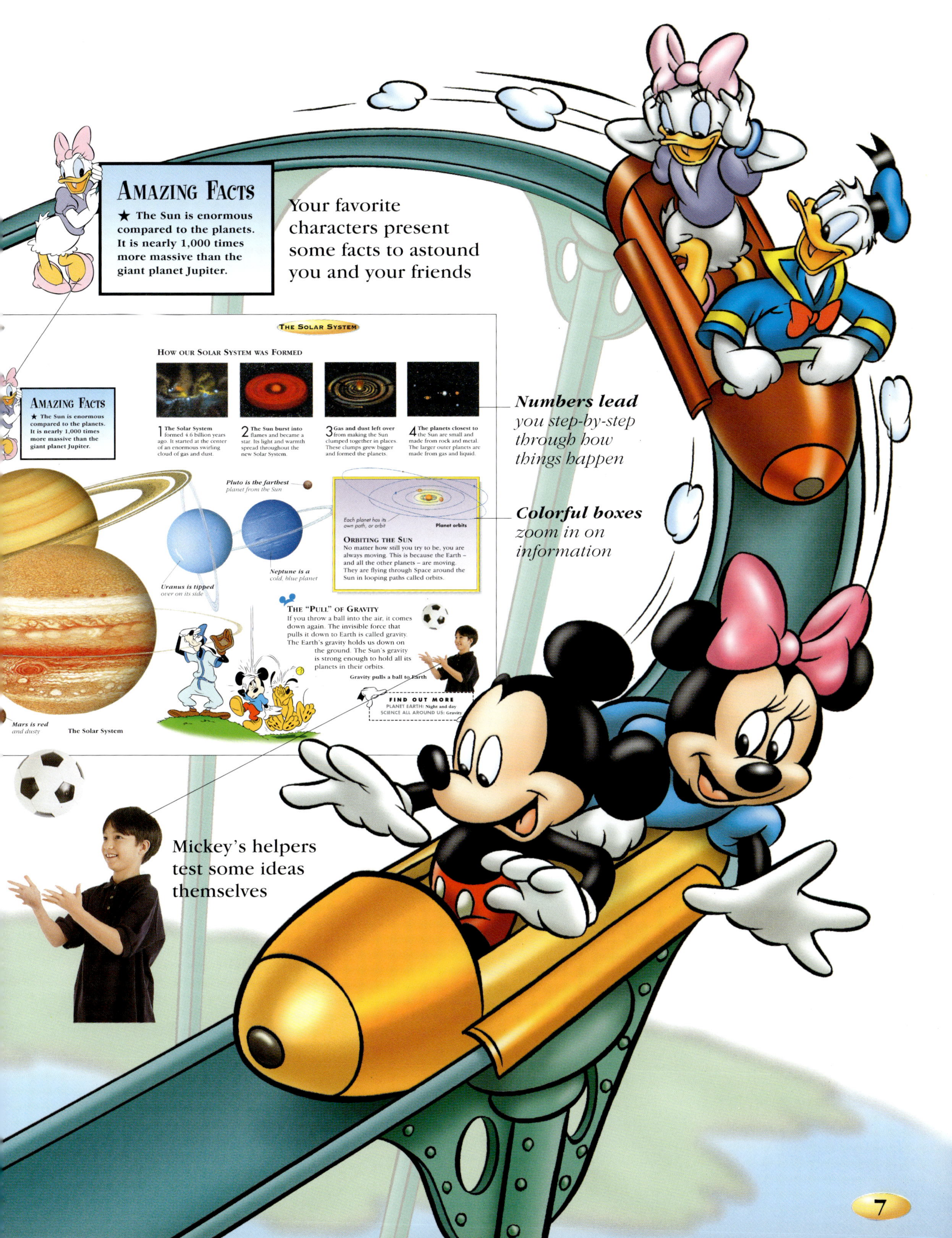

Amazing Facts

★ The Sun is enormous compared to the planets. It is nearly 1,000 times more massive than the giant planet Jupiter.

Your favorite characters present some facts to astound you and your friends

THE SOLAR SYSTEM

How our Solar System was Formed

1 The Solar System formed 4.6 billion years ago. It started at the center of an enormous swirling cloud of gas and dust.

2 The Sun burst into flames and became a star. Its light and warmth spread throughout the new Solar System.

3 Gas and dust left over from making the Sun clumped together in places. These clumps grew bigger and formed the planets.

4 The planets closest to the Sun are small and made from rock and metal. The larger outer planets are made from gas and liquid.

Amazing Facts

★ The Sun is enormous compared to the planets. It is nearly 1,000 times more massive than the giant planet Jupiter.

Pluto is the farthest planet from the Sun

Uranus is tipped over on its side

Neptune is a cold, blue planet

Each planet has its own path, or orbit

Planet orbits

Orbiting the Sun

No matter how still you try to be, you are always moving. This is because the Earth – and all the other planets – are moving. They are flying through Space around the Sun in looping paths called orbits.

The "Pull" of Gravity

If you throw a ball into the air, it comes down again. The invisible force that pulls it down to Earth is called gravity. The Earth's gravity holds us down on the ground. The Sun's gravity is strong enough to hold all its planets in their orbits.

Gravity pulls a ball to Earth

FIND OUT MORE
PLANET EARTH: Night and day
SCIENCE ALL AROUND US: Gravity

Mars is red and dusty

The Solar System

***Numbers lead** you step-by-step through how things happen*

***Colorful boxes** zoom in on information*

Mickey's helpers test some ideas themselves

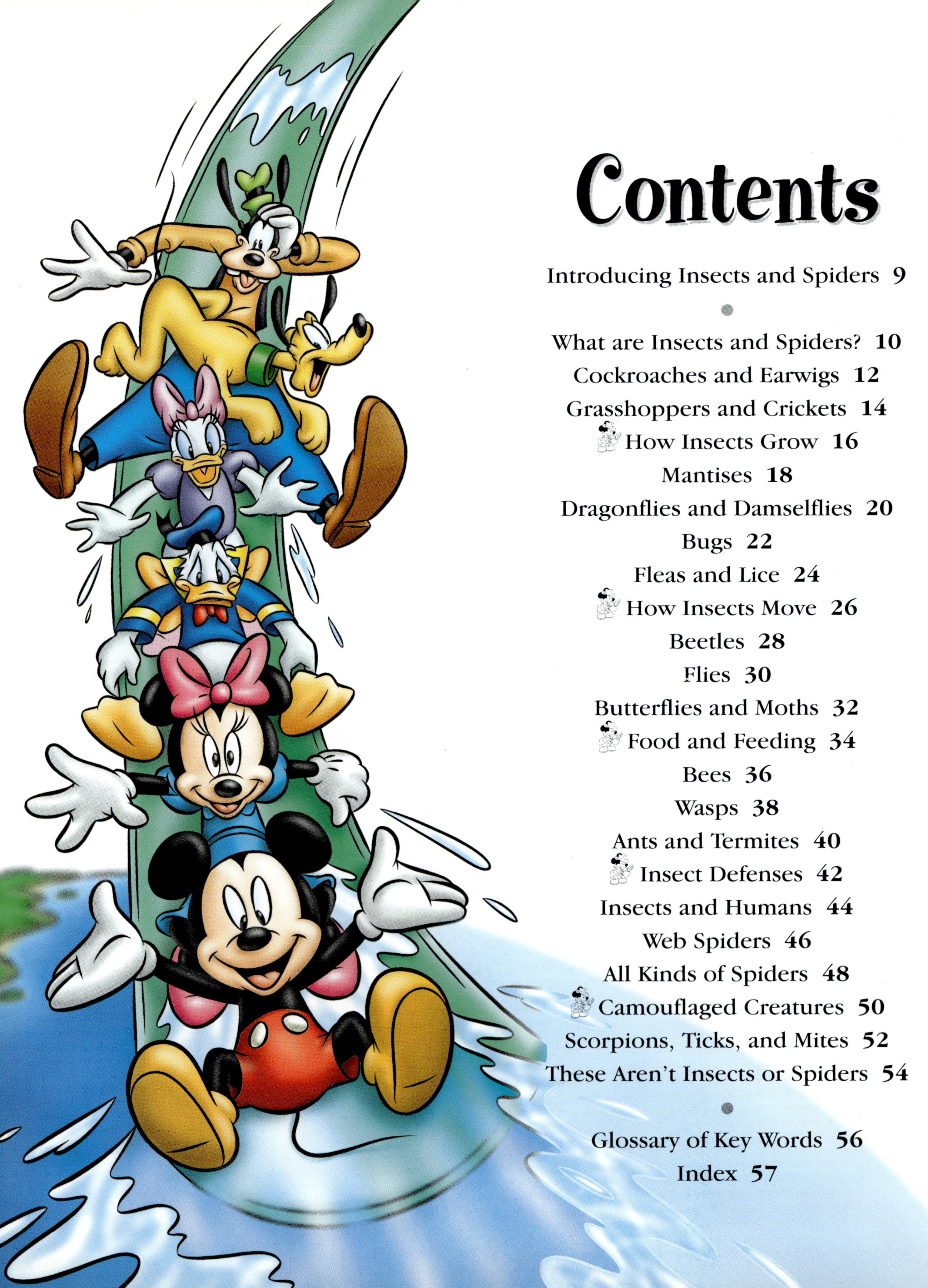

Contents

Introducing

Insects and Spiders

There are more types of insects than of all other animals put together. Among them are fierce hunters and masters of disguise. There are insects that sting, bite, and poison. Spiders and their relatives can also have deadly ways of catching prey and defending themselves.

Not all insects are pests. Many are useful, such as caterpillars that make silk and bees that make honey. Insects also carry pollen from one flower to another, helping the flowers' seeds to form.

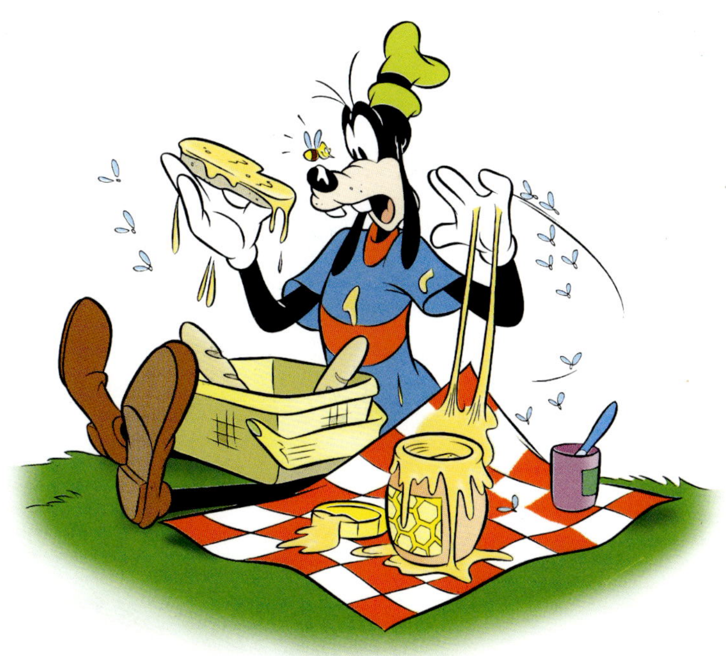

What are Insects and Spiders?

Insects and spiders are invertebrate animals. This means that they do not have bony skeletons inside their bodies. More than a million kinds of insects are known, but scientists believe there may be as many as 30 million. Spiders and their relatives belong to a group called arachnids. There are about 70,000 kinds of arachnids known.

A TYPICAL SPIDER

It is easy to tell a spider from an insect. Spiders only have two parts to their bodies – a head and thorax joined together, and a large abdomen. They have eight legs and do not have wings or antennae.

AMAZING FACTS

★ **Giant insects lived on Earth millions of years ago. They included a huge dragonfly with wings measuring an incredible 60 cm (24 in) across.**

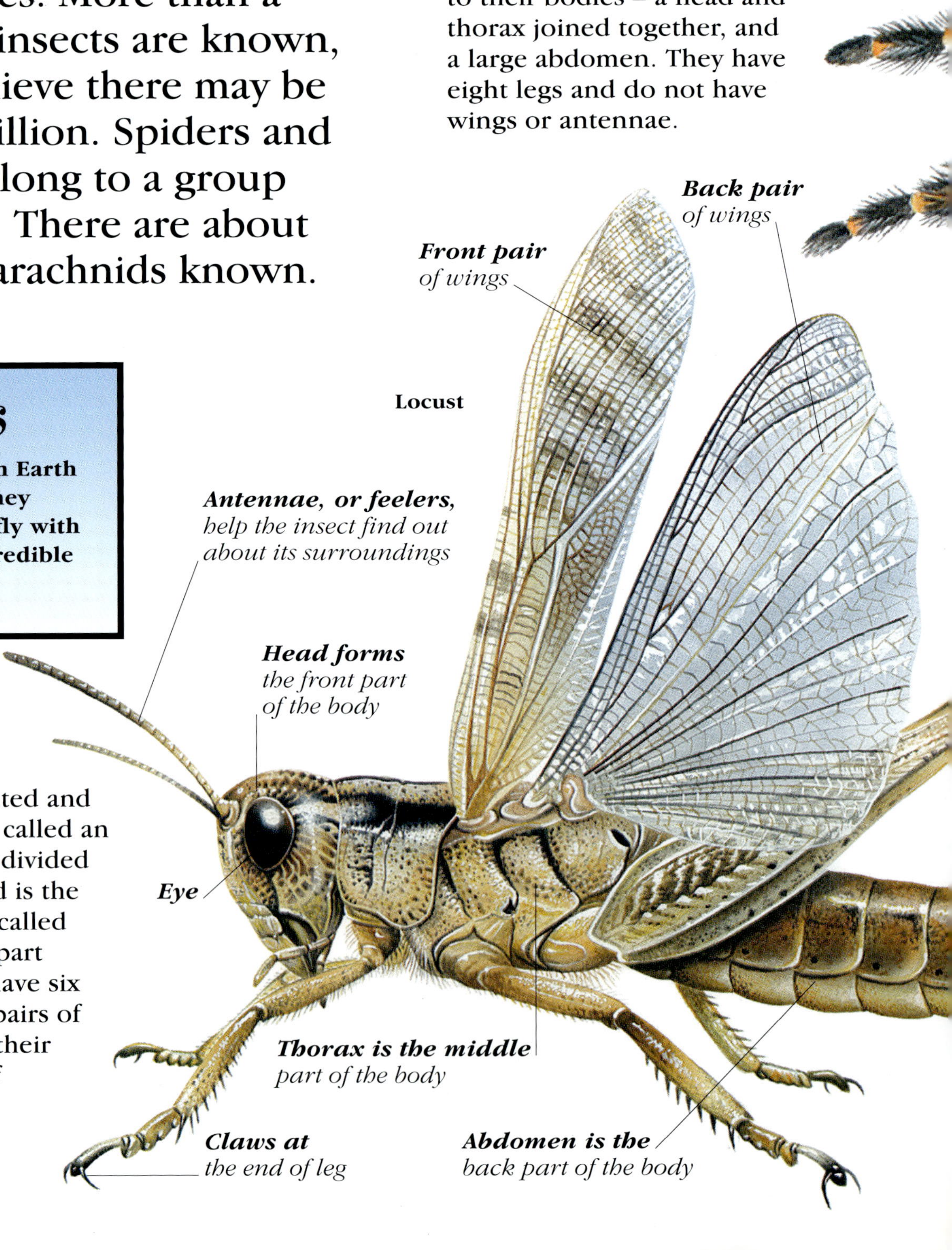

A TYPICAL INSECT

An insect's body is protected and supported by a hard case called an exoskeleton. The body is divided into three parts. The head is the front part. The middle is called the thorax, and the back part is the abdomen. Insects have six legs, and most have two pairs of wings on the thorax. On their heads, they have a pair of antennae, or feelers.

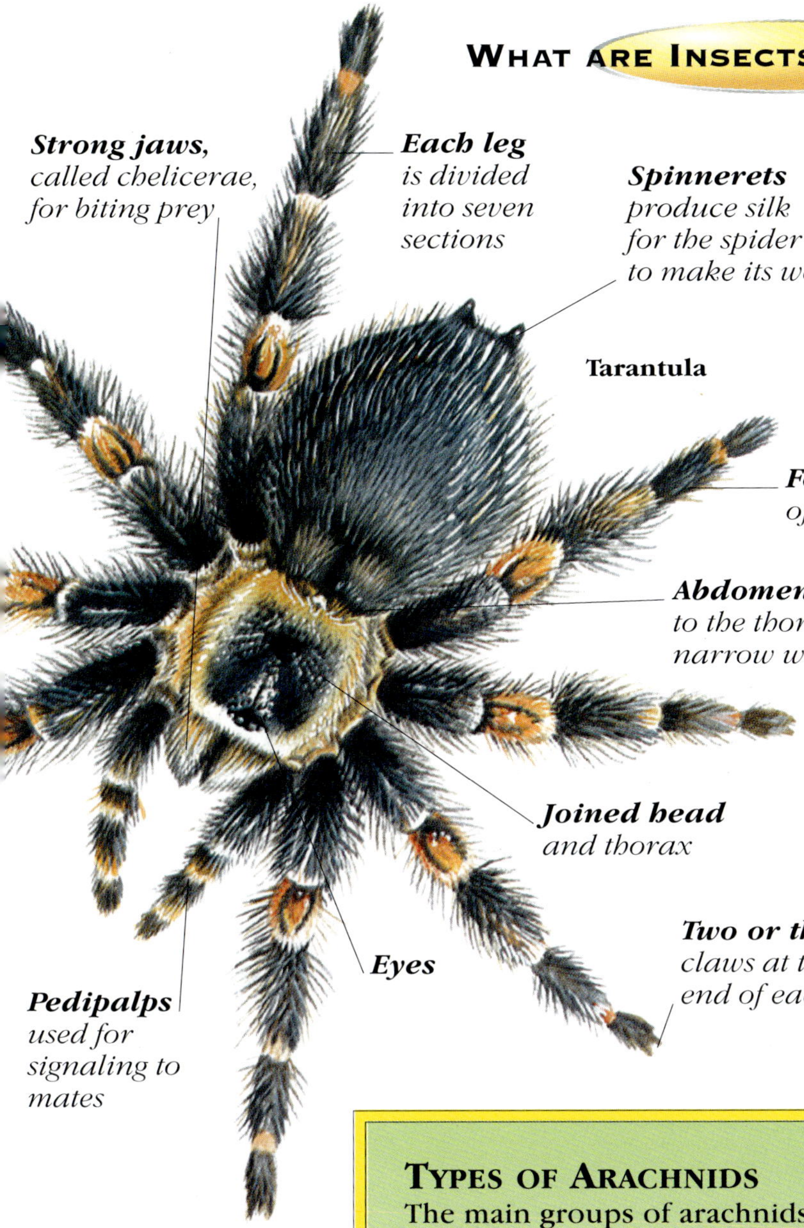

Strong jaws, *called chelicerae, for biting prey*

Each leg *is divided into seven sections*

Spinnerets *produce silk for the spider to make its web*

Tarantula

Four pairs *of legs*

Abdomen linked *to the thorax by a narrow waist*

Joined head *and thorax*

Eyes

Two or three *claws at the end of each leg*

Pedipalps *used for signaling to mates*

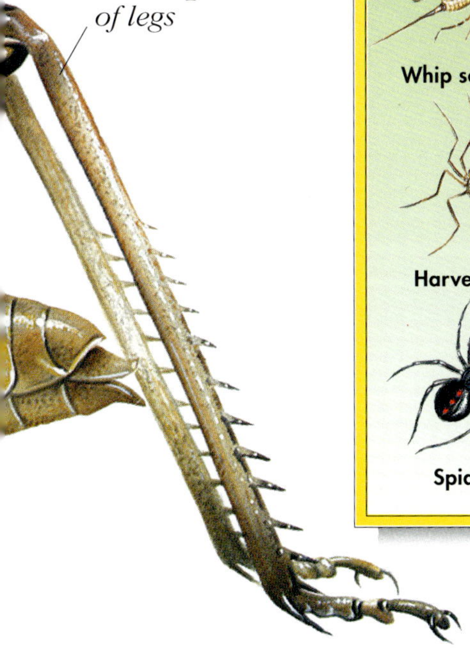

Three pairs *of legs*

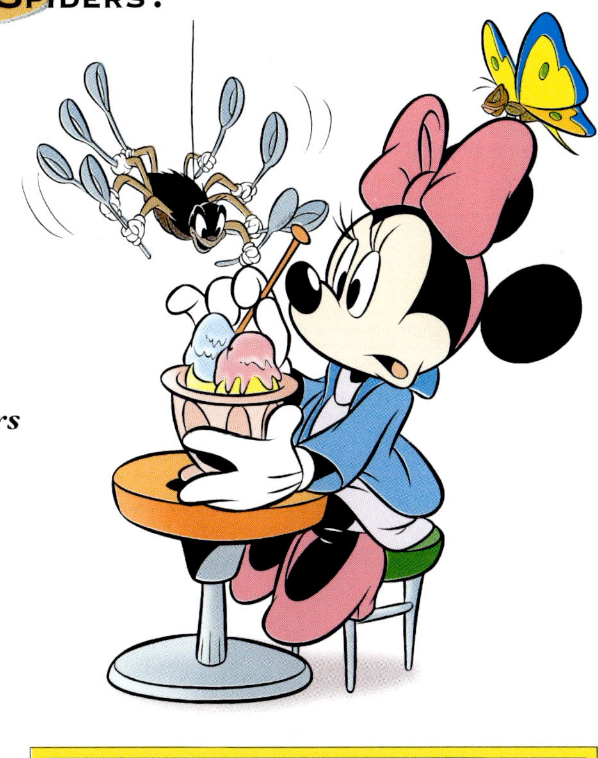

Types of Arachnids

The main groups of arachnids.

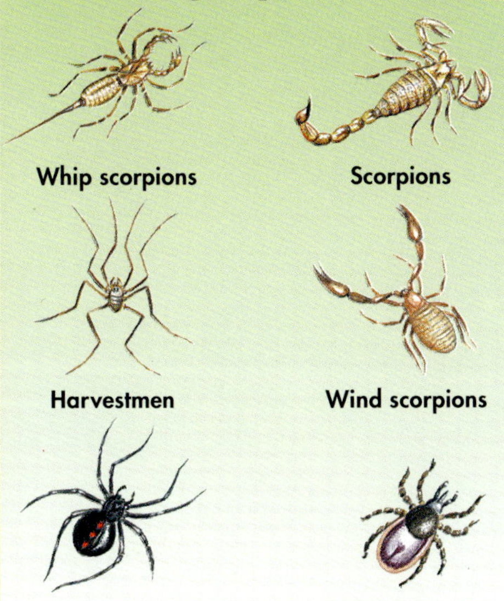

Whip scorpions

Scorpions

Harvestmen

Wind scorpions

Spiders

Ticks and mites

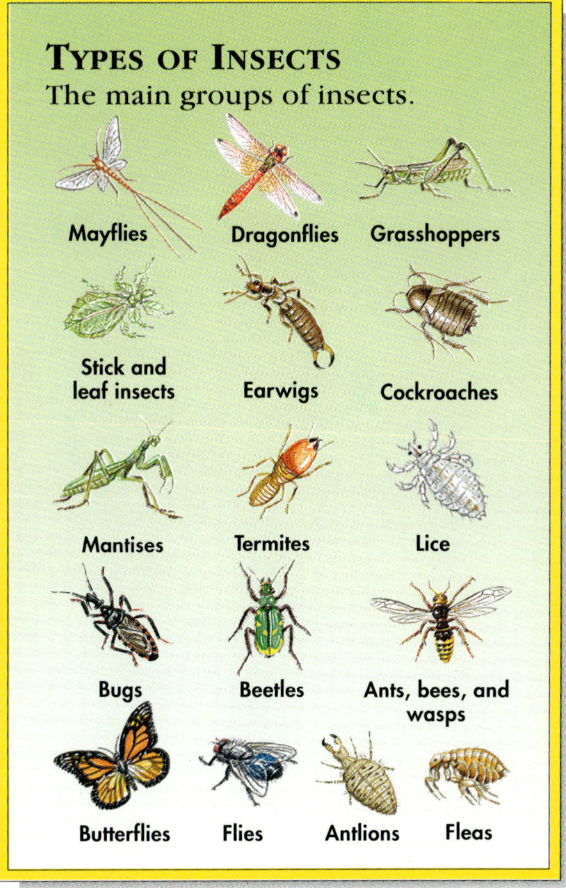

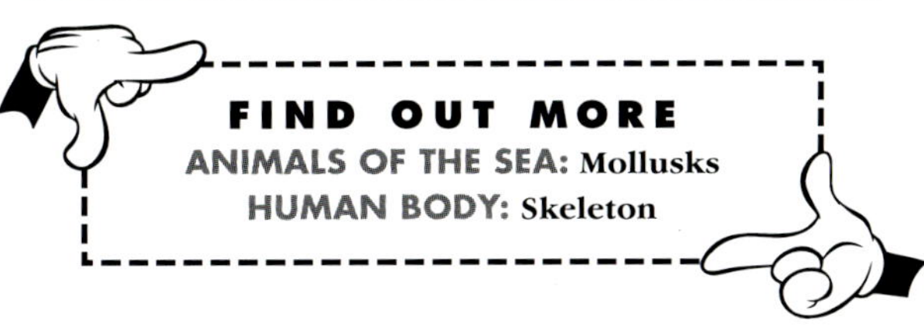

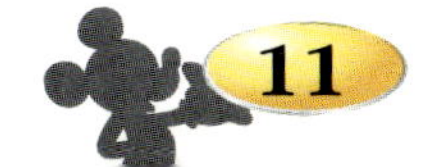

Cockroaches and Earwigs

Cockroaches live all over the world, even in people's homes. During the day, their flattened bodies help them hide in tiny cracks and holes. At night, these fast-running insects hurry out to look for any food they can find. Earwigs hide under stones by day, but at night they come out to feed on plants and smaller insects.

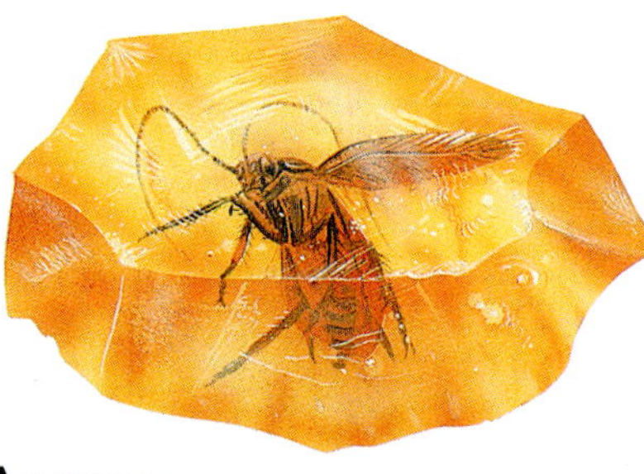

Cockroach trapped in a piece of amber

Insect in Amber

Cockroaches first lived on Earth 350 million years ago. Scientists have found long-dead cockroaches trapped inside pieces of amber. Amber is a fossil made of lumps of a sticky fluid called resin, which oozed from prehistoric pine trees. It can be made into jewelry.

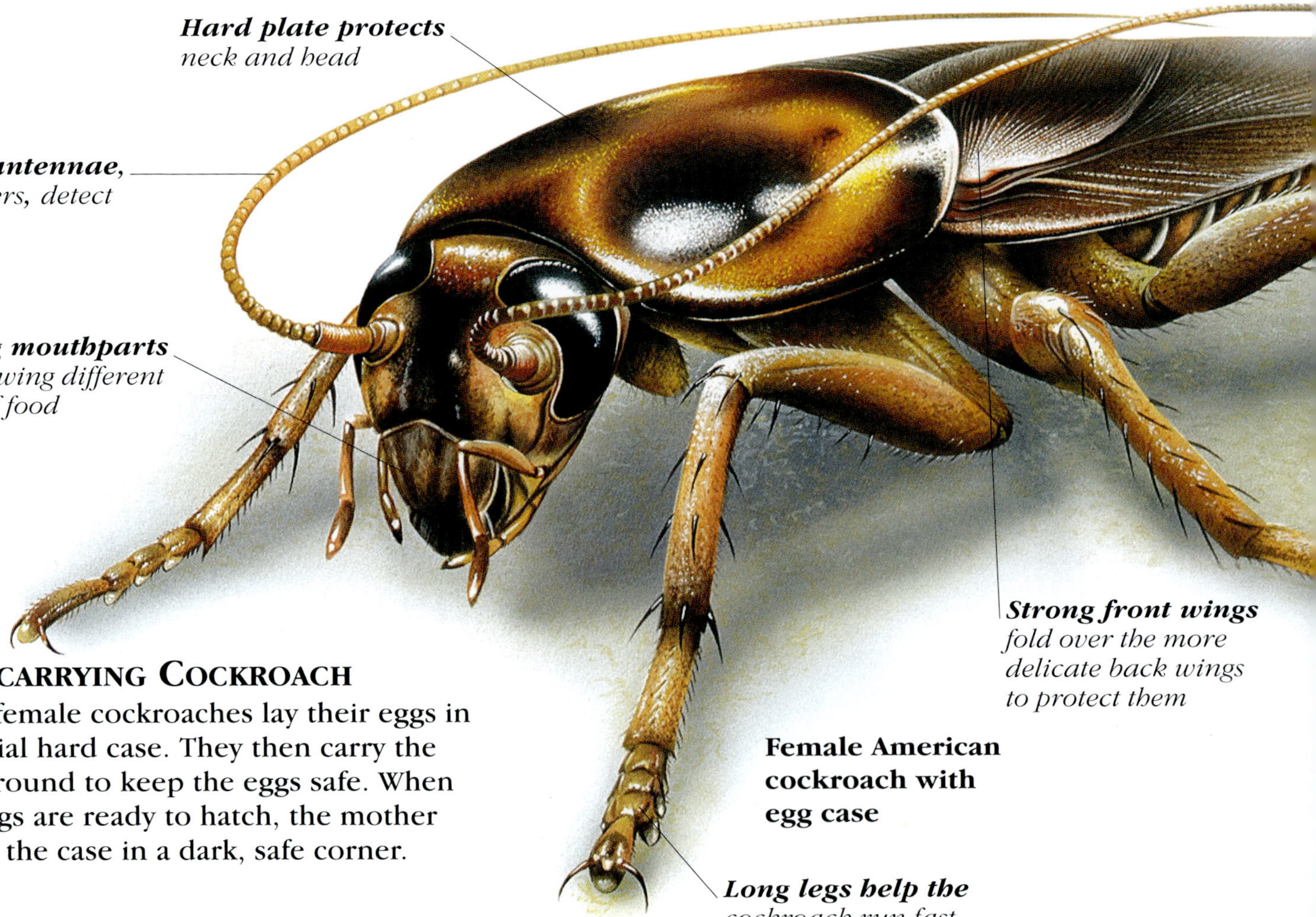

Hard plate protects *neck and head*

Long antennae, *or feelers, detect smells*

Strong mouthparts *for chewing different sorts of food*

Strong front wings *fold over the more delicate back wings to protect them*

Female American cockroach with egg case

Long legs help the *cockroach run fast*

Egg-carrying Cockroach

Many female cockroaches lay their eggs in a special hard case. They then carry the case around to keep the eggs safe. When the eggs are ready to hatch, the mother places the case in a dark, safe corner.

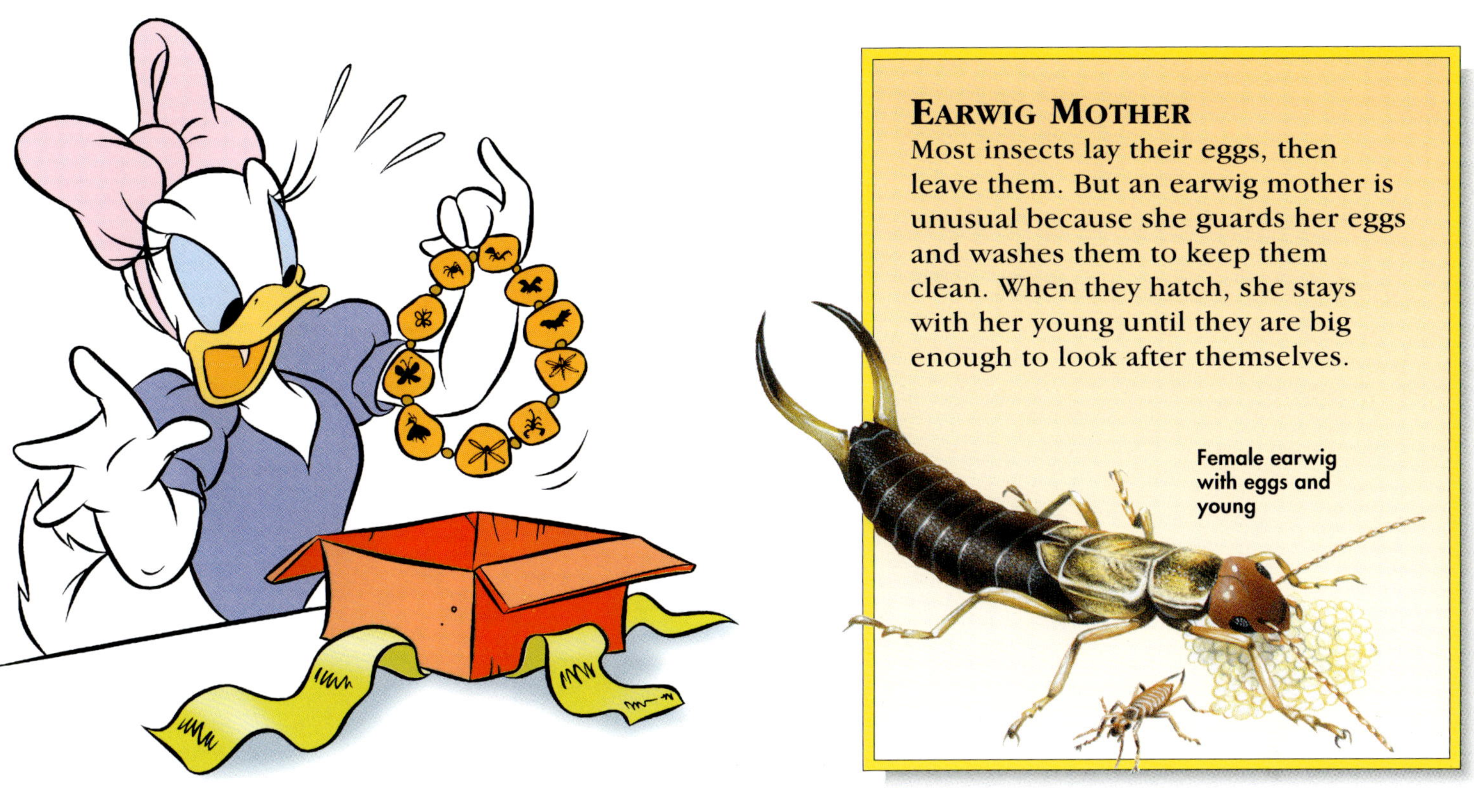

Earwig Mother

Most insects lay their eggs, then leave them. But an earwig mother is unusual because she guards her eggs and washes them to keep them clean. When they hatch, she stays with her young until they are big enough to look after themselves.

Female earwig with eggs and young

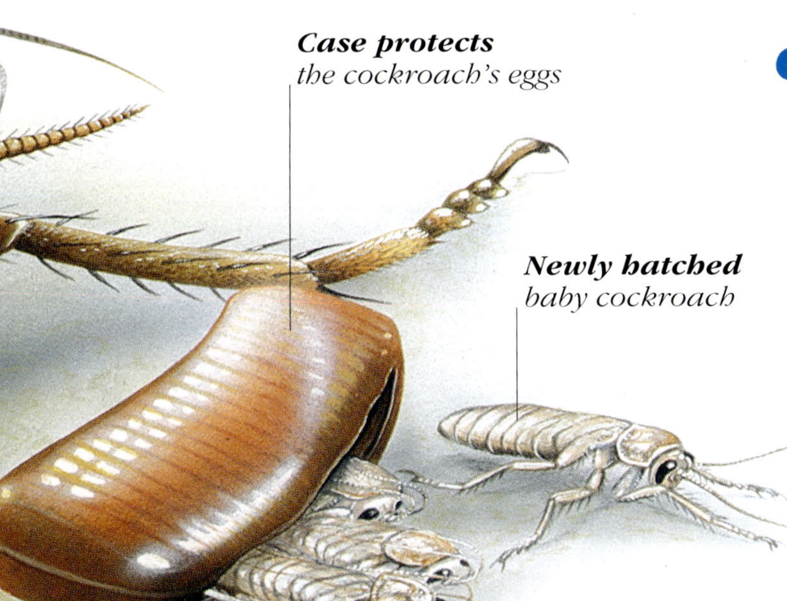

Case protects *the cockroach's eggs*

Newly hatched *baby cockroach*

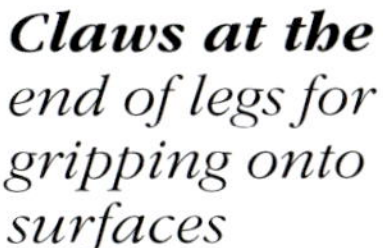

Claws at the *end of legs for gripping onto surfaces*

Winged and Wingless

Most cockroaches have two pairs of wings, although they are not strong fliers. They cannot fly far or very fast. Burrowing cockroaches do not grow wings. They spend their lives underground and so do not need to fly.

Strong *front wings*

Light back *wings*

Cockroach in flight

Amazing Facts

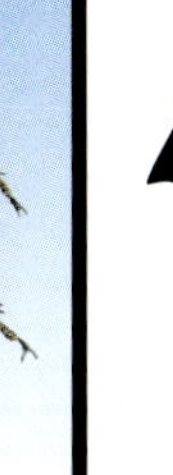

★ The giant cockroach is almost 10 cm (4 in) long, more than twice as long as a child's thumb.

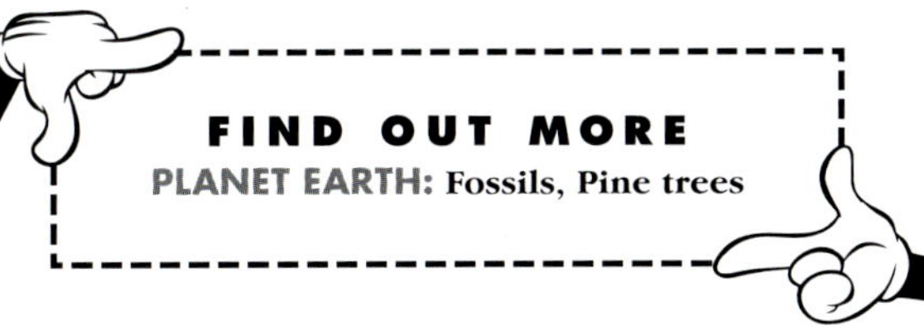

FIND OUT MORE
PLANET EARTH: Fossils, Pine trees

Grasshoppers and Crickets

Grasshoppers and crickets are famous for the chirping songs that males use to find a mate. Each has his own special call, which only attracts females of his own type. These insects do not use their voices for singing. Instead, they make sounds with their wings and legs. There are two groups of grasshoppers. The short-horned ones have short antennae, and the long-horned ones and crickets have long antennae.

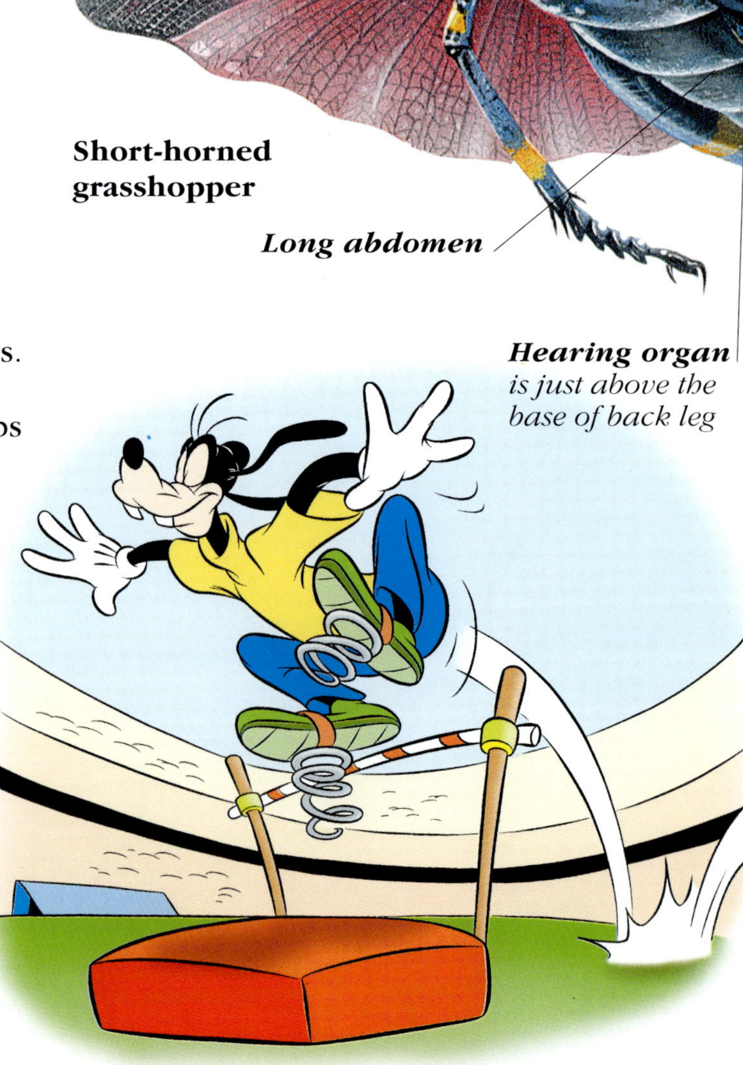

Short-horned grasshopper

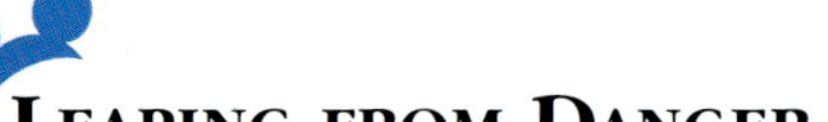

Leaping from Danger

Grasshoppers have strong back legs, which help them escape from enemies. As they jump, they spread out their brightly colored back wings. This helps to scare off their enemies. They fly a short distance, then land again.

Digging a Burrow

Mole crickets live under the ground, where they feed on plant roots. They use their broad front legs as spades for digging. Mole crickets have tiny wings and cannot fly.

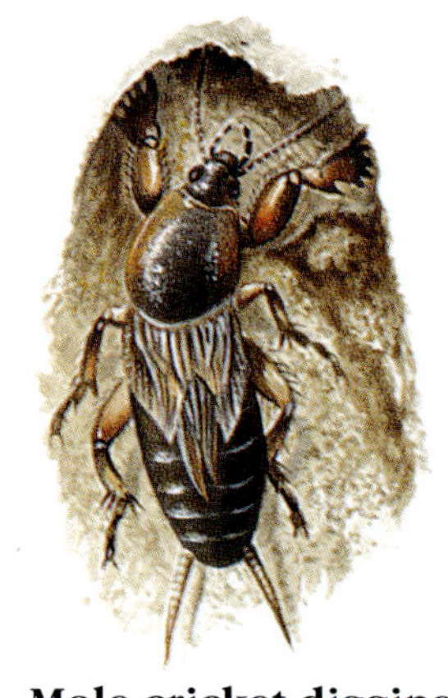

Mole cricket digging a burrow

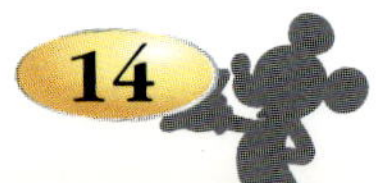

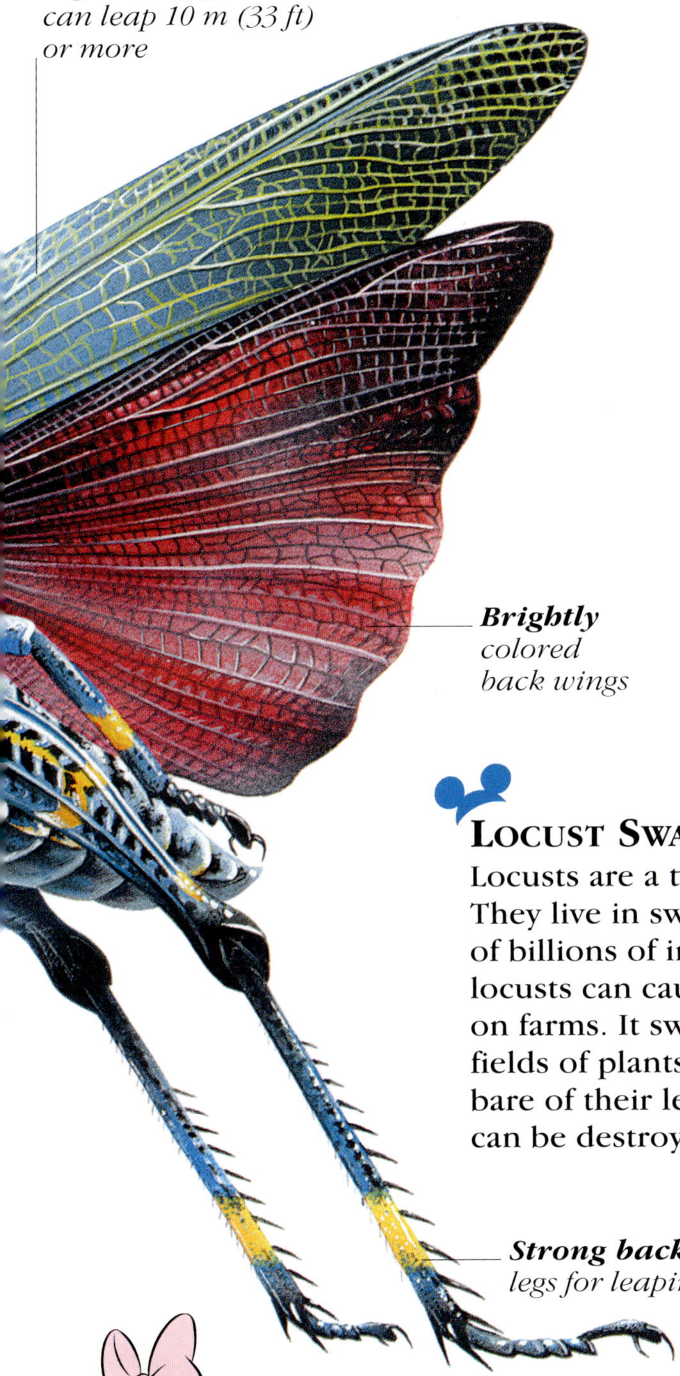

A grasshopper *can leap 10 m (33 ft) or more*

Brightly *colored back wings*

Strong back *legs for leaping*

MAKING SOUNDS

Male short-horned grasshoppers "sing" by rubbing a ridge or file on the inside of their back legs against their front wings. Crickets and long-horned grasshoppers sing by rubbing together special areas on their front wings.

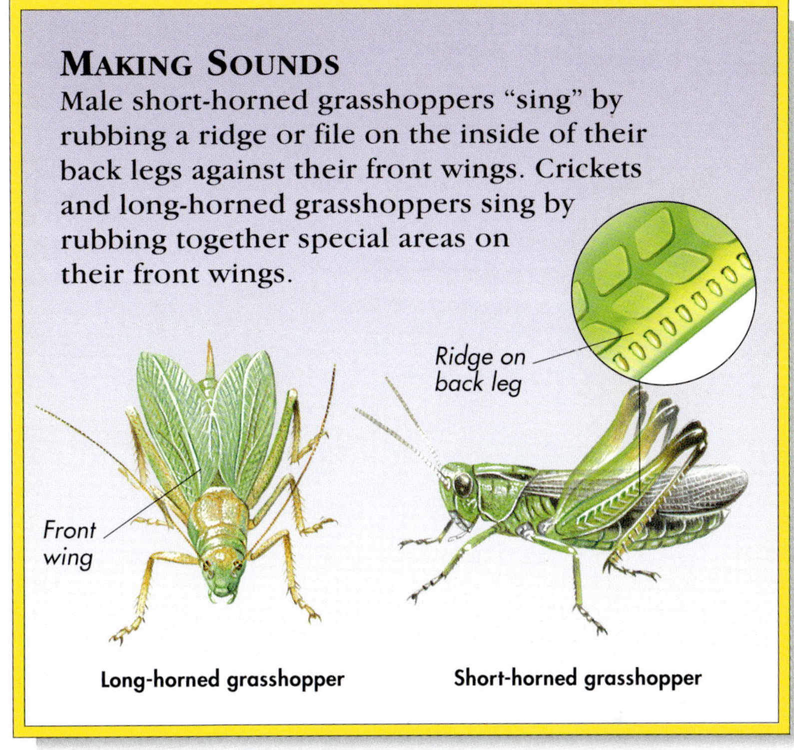

LOCUST SWARMS

Locusts are a type of grasshopper. They live in swarms, or groups, of billions of insects. A swarm of locusts can cause terrible damage on farms. It swoops down on fields of plants, stripping them bare of their leaves. Whole fields can be destroyed.

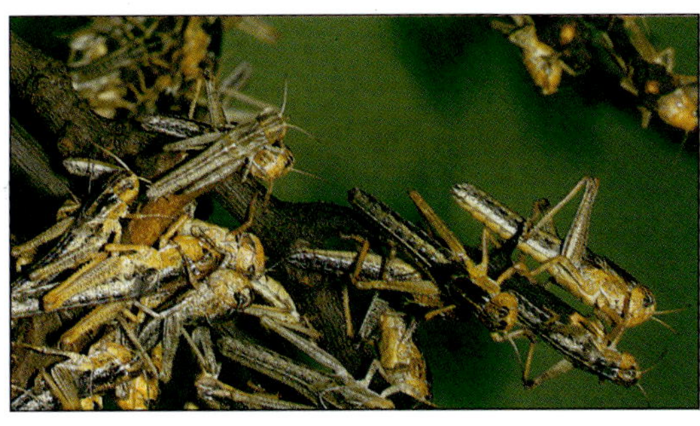

Swarm of locusts feeding on a plant

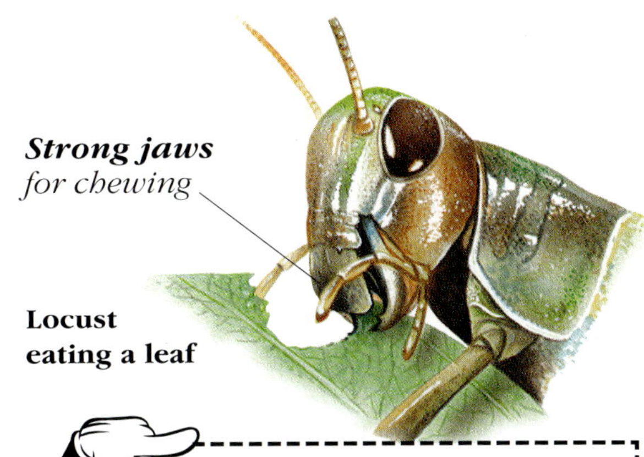

Locust eating a leaf

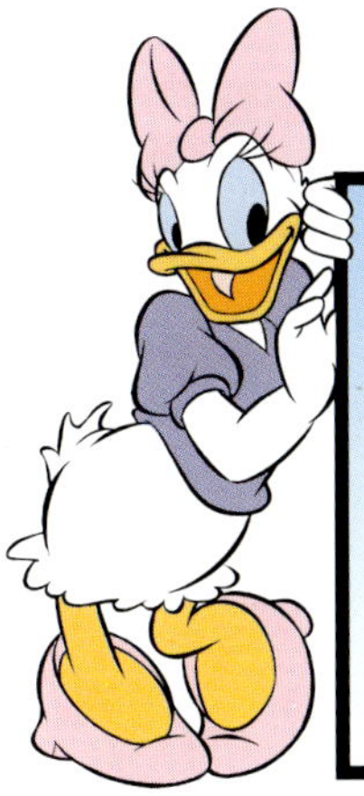

AMAZING FACTS

★ **The biggest swarm of locusts ever seen in Africa contained an incredible 75 billion insects. The swarm covered an area of about 1,300 sq km (500 sq miles).**

FIND OUT MORE
HUMAN BODY: Hearing
SCIENCE ALL AROUND US: Sound

How Insects Grow

All insects start life as tiny eggs. They hatch into young that look different from their parents. To become adults, the young go through a series of amazing changes in a process called metamorphosis.

As an insect grows, it becomes too big for its hard skin and has to molt, or shed its skin, and grow a new one. In some insects this happens many times before the insect becomes an adult. For other insects metamorphosis is more dramatic. These insects make a hard case called a pupa around themselves. Inside, the whole body is rearranged into an adult insect.

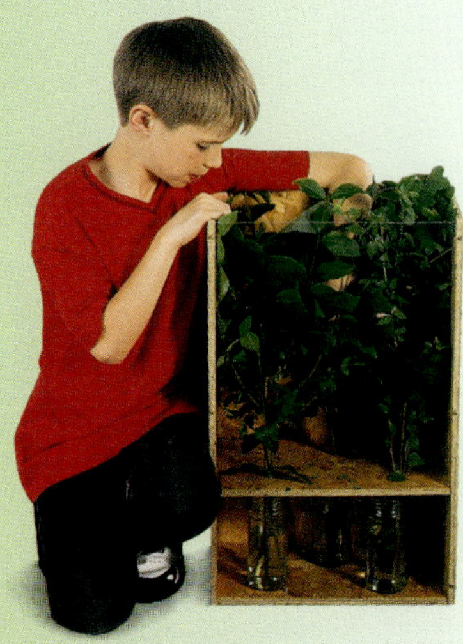

The growth and development of caterpillars can be seen if they are kept in a box, with plenty of food

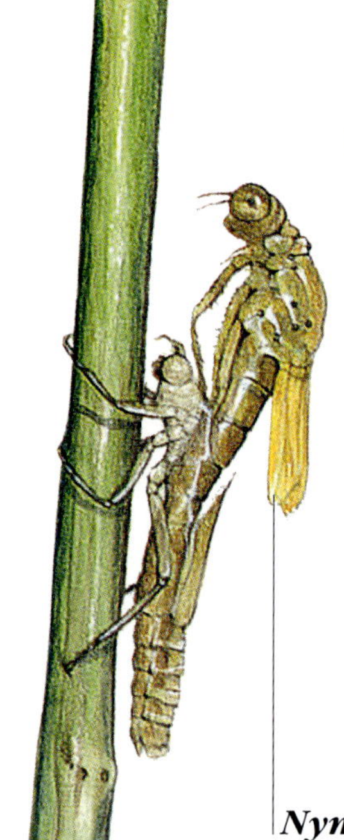

LIFE OF A DAMSELFLY

Damselfly eggs hatch into young called nymphs, which live and feed in water. As a nymph grows, it sheds its old skin and grows a new one. This happens several times. After about two years, the nymph is ready to climb out of the water and make its final molt into an adult.

Nymph climbs out of water *and up a plant stem. Its skin splits, and the adult damselfly starts to crawl out*

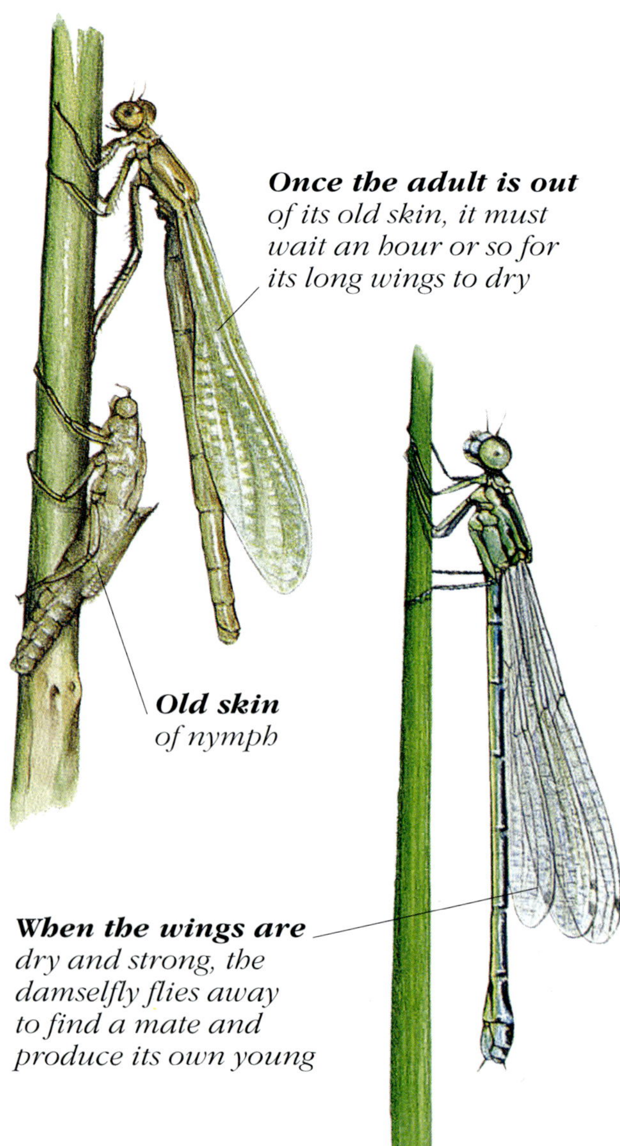

Once the adult is out *of its old skin, it must wait an hour or so for its long wings to dry*

Old skin *of nymph*

When the wings are *dry and strong, the damselfly flies away to find a mate and produce its own young*

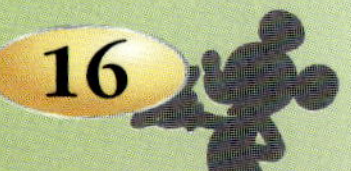

Egg to Butterfly

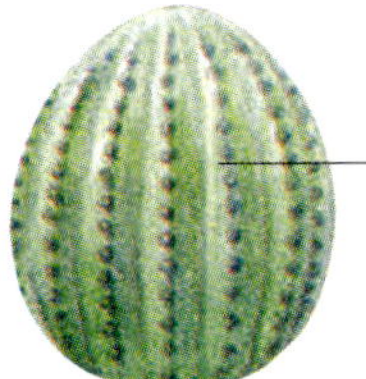

Egg measures *up to 2 mm (1/16 in) across*

1 Butterfly lays eggs on a leaf. Each egg takes about a week to hatch into a larva called a caterpillar.

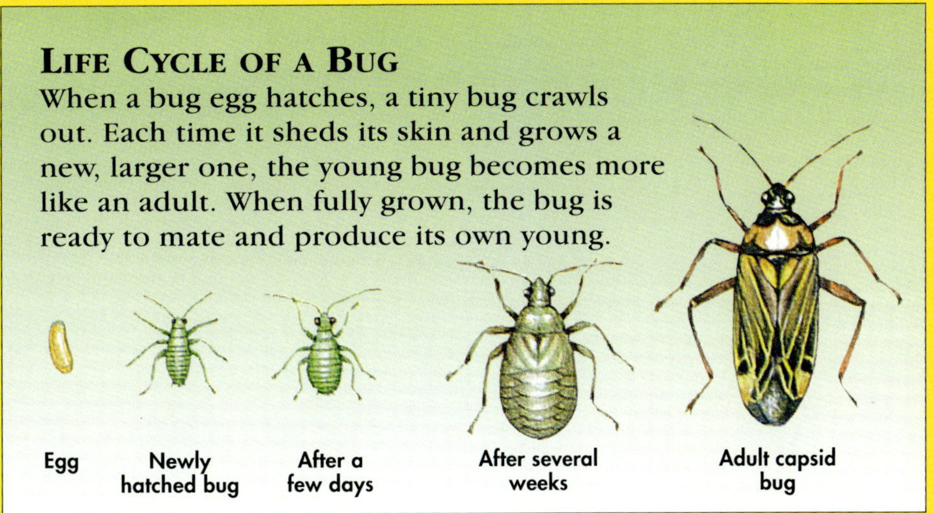

Life Cycle of a Bug

When a bug egg hatches, a tiny bug crawls out. Each time it sheds its skin and grows a new, larger one, the young bug becomes more like an adult. When fully grown, the bug is ready to mate and produce its own young.

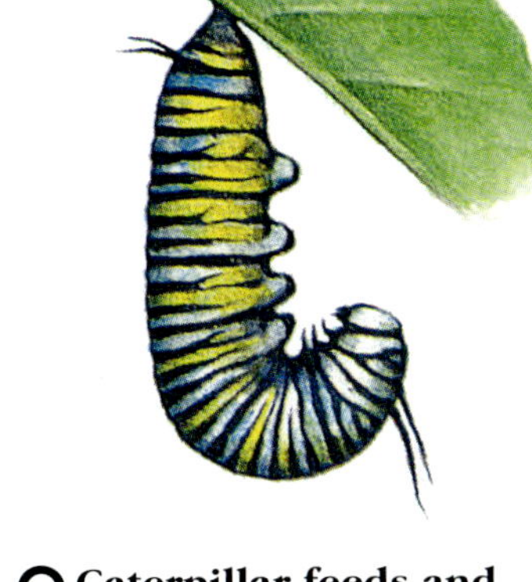

2 Caterpillar feeds and grows. When fully grown, it stops eating and anchors itself to a leaf, using silk from its own body.

3 Caterpillar builds a hard case called a pupa around its body. Inside, the larva begins to change into an adult.

Adult *butterfly*

Butterfly's wings *gradually unfold*

4 A few weeks later, the skin of the pupa splits, and a beautiful adult butterfly comes out. It will now fly off to find a mate.

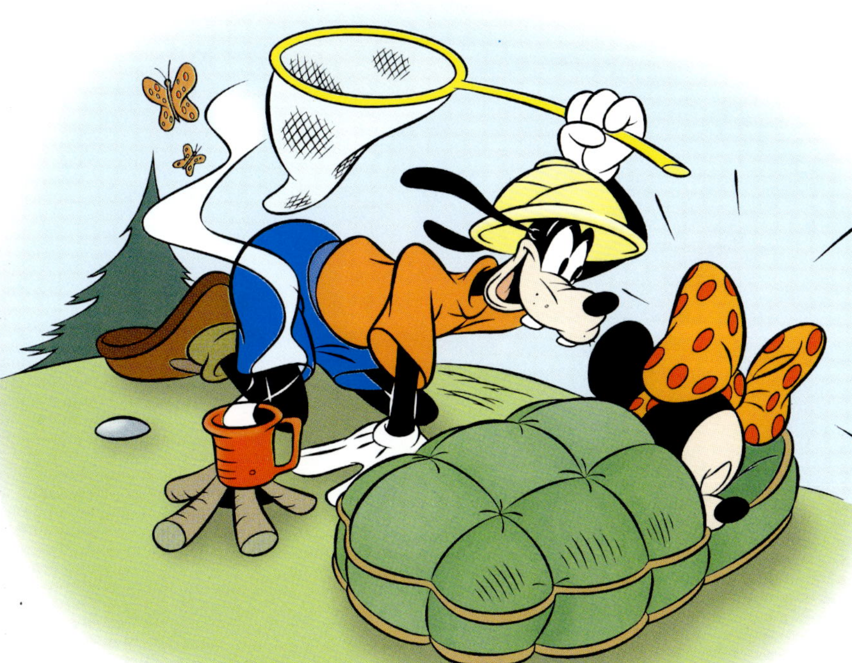

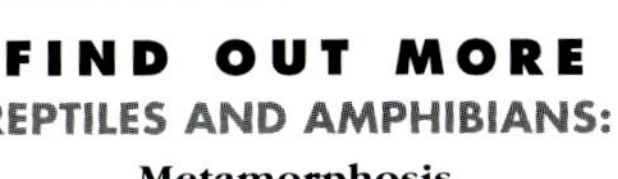

FIND OUT MORE
REPTILES AND AMPHIBIANS:
Metamorphosis

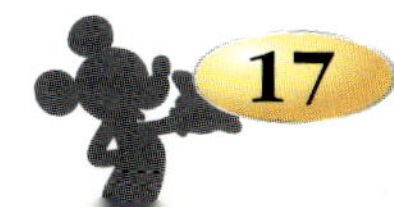

Mantises

Mantises are some of the fiercest hunters in the insect world. With lightning speed, they shoot out their long front legs to catch their prey, or food. There are about 1,800 different kinds of mantises. Many are colored to match the flowers or leaves on which they usually live. This helps keep them hidden as they lie in wait for their prey.

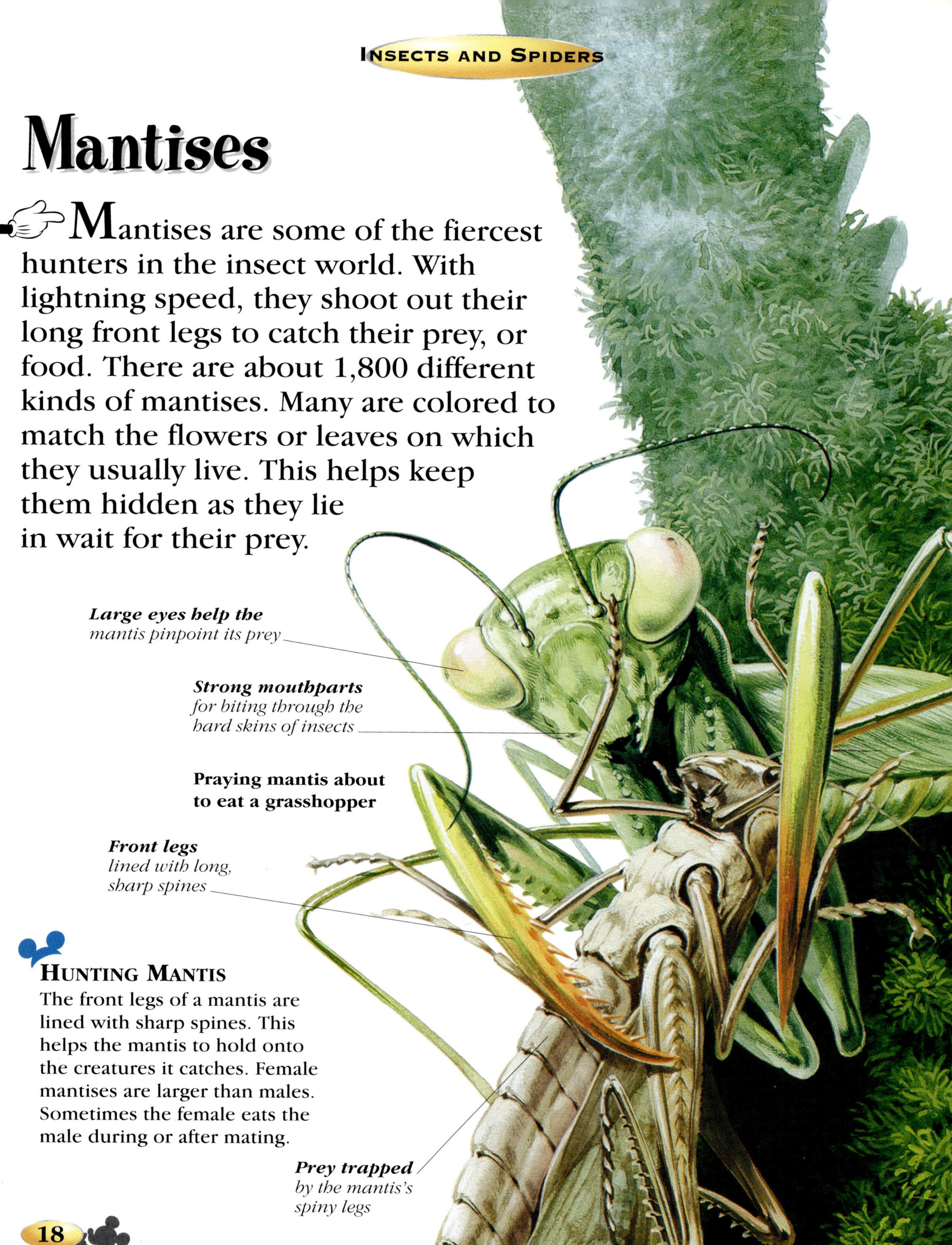

HUNTING MANTIS

The front legs of a mantis are lined with sharp spines. This helps the mantis to hold onto the creatures it catches. Female mantises are larger than males. Sometimes the female eats the male during or after mating.

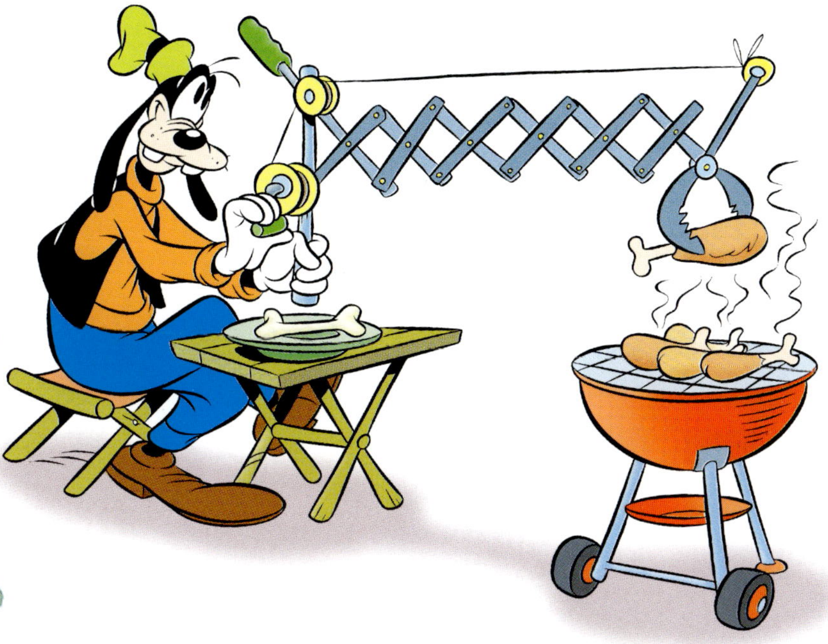

CLEVER DISGUISE

The back legs of the flower mantis are flattened to look like flower petals. This helps the insect hide while watching for prey and also camouflages it from its own enemies, such as birds and lizards.

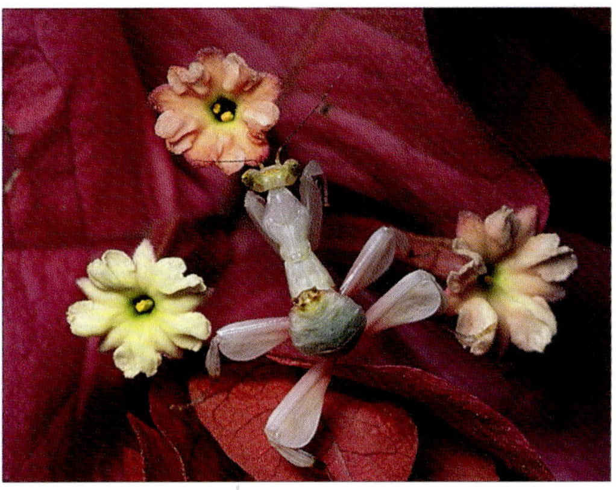

Flower mantis with legs like petals

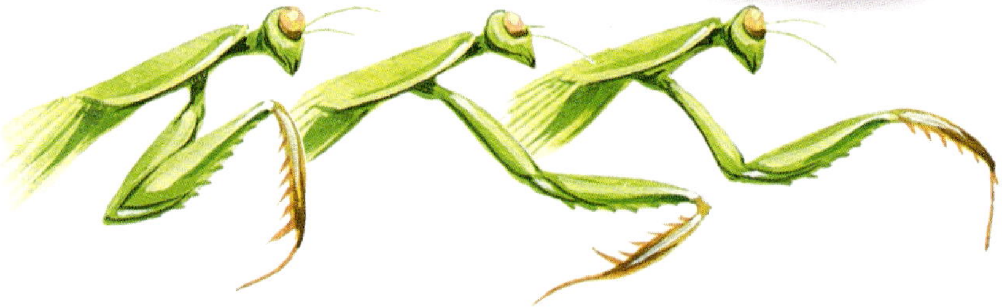

How the mantis shoots out its front legs to catch prey

CATCHING PREY

While it watches for prey, a mantis sits with its front legs folded. It stays still until an insect passes, then it shoots out its legs, quick as a flash. It grips the prey between its spiny legs and chews with its powerful mouthparts.

MANTIS LOOKALIKE

The mantisfly is a type of lacewing, not a mantis, but it looks and behaves very like one. Like a proper mantis, it reaches out with its long front legs to trap prey such as small insects and mites.

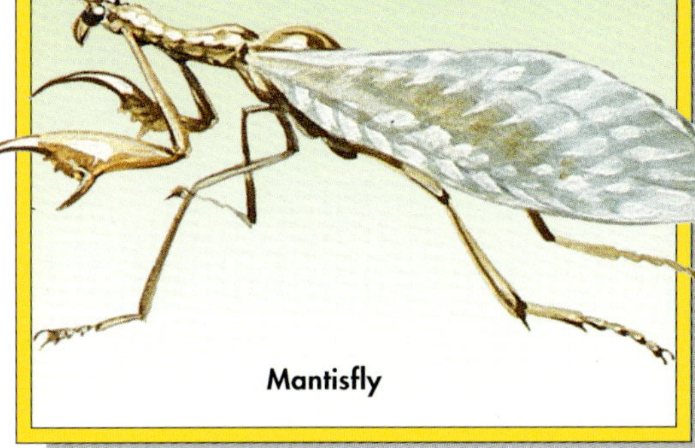

Mantisfly

AMAZING FACTS

★ It takes less than one thirty-thousandth of a second for a mantis to reach out its front legs, grab prey, and bring the prey back to its mouth.

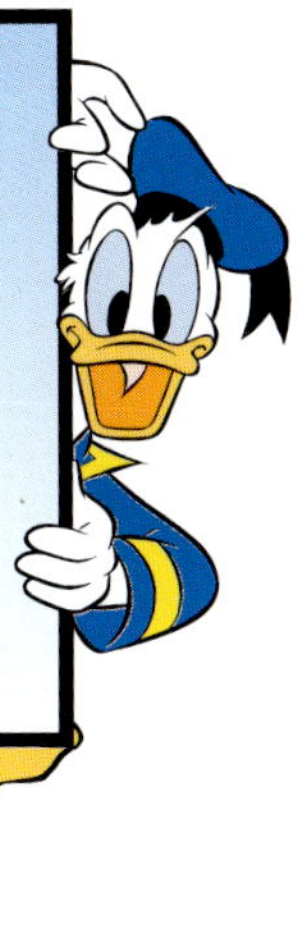

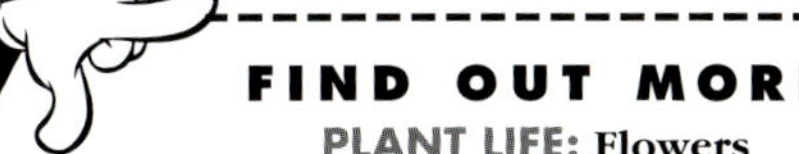

FIND OUT MORE
PLANT LIFE: Flowers
REPTILES AND AMPHIBIANS: Camouflage

Dragonflies and Damselflies

With their large shimmering wings, dragonflies are among the fastest-flying insects. They use their speed and acrobatic skills for hunting other insects in midair. Their cousins, the damselflies, are smaller and fly more slowly. Dragonflies and damselflies live near rivers, ponds, and streams. They lay their eggs in water. Young dragonflies and damselflies are called nymphs. Like their parents, they are fierce hunters.

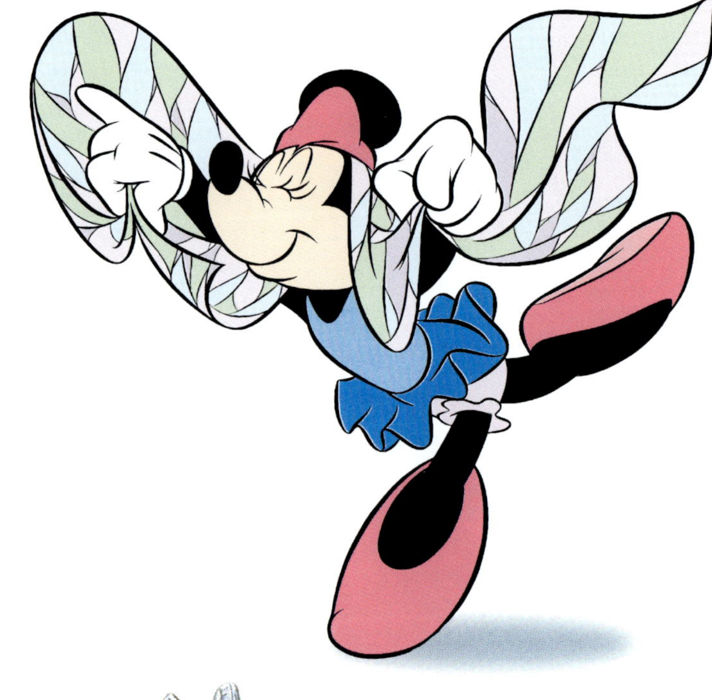

Underwater Nymphs

Wingless dragonfly and damselfly nymphs live and hunt in water. A nymph's long lower lip is tipped with sharp claws. It shoots its lip forward to grab other creatures to eat.

Dragonfly nymph

Prey caught in claws on lower lip

Damselfly nymph

Sharp claws on lower lip

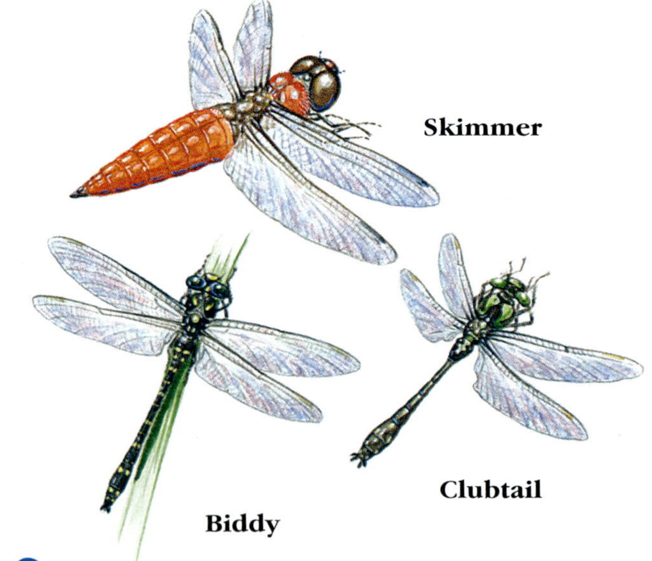

Types of Dragonflies

There are about 5,000 types of dragonflies. Clubtails sit on a perch, then dart out to catch prey. Biddies are large dragonflies that live near woodland streams. Skimmers usually hunt near still or slow-moving water.

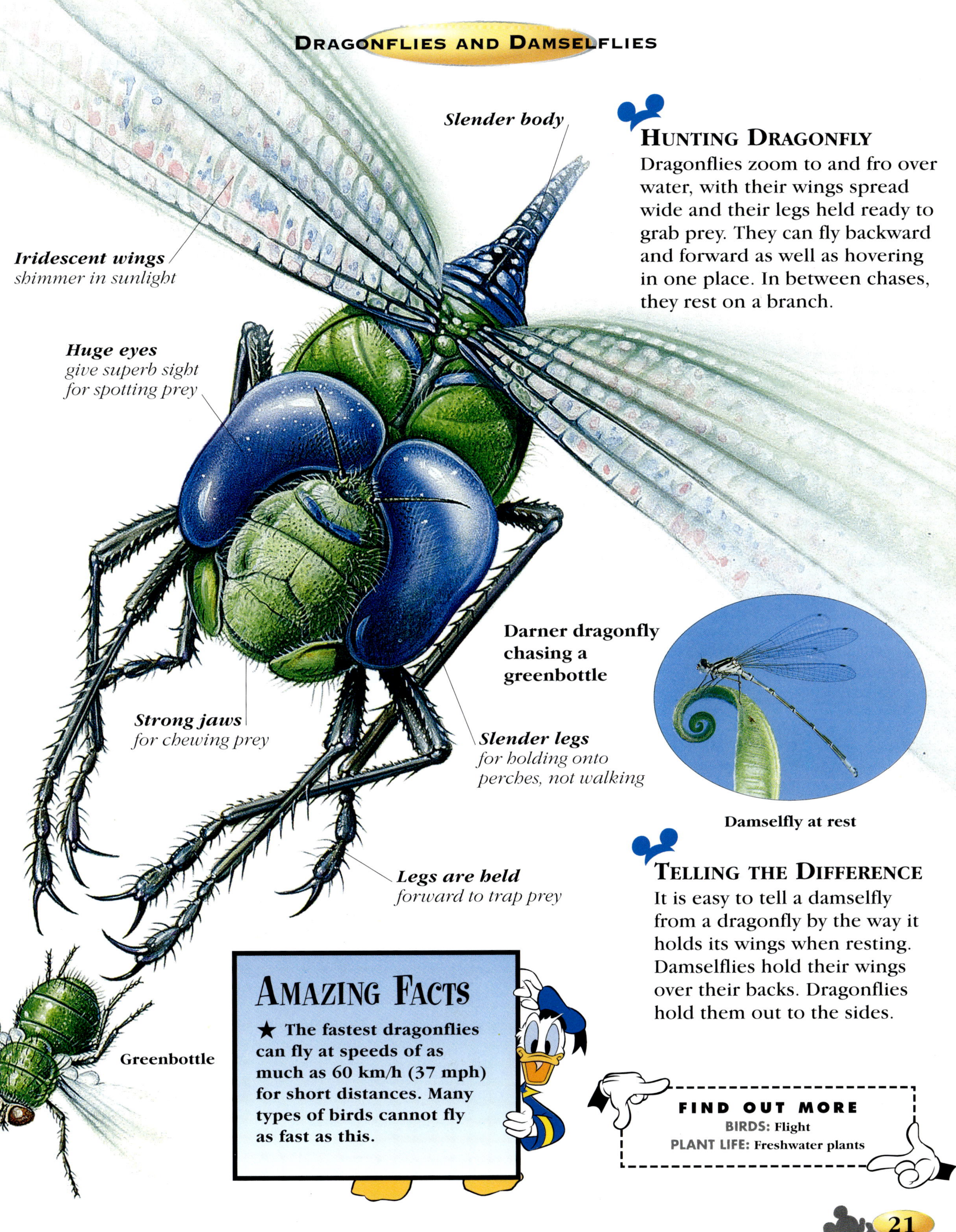

Darner dragonfly chasing a greenbottle

Damselfly at rest

HUNTING DRAGONFLY

Dragonflies zoom to and fro over water, with their wings spread wide and their legs held ready to grab prey. They can fly backward and forward as well as hovering in one place. In between chases, they rest on a branch.

TELLING THE DIFFERENCE

It is easy to tell a damselfly from a dragonfly by the way it holds its wings when resting. Damselflies hold their wings over their backs. Dragonflies hold them out to the sides.

AMAZING FACTS

★ **The fastest dragonflies can fly at speeds of as much as 60 km/h (37 mph) for short distances. Many types of birds cannot fly as fast as this.**

FIND OUT MORE
BIRDS: Flight
PLANT LIFE: Freshwater plants

Bugs

Bugs are a group of insects with special mouths like long tubes. They use these tubes for piercing holes in food and sucking out the juices. Some, such as greenflies and shield bugs, suck plant juices. Others, such as water bugs, hunt small animals, including frogs, fish, and snails. Some bugs even drink human blood. These can be dangerous because they spread diseases.

Plant-eating Bug

Shield bugs are plant-eaters. They live among trees and bushes, feeding on plant juices and fruit. They take their name from their flattened bodies, which look like a warrior's shield. They are often brightly colored and patterned.

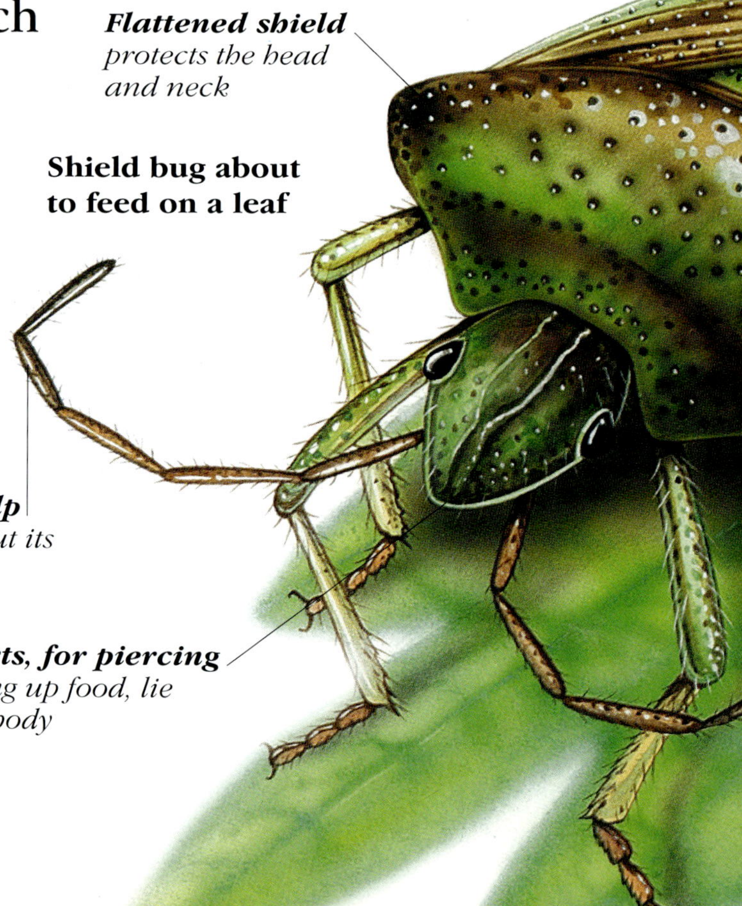

Flattened shield *protects the head and neck*

Shield bug about to feed on a leaf

Long antennae help *the bug find out about its surroundings*

Mouthparts, for piercing *and sucking up food, lie under the body*

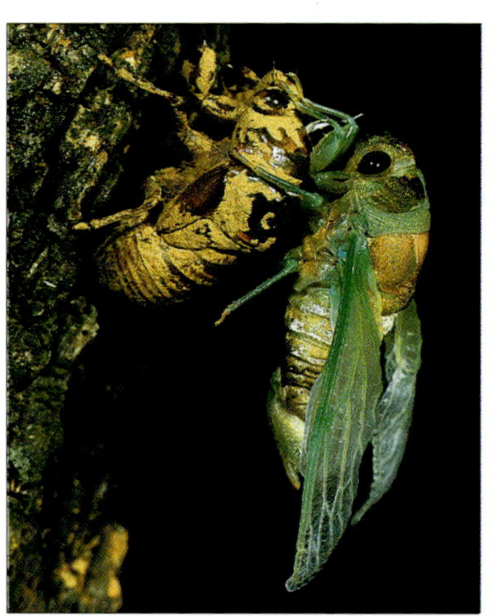

Adult cicada emerging from nymph

Cicada Call

Male cicadas sit high up in the trees and sing loudly to attract mates. The females lay their eggs in slits in twigs. When the young, called nymphs, hatch, they live underground. Some cicadas stay as nymphs for as long as 17 years before changing into adult insects.

Blood Feeder

Bedbugs hide during the day and come out at night to feed. They live by sucking the blood of birds and mammals, including humans. They do not live on the animal but in its home or nest.

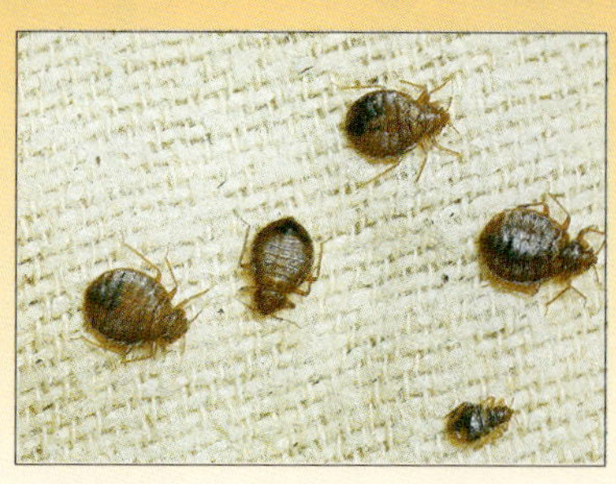

Bedbugs on a mattress

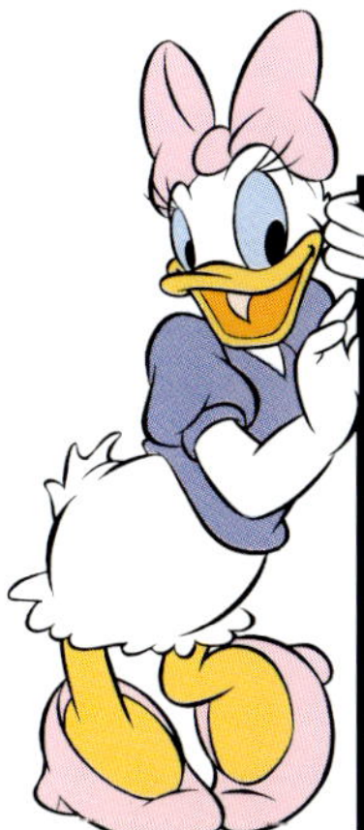

Amazing Facts

★ **The cicada makes the loudest sound of any insect. Its song can reach 112 decibels – louder than the sound of a chainsaw.**

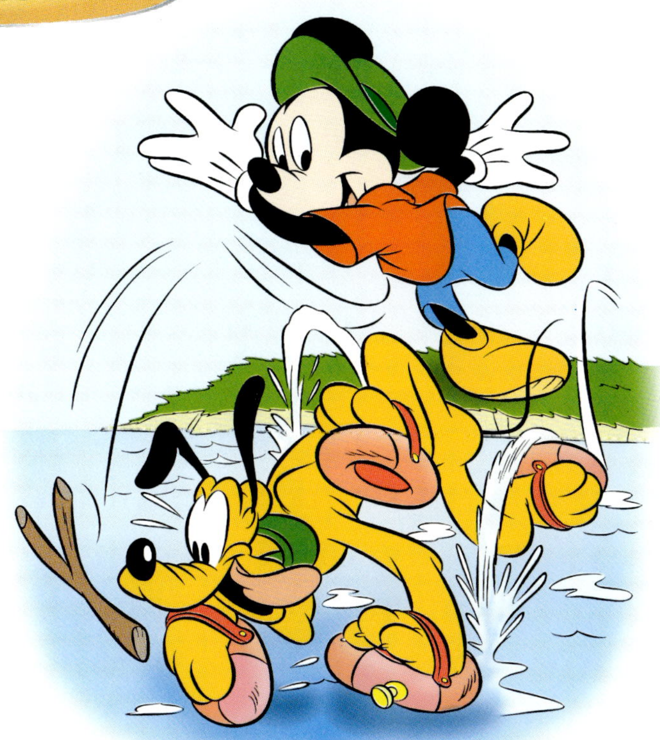

Transparent *tips of front wings*

Tough front wings *protect the abdomen and back wings*

Tiny waterproof hairs on *the water strider's feet help it move on the water surface*

Water strider

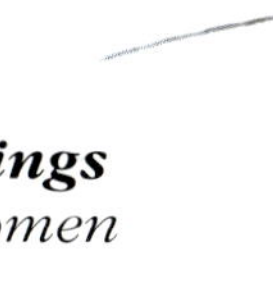

Water Bugs

Many kinds of water bugs live in lakes, ponds, and rivers. Some are so light they can walk on the water without breaking the film on the surface. Others, such as the water boatman, swim using their middle and back legs. Giant water bugs are up to 6 cm (2½ in) long and are the biggest of all bugs. They dive underwater to catch prey.

Water boatman feeds on tiny plants and algae

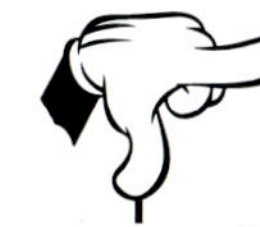

FIND OUT MORE
HUMAN BODY: Blood
REPTILES AND AMPHIBIANS: Frogs

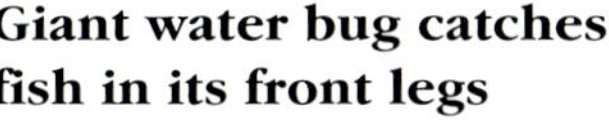

Giant water bug catches fish in its front legs

Fleas and Lice

Fleas and lice are parasites. This means that they live and feed on other animals, called their hosts. Fleas pierce the skin of birds and mammals and drink their blood. Fleas cannot fly, but for their size, they can jump higher and farther than any other animal. Sucking lice also live on blood. They include several types that feed on humans. Chewing lice use their jaws to chew their victim's skin, hair, or feathers.

Champion Jumper

A cat flea can jump more than 200 times its own length. This means a flea can leap from an animal's nest or bed onto its fur. Tiny, spiny combs on the flea's head help it stay in the fur as it sucks the cat's blood. The flea also uses its hooked claws to hold onto the cat's skin.

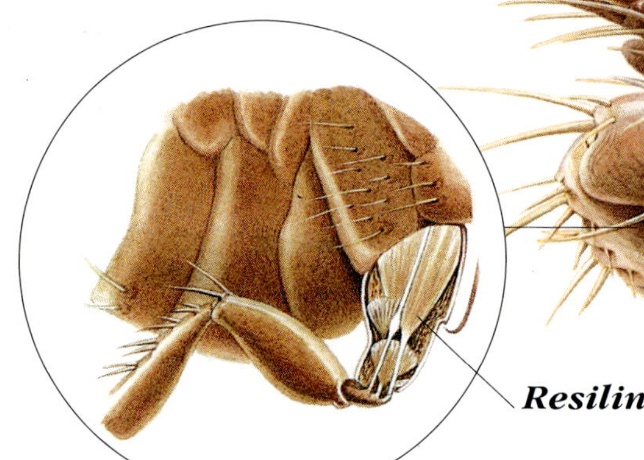

Jumping Power

A special elastic material, called resilin, inside the flea's back legs powers its jump. The resilin acts like a spring to catapult the flea into the air.

Fleas and the Plague

The Black Death was a terrible disease that killed millions of people in the 14th century. It was spread by blood-sucking fleas, which lived on infected rats. The fleas then bit humans and passed on the disease.

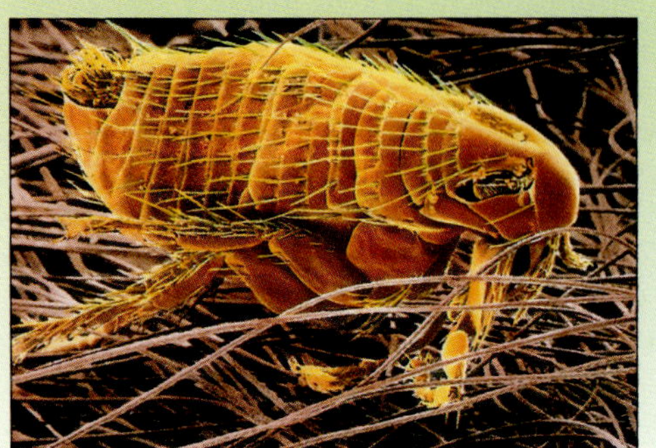

Rat flea shown at 30 times its actual size

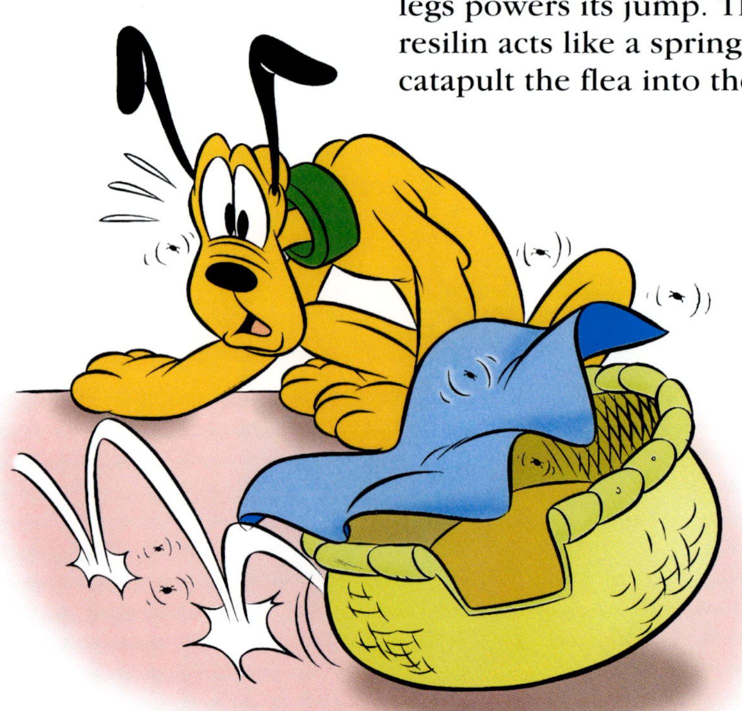

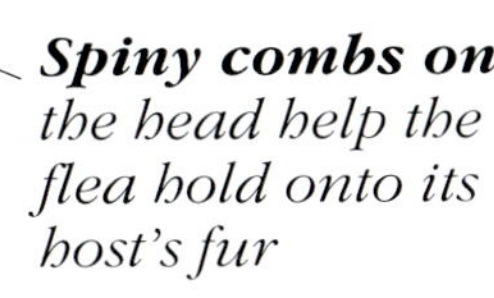

Spiny combs on the head help the flea hold onto its host's fur

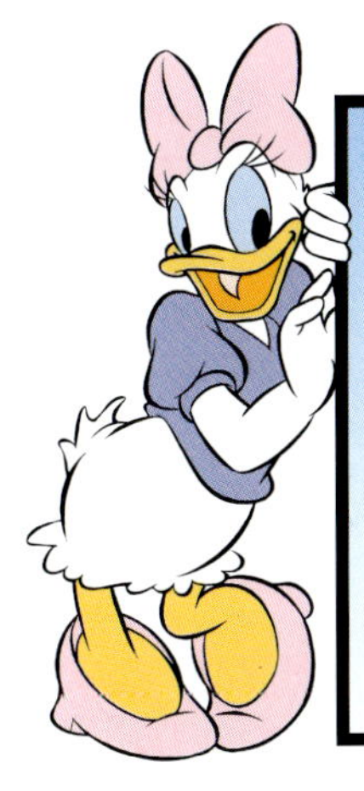

AMAZING FACTS

★ **The biggest kind of flea is the beaver flea. It can grow up to 8 mm (⅓ in) long, about half the size shown here.**

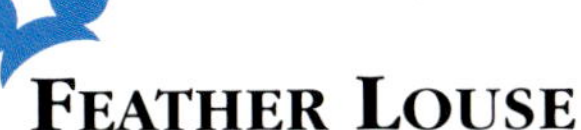

FEATHER LOUSE

Feather lice feed on birds' feathers. They cling on tightly with two strong claws. Tiny feather lice even live on hummingbirds, the smallest type of bird.

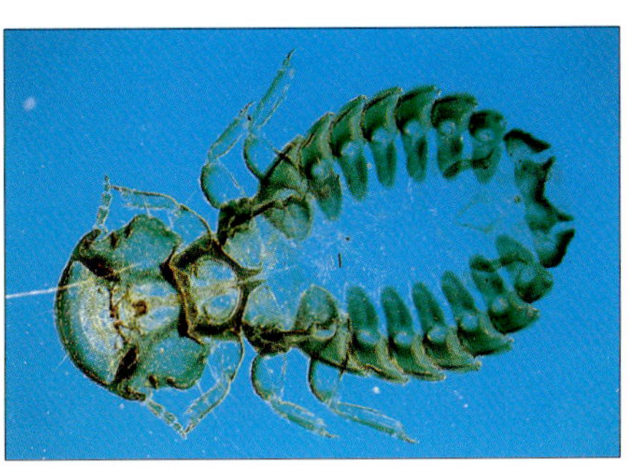

Feather louse shown at 40 times its actual size

Bristles are *highly sensitive to movements*

Leaping cat flea

Mouthparts for *piercing skin and sucking up blood*

Long back legs *for leaping up onto a host animal*

Claws for holding *onto a host animal's skin*

Hair

Strong claws for *holding onto hair*

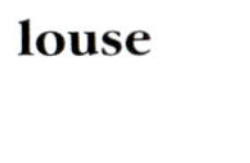

Head louse

Louse can change *color to match the hair it lives on*

AT HOME IN HAIR

The head louse lives on some people's heads. It grips onto hair with its strong legs and claws while sucking blood. Female lice lay their eggs in hair, fixing them on with a sticky liquid they make in their bodies.

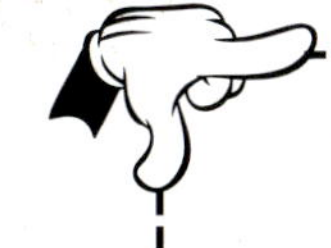

FIND OUT MORE
BIRDS: Feathers
HUMAN BODY: Hair

How Insects Move

Insects need to move around to find food, mates, and places to hide from danger. Nearly all can walk or crawl, most can fly, and some can jump or swim.

A typical insect walks on its three pairs of legs, moving the legs in each pair separately one after the other. All insect legs are made up of the same basic parts. These are adapted for different purposes such as swimming or jumping. Flying insects have strong thoracic muscles to help them move their wings. They need to beat their wings very fast to stay in the air. Hover flies, for example, beat their wings up to 1,000 times a second.

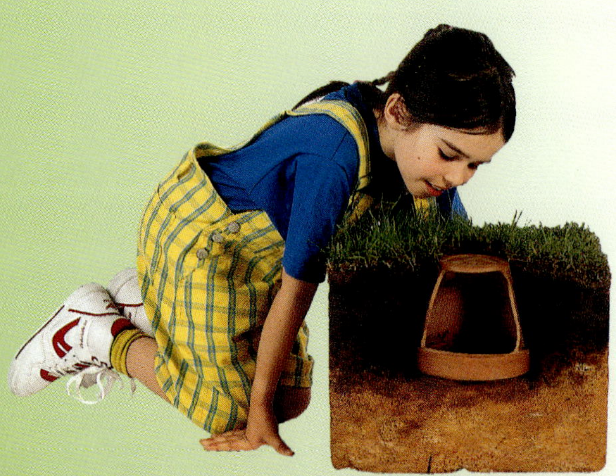

Insects can be collected in a plant pot sunk into the earth and observed as they move around

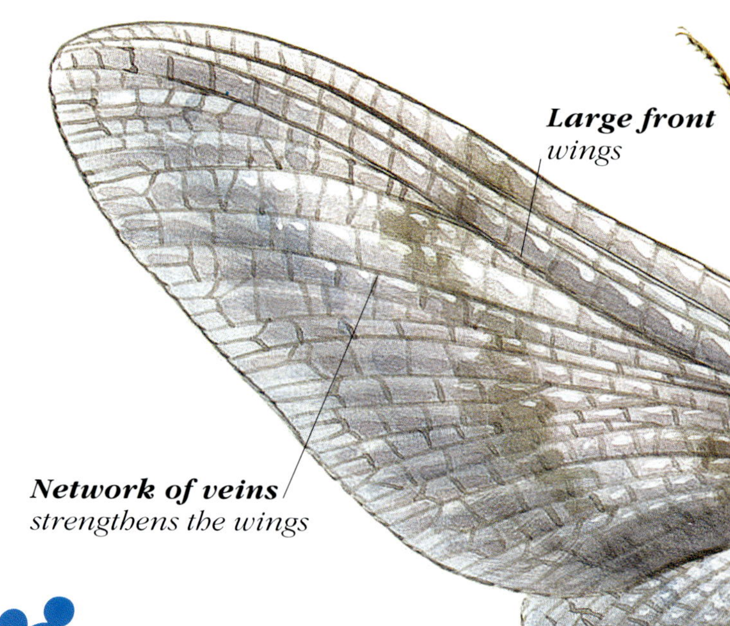

THE STRUCTURE OF WINGS

An insect's wings are attached to the sides of the thorax, the middle part of the body. Most are made of a fine, delicate material called membrane and are strengthened by hollow tubes called veins. The veins contain nerves and blood.

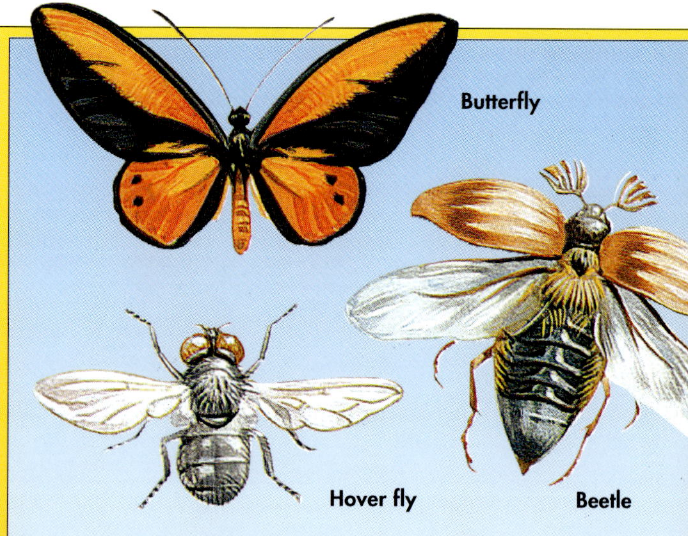

INSECT WINGS

Butterflies, beetles, and many other insects have two pairs of wings. Flies have only one pair. The front wings of some insects, such as beetles, are hard and tough. They cover and protect the delicate back wings when they are not in use.

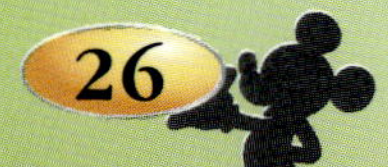

Crawl, Swim, or Jump

Like most insects, the silverfish moves fast on its six legs. Many caterpillars have extra "false legs," like little rods, at the back of their bodies. These help them to pull their bodies forward with wavelike movements. Some insects, such as diving beetles, are expert swimmers, and others jump away from danger.

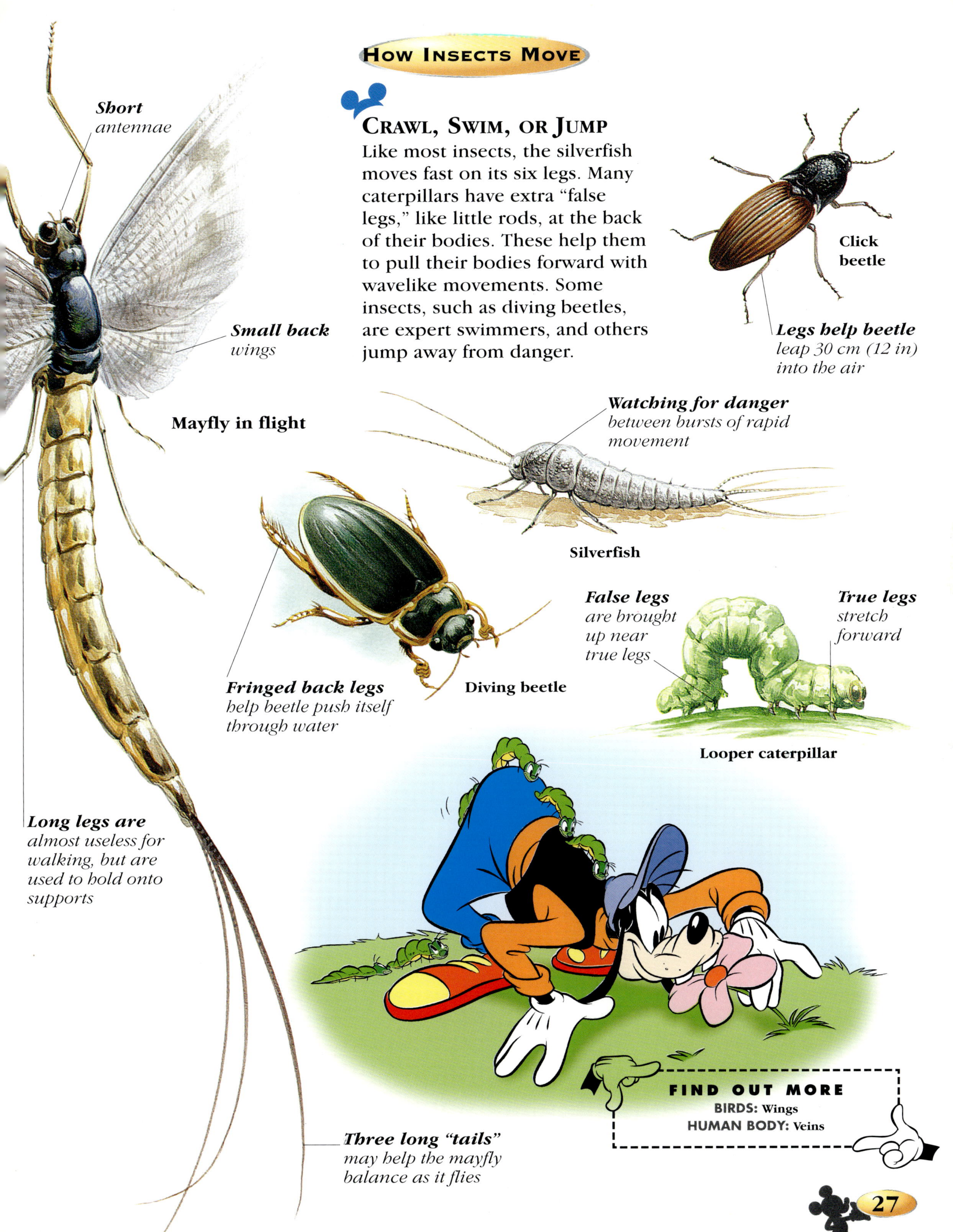

FIND OUT MORE
BIRDS: Wings
HUMAN BODY: Veins

Beetles

Beetles are the largest group of insects. At least a quarter of a million kinds are known, and there are many more still to be discovered. Beetles live all over the world, everywhere from the driest deserts to tropical rain forests. They have strong, chewing mouthparts and eat almost every type of plant and animal food.

Amazing Facts

★ The whirligig beetle's eyes are divided in two so it can see above and below the water at the same time.

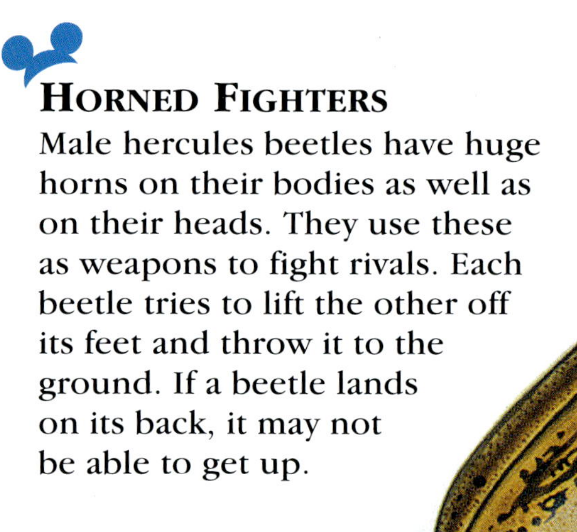

Rival male hercules beetles fighting to win mates

Horned Fighters

Male hercules beetles have huge horns on their bodies as well as on their heads. They use these as weapons to fight rivals. Each beetle tries to lift the other off its feet and throw it to the ground. If a beetle lands on its back, it may not be able to get up.

Shiny Beetles

Jewel beetles have shiny, colorful bodies. Adults eat leaves and nectar. Their larvae eat dead or living wood. They bore through the wood, causing damage.

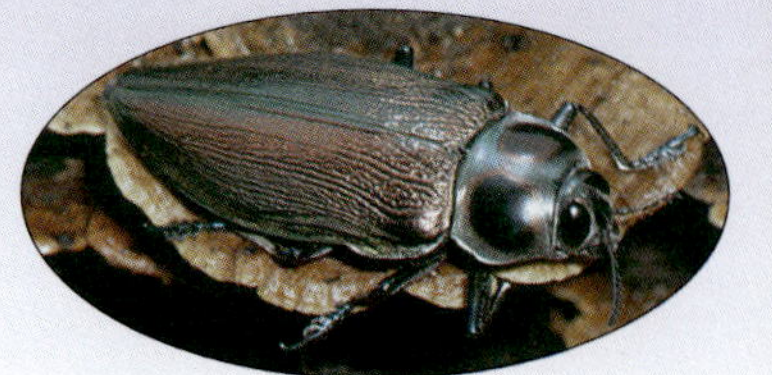

Jewel beetle

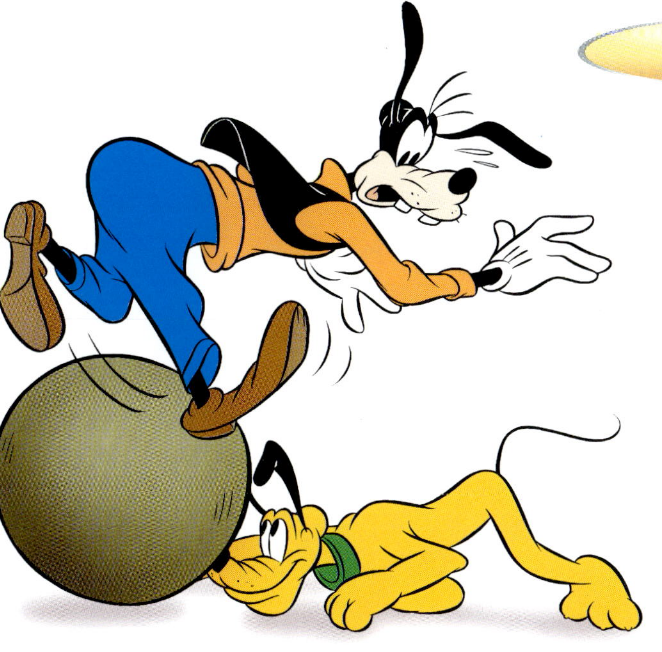

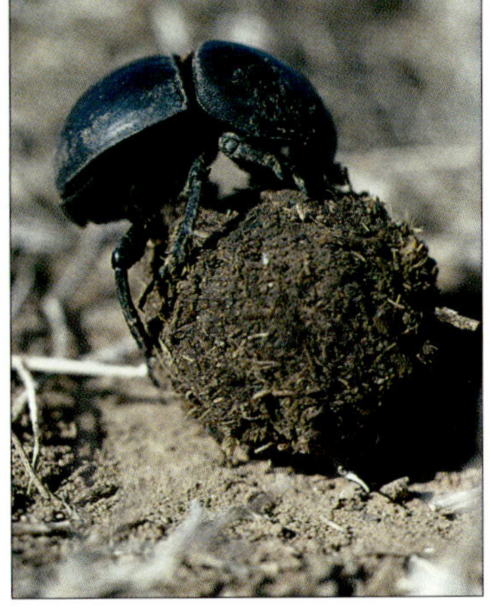

Female scarab beetle rolling a ball of dung

DUNG ROLLER

A female scarab beetle collects a lump of animal dung and makes it into a ball. Then she rolls it to her burrow and lays an egg in the middle. When the larva hatches out, it feeds on the nourishing dung.

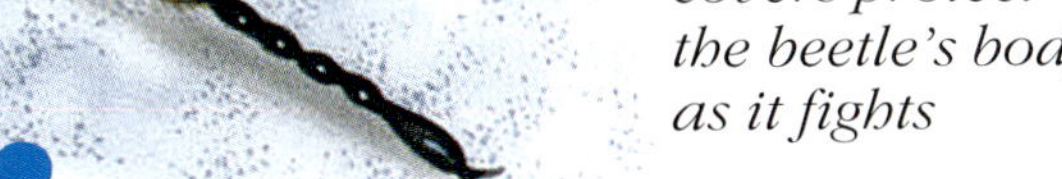

Hard wing *covers protect the beetle's body as it fights*

Male goliath beetle

SPEEDY HUNTERS

Tiger beetles are fast-running hunters that catch small prey in their jaws. Their larvae are hunters, too. They dig a burrow in the ground, then lie in wait for other insects to pass by.

GIANT BEETLE

The huge goliath beetle of Africa is one of the biggest and heaviest of all insects. Males weigh up to 100 g (3½ oz), about three times as much as a mouse, and grow up to 12.5 cm (5 in) long. Female beetles are smaller than males.

Adult tiger beetle with prey

FIND OUT MORE
DINOSAURS: Horned dinosaurs
PLANT LIFE: Tropical rain forest

Flies

Flies are common all over the world. One of the few land creatures to live in the Antarctic is a type of fly. Unlike most insects, flies have only one pair of wings. The back wings have become reduced to two small, knobbed rods, called halteres, which help them balance as they fly. There are more than 90,000 types of flies, including house flies, mosquitoes, and horse flies.

Claws at *the end of each leg*

Mouthparts *for soaking up liquid food*

House fly walking on ceiling

Fly's compound *eyes pick up the tiniest movements of prey or enemies*

Special mouthparts *for piercing victim's skin*

Mosquito feeding on blood

UPSIDE-DOWN HOUSE FLY

House flies have tiny claws and special sticky pads on their feet, which help them grip even the smoothest, shiniest surfaces. This is how house flies can walk upside down on the ceiling.

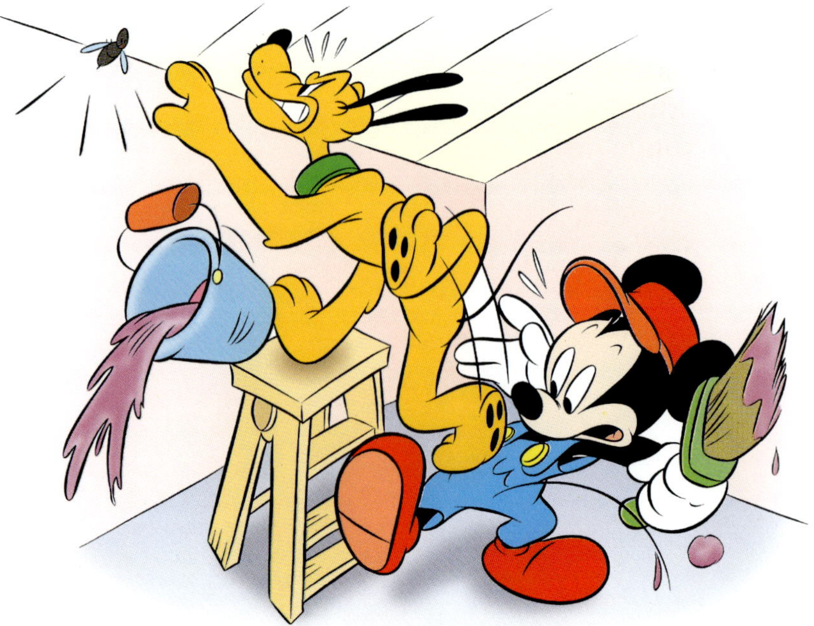

BLOOD FEEDER

Female mosquitoes feed on animal blood, which they suck from under the skin. As they bite they can spread diseases such as malaria and yellow fever. Male mosquitoes do not suck blood. They feed on sweet nectar from plants.

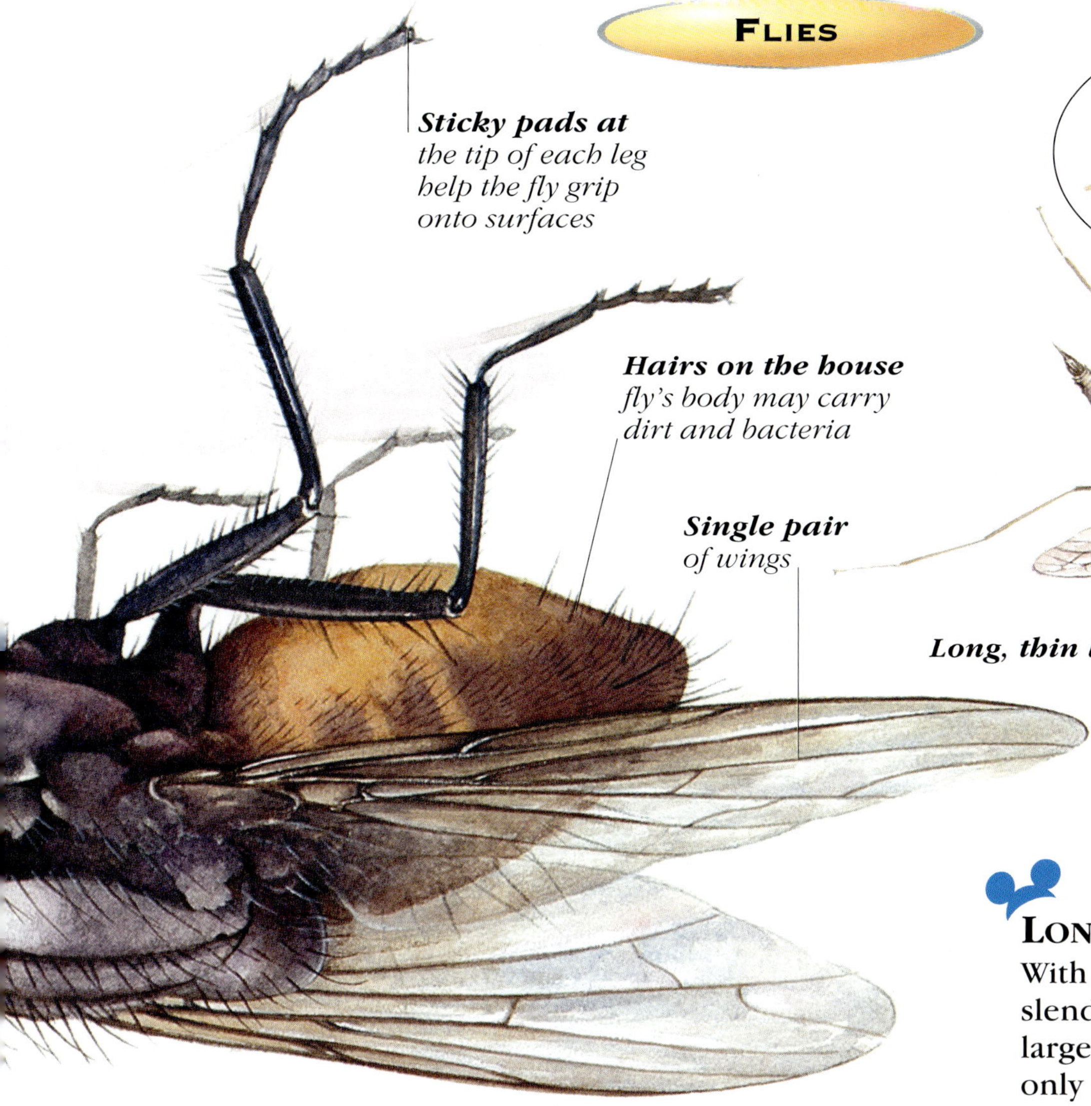

***Sticky pads at** the tip of each leg help the fly grip onto surfaces*

***Hairs on the house** fly's body may carry dirt and bacteria*

***Single pair** of wings*

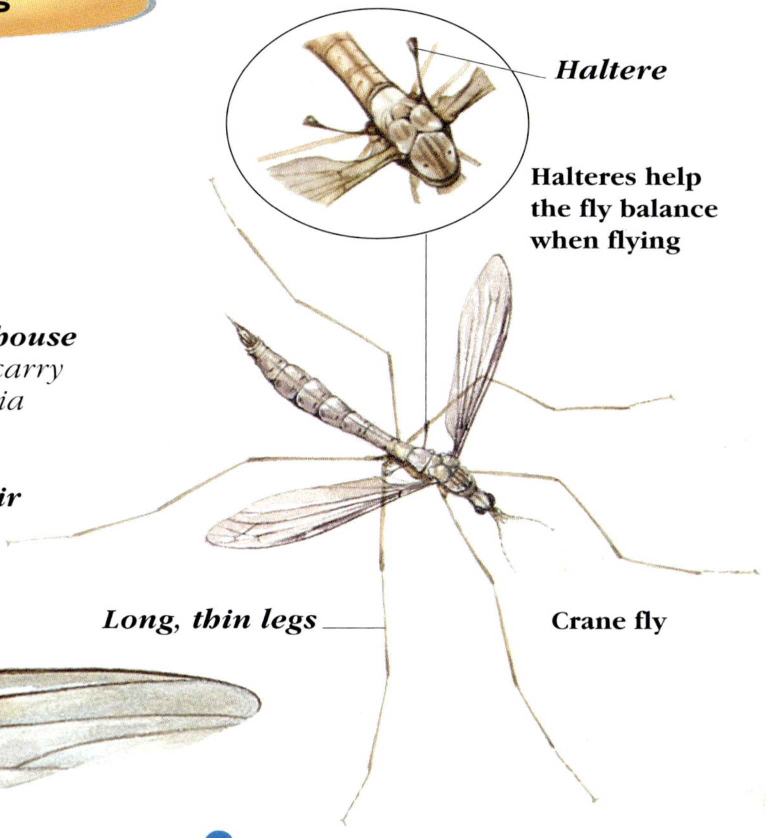

Haltere

Halteres help the fly balance when flying

Long, thin legs

Crane fly

LONG-LEGGED FLY

With their long, thin legs and slender wings, crane flies look like large mosquitoes. Most adults live only a few days and probably do not eat. Their larvae feed mainly on plant roots and rotting plants.

HORSE BITER

Horse flies have particularly large eyes, which shine red, gold, and green. Males feed on nectar, a sweet liquid in flowers. Females bite horses, cattle, and other mammals and lap up their blood.

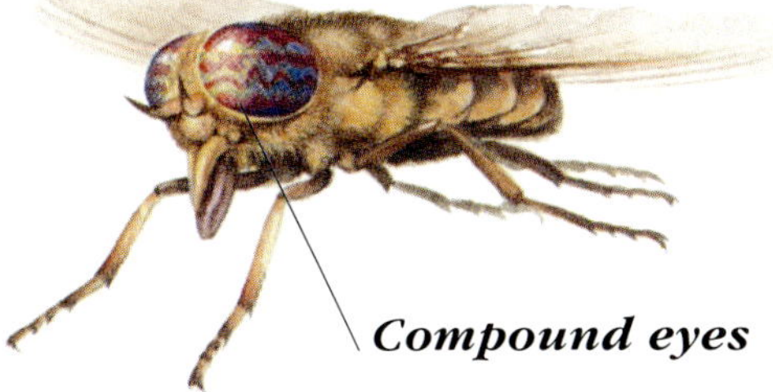

Compound eyes

Horse fly

AMAZING FACTS

★ The larvae of the petroleum fly live in pools of thick, sticky oil in California. They eat any insects that become trapped on the surface.

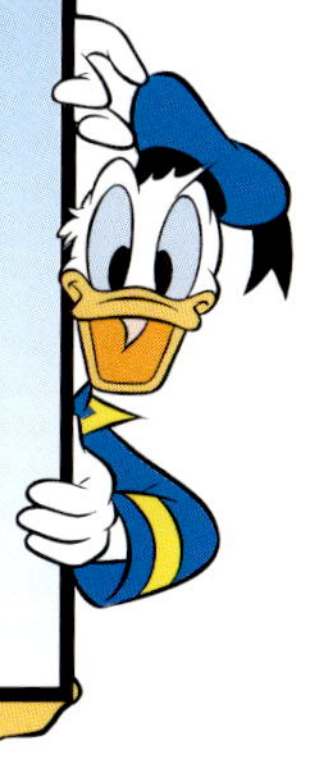

FLY EYE

A fly's bulging eyes are called compound eyes. They are made up of thousands of tiny lenses, called facets, and are particularly sensitive to movement.

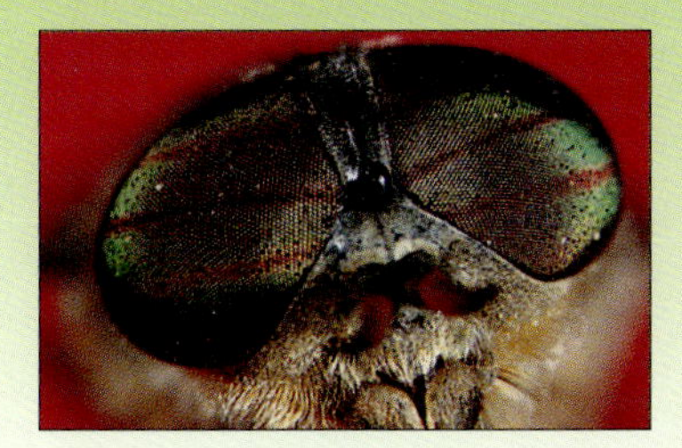

A fly's compound eyes

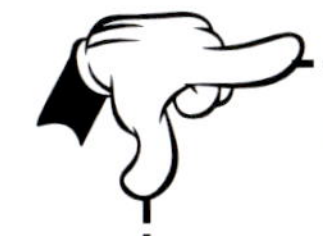

FIND OUT MORE
HUMAN BODY: Blood
PLANT LIFE: Nectar

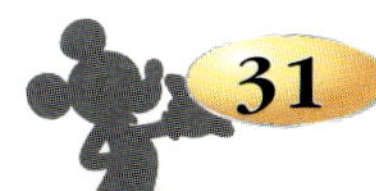

Butterflies and Moths

There are about 200,000 kinds of butterflies and moths. They range from tiny creatures less than a centimeter long to giant moths bigger than some birds. Butterflies and moths have two pairs of wings and special mouthparts, including a long, coiled tube for feeding on liquids. Their young are called caterpillars. They have chewing mouthparts and feed on plants.

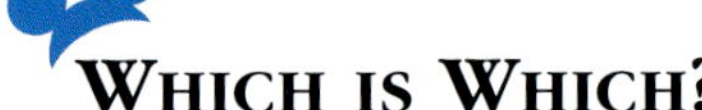

WHICH IS WHICH?

Butterflies fly by day and are often brightly colored. Moths are usually duller in color and fly at night. Most moths have straight or feathery antennae. A butterfly's antennae are like tiny clubs.

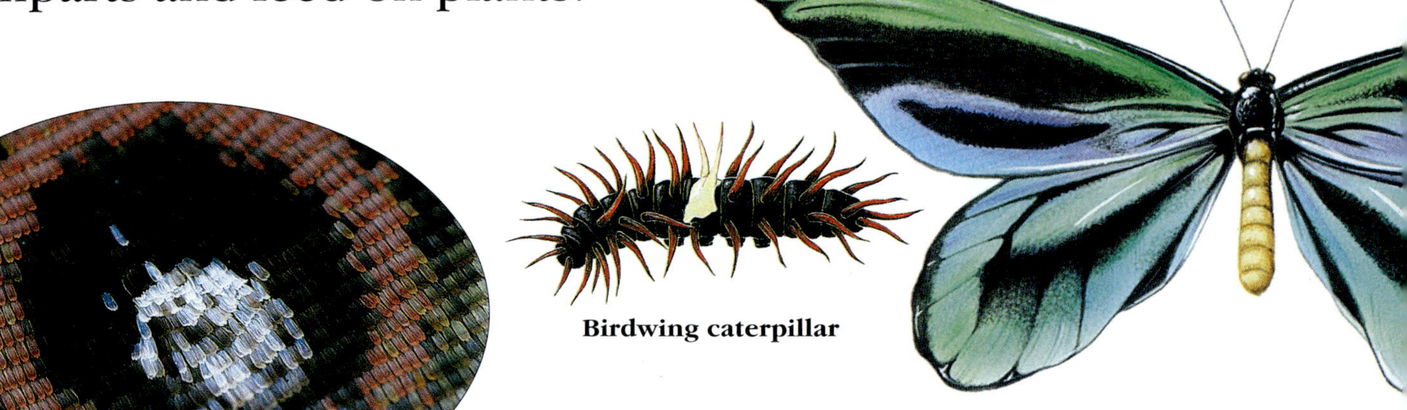

Birdwing caterpillar

Queen Alexandra's birdwing butterfly

Close-up of scales on a butterfly's wing

SCALY WINGS

Butterfly and moth wings are covered in colored scales, which are actually tiny, flat hairs. These overlap, like the tiles on the roof of a house. Each scale has its own flexible fixing and can move up and down. The scales form beautiful patterns and colors that shimmer in the sun.

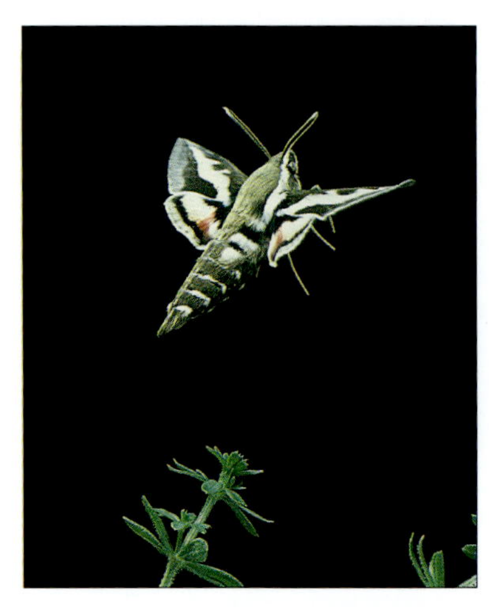

Hawkmoth in flight

FAST FLIERS

Hawkmoths are strong and speedy fliers. They reach speeds of 40 km/h (25 mph), faster than any other moth or butterfly. Hawkmoths can also hover in midair as they feed on flower nectar.

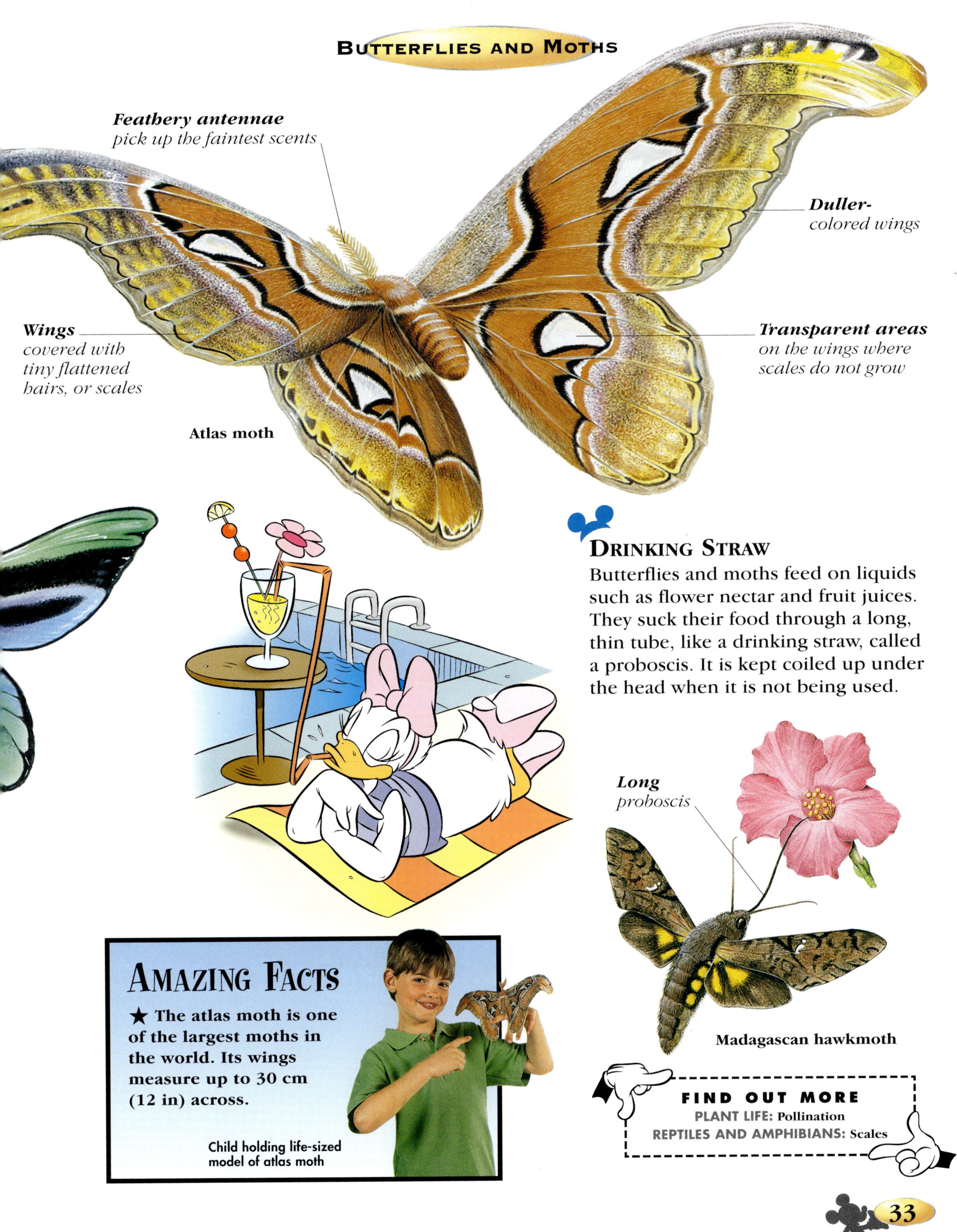

Atlas moth

Madagascan hawkmoth

DRINKING STRAW

Butterflies and moths feed on liquids such as flower nectar and fruit juices. They suck their food through a long, thin tube, like a drinking straw, called a proboscis. It is kept coiled up under the head when it is not being used.

AMAZING FACTS

★ The atlas moth is one of the largest moths in the world. Its wings measure up to 30 cm (12 in) across.

Child holding life-sized model of atlas moth

FIND OUT MORE
PLANT LIFE: Pollination
REPTILES AND AMPHIBIANS: Scales

Food and Feeding

Almost everything is food to some kind of insect. Plant-eaters feed on leaves, stems, and flowers as well as sap and nectar. Meat-eaters catch living creatures or eat the bodies of animals that are already dead. Some insects even suck blood or eat paper, wool, and wood.

The mouthparts of insects are specially adapted for the way they eat. Insects that take liquid food, such as nectar, have a mouth like a sucking tube, called a proboscis. Those that feed on blood or sap also have a special part for piercing the food source. Beetles and other insects that eat solid food have strong jaws for biting and chewing.

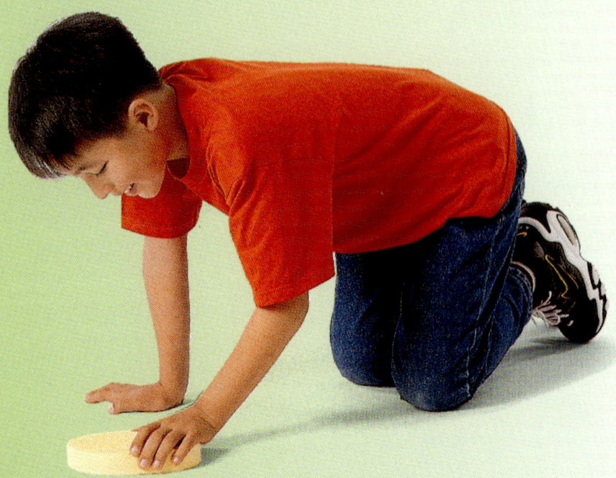

A house fly uses a pad a little like a sponge to soak up food in liquid form

PLANT-EATER

The plant bug's mouth is like a long, jointed tube. It pierces a hole in a leaf or stem, then sucks out the juicy sap inside. Plant bugs are often green to help them hide among leaves.

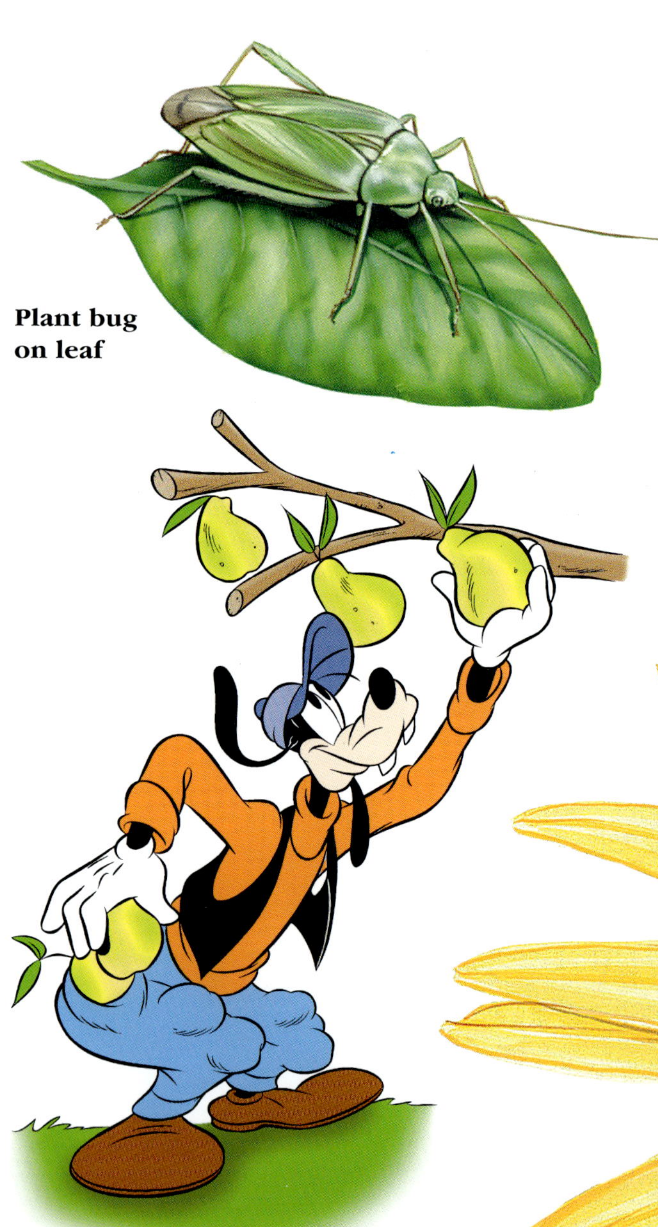

Plant bug on leaf

COLLECTING FOOD STORES

Honeybees gather nectar and pollen from flowers to take back to their nests. When a bee lands on a flower, pollen sticks to its body. The bee sweeps the pollen off with its middle legs and packs it into special areas on the back legs. The pollen is held in place by tiny bristles.

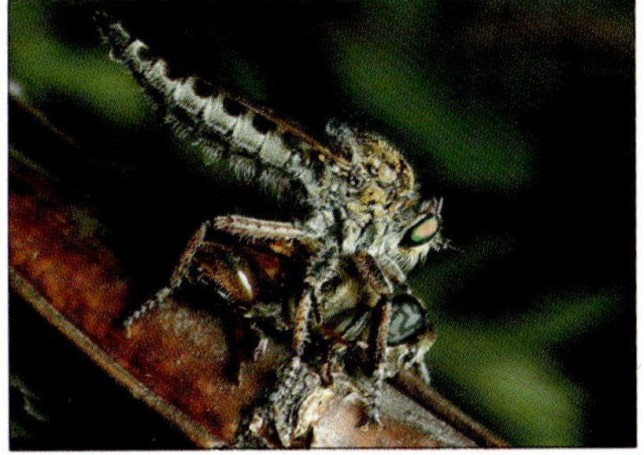

Robber fly and its prey

Antlion at the bottom of trap

Antlion Trap

An antlion larva digs a funnel-shaped pit in the soil. Then it lies in wait at the bottom, with its sharp jaws held ready. If an ant tumbles into the pit, the antlion is quick to pounce.

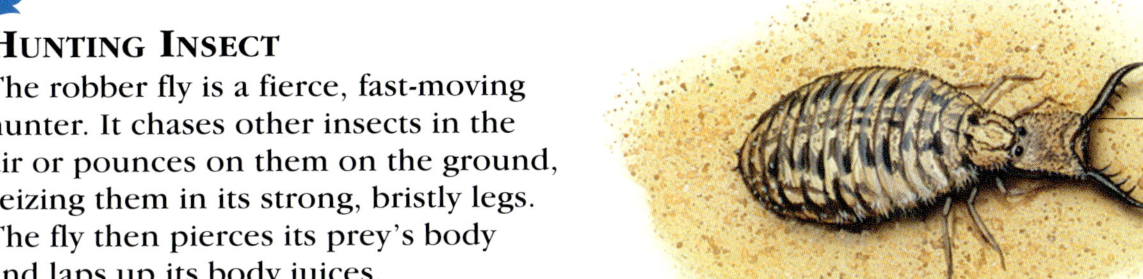

Hunting Insect

The robber fly is a fierce, fast-moving hunter. It chases other insects in the air or pounces on them on the ground, seizing them in its strong, bristly legs. The fly then pierces its prey's body and laps up its body juices.

Spiny jaws held open to catch prey

Antlion waiting for prey

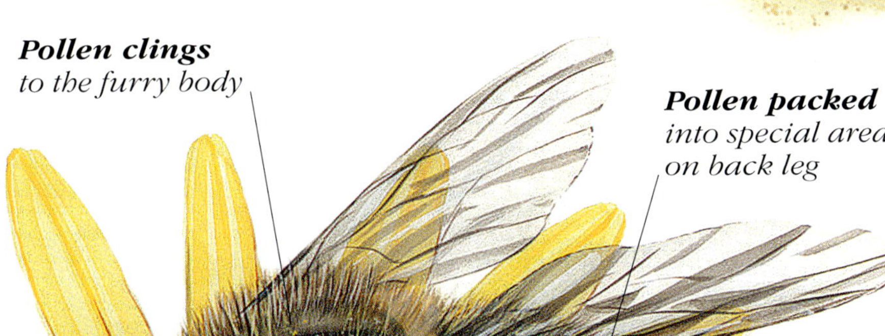

Pollen clings to the furry body

Pollen packed into special area on back leg

Hairs on middle legs for removing pollen from the body

Bee sucks up nectar

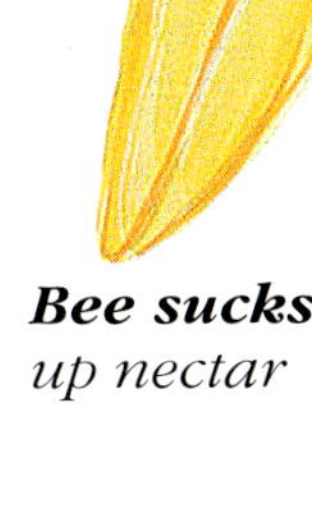

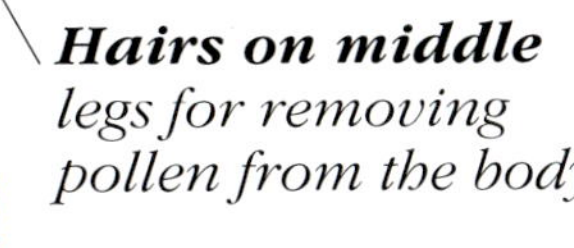

Honeybee gathering pollen

Meat-Eaters

Carrion beetles feed on the dead bodies of mice and birds. Some bury the bodies in the ground. They lay their eggs on the rotting meat so their larvae have plenty of food to eat when they hatch.

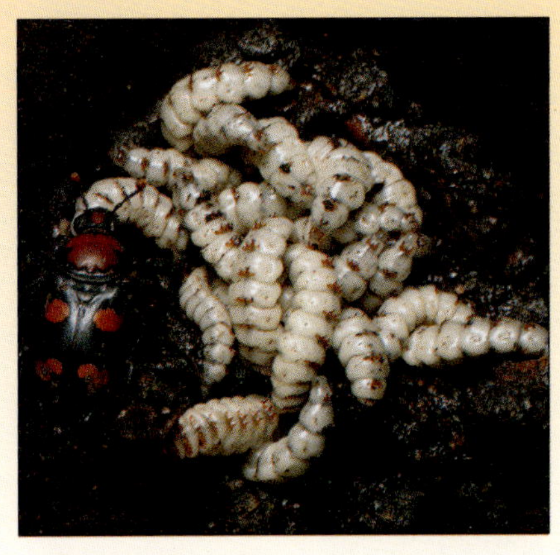

Carrion beetle and larvae on dead flesh

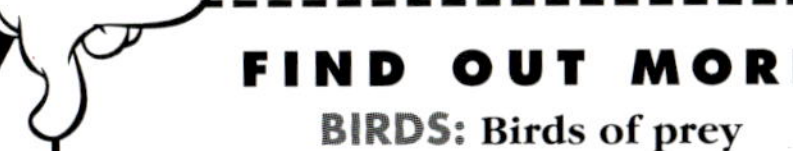

FIND OUT MORE
BIRDS: Birds of prey
PLANT LIFE: Pollination

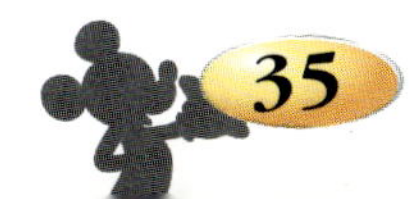

Bees

Some kinds of bees, such as honeybees and bumblebees, live in huge groups called colonies. These contain many thousands of insects. A large female, called the queen, is head of the colony. Worker bees look after the nest, gather nectar and pollen to use as food stores, and care for the young. Other kinds of bees live by themselves and do not build large nests.

Worker bee filling *a cell with pollen which is fed to larvae*

Honeybees' Nest

Honeybees build their nests in trees or beehives. The nests contain lots of hexagonal, or six-sided, cells made of wax from the bees' bodies. Some of the cells are used for storing honey. Others are nurseries for eggs and larvae.

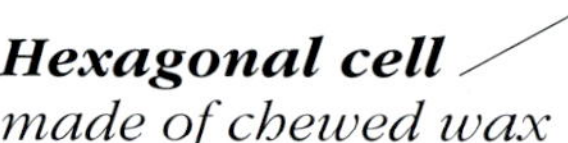

Hexagonal cell *made of chewed wax*

Dancing Bees

Inside their hive, worker bees perform a special dance to tell each other where to find food. The speed and direction of the dance shows the other workers where the best food is to be found. A fast dance means a good food source.

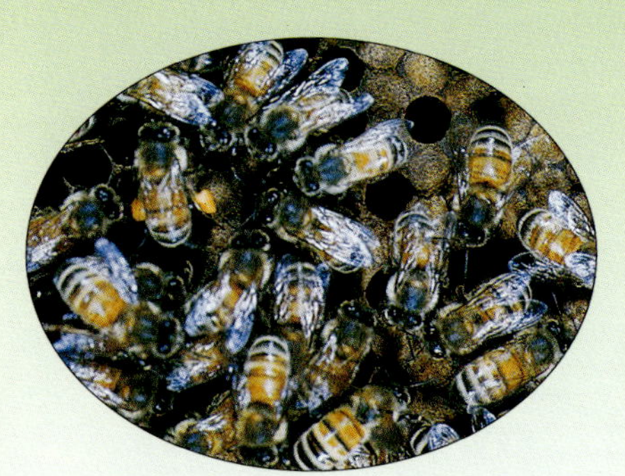

Honeybees performing their dance

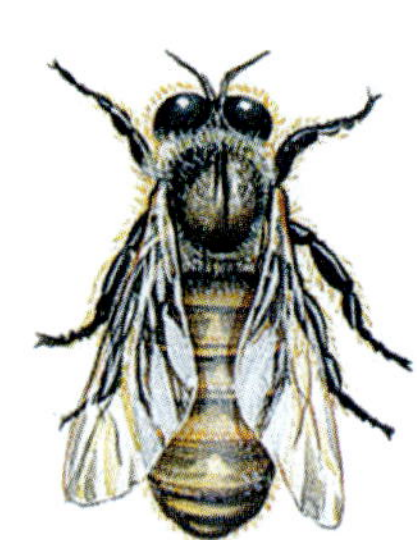

Drone

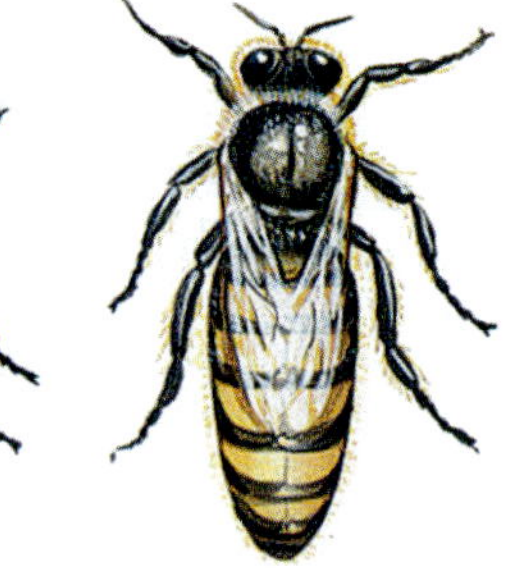

Queen bee

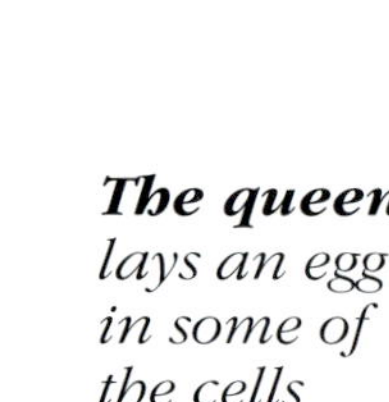

The queen *lays an egg in some of the cells*

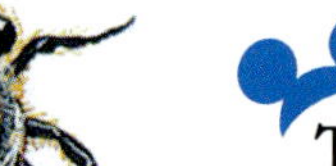

Worker bee

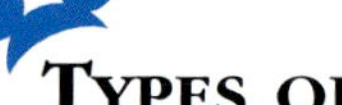

Types of Bees

In a honeybee colony, there are several different types of bees. The queen is larger than the others and lays all the eggs. Worker bees are females, too, but they do not lay eggs. Male bees, called drones, mate with new queens and make new nests.

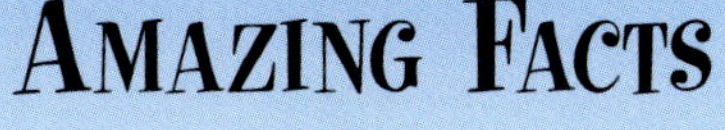

AMAZING FACTS

★ **In its lifetime, a worker bee collects enough nectar to make about 7 g (¼ oz) of honey. It would take about 57 bees to fill a 400 g (14 oz) jar of honey.**

Honey is made from *nectar and is stored in cells to feed the colony in winter*

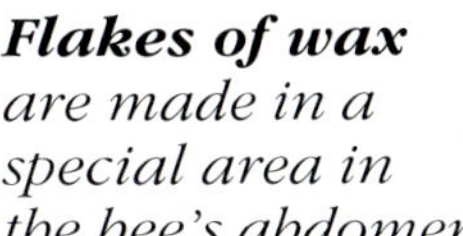

Flakes of wax *are made in a special area in the bee's abdomen*

Queen and worker bees on nest cells

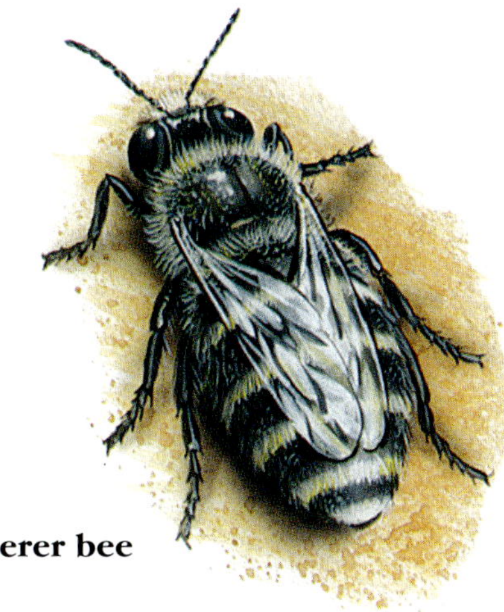

Plasterer bee

UNDERGROUND BEE

The plasterer bee lives alone. It digs a small nest in the ground and lines the walls with a clear, waterproof liquid from its abdomen. This sets smooth and hard, like plaster.

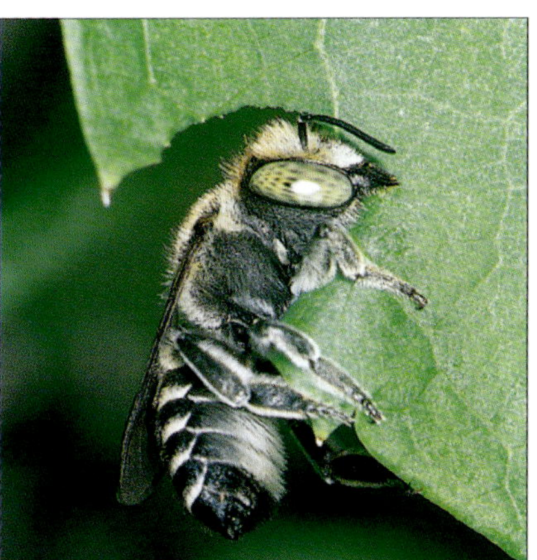

Leafcutter bee at work on a leaf

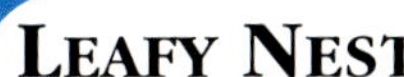

LEAFY NEST

Using its large jaws, the leafcutter bee cuts out pieces from leaves and uses them to divide and line the cells in its nest. It fills the cells with pollen and lays an egg in each one. When the young bees hatch, they feed on the pollen.

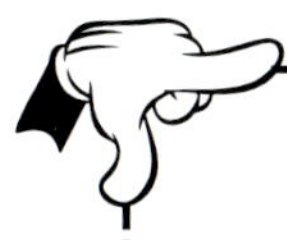

FIND OUT MORE
BIRDS: Nests
PLANT LIFE: Bee vision

Wasps

Like bees, many types of wasps live in large groups called colonies. Some of these, such as paper wasps, build amazing nests out of chewed-up wood. Others, such as spider wasps and gall wasps, live alone. Adult wasps feed on nectar and ripe fruit, but they hunt other insects to feed to their young. Most wasps have a sting at the end of their body, which they use to kill prey and to defend themselves.

AMAZING FACTS

★ **The biggest nest ever made by paper wasps was found in New Zealand. It was as tall as two people and was so heavy it had fallen and broken in two.**

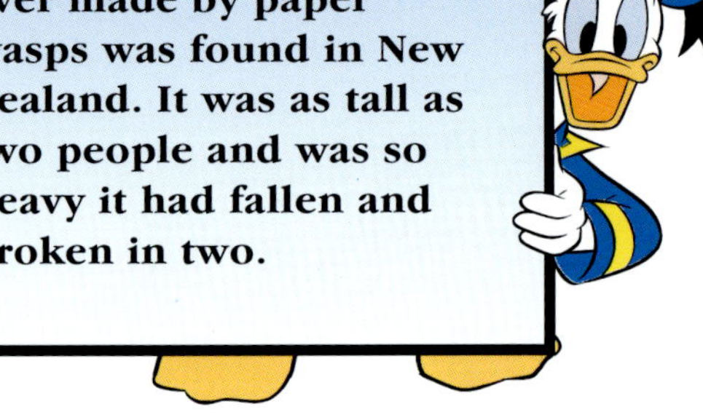

Long body

Sting at the *end of the body*

Narrow waist *between thorax and abdomen*

PAPER NESTS

To build their nests, paper wasps chew up tiny pieces of wood and mix it with their own spit. They use this papery material to make the six-sided cells that form the body of the nest and wrap several layers around the outside. The nest usually hangs from a branch.

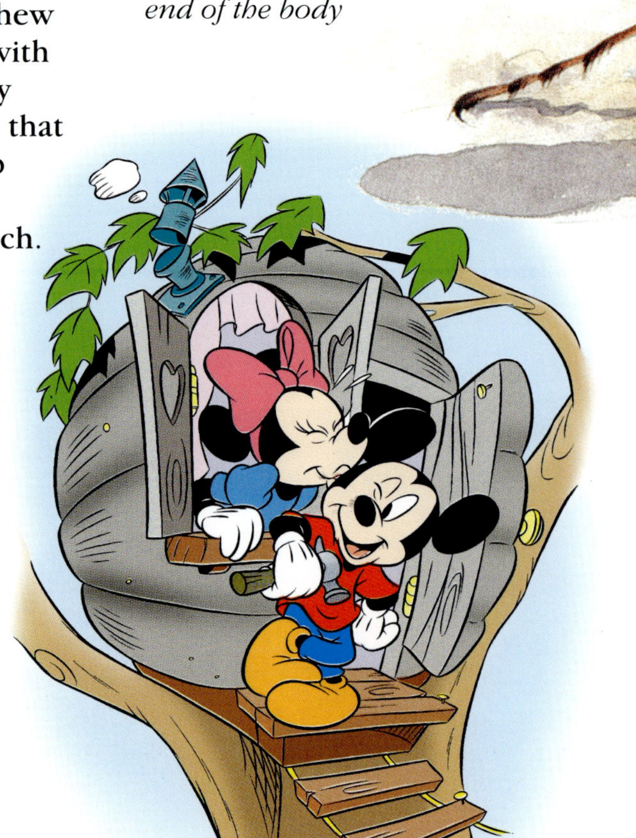

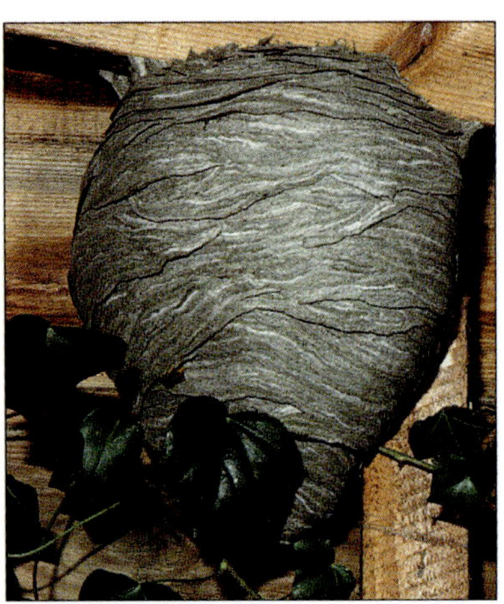

Paper wasps' nest

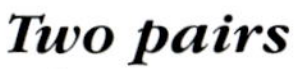

BURIED ALIVE

Female hunting wasps catch other insects and spiders. The wasp stings her prey so it cannot move but is still alive. Then she buries it in a small burrow and lays an egg on its body. When the larva hatches, it has fresh meat to eat.

FOOD FOR YOUNG

Gall wasps lay their eggs on the buds, roots, or leaves of trees. The plant grows a ball-shaped swelling, called a gall, around each egg. When the wasp larva hatches, it feeds on the fleshy gall.

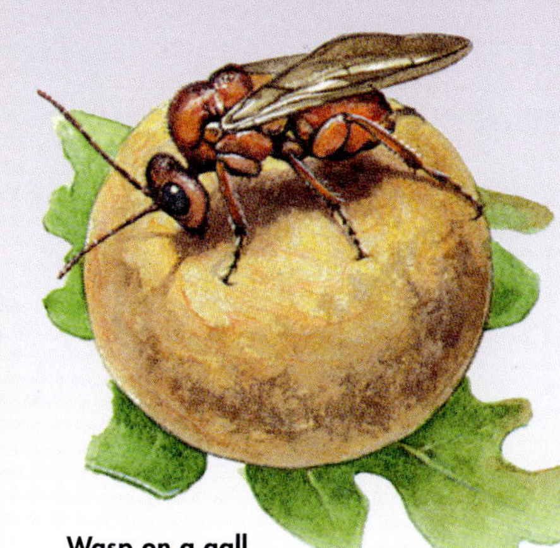

Wasp on a gall

***Two pairs** of wings*

Strong jaws

***Caterpillar** will be food for the wasp's young*

Hunting wasp burying her prey

Female wood-boring wasp laying eggs

***Egg-laying** tube*

Insect larva

DRILLING INTO WOOD

Wood-boring wasps lay their eggs on the larvae of other insects that live under tree bark. The female finds a larva by smell or by sensing its movements. She drills a hole in the wood, using the long, pointed tube at the end of her body, and lays her eggs. When her eggs hatch, the young eat the larva.

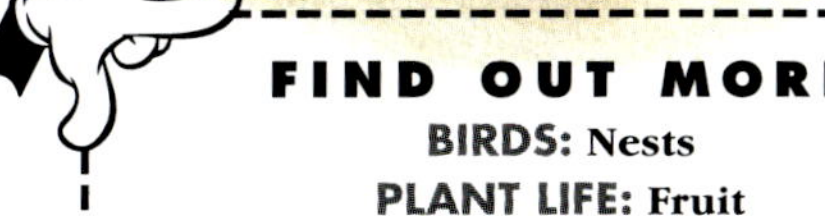

FIND OUT MORE
BIRDS: Nests
PLANT LIFE: Fruit

Ants and Termites

Closely related to bees and wasps, ants live in huge colonies of as many as 100,000 insects. Ants build nests in trees or underground. Termites live like ants, but they are not related to them. These tiny insects are famous for building tower-shaped nests which can stand several meters tall.

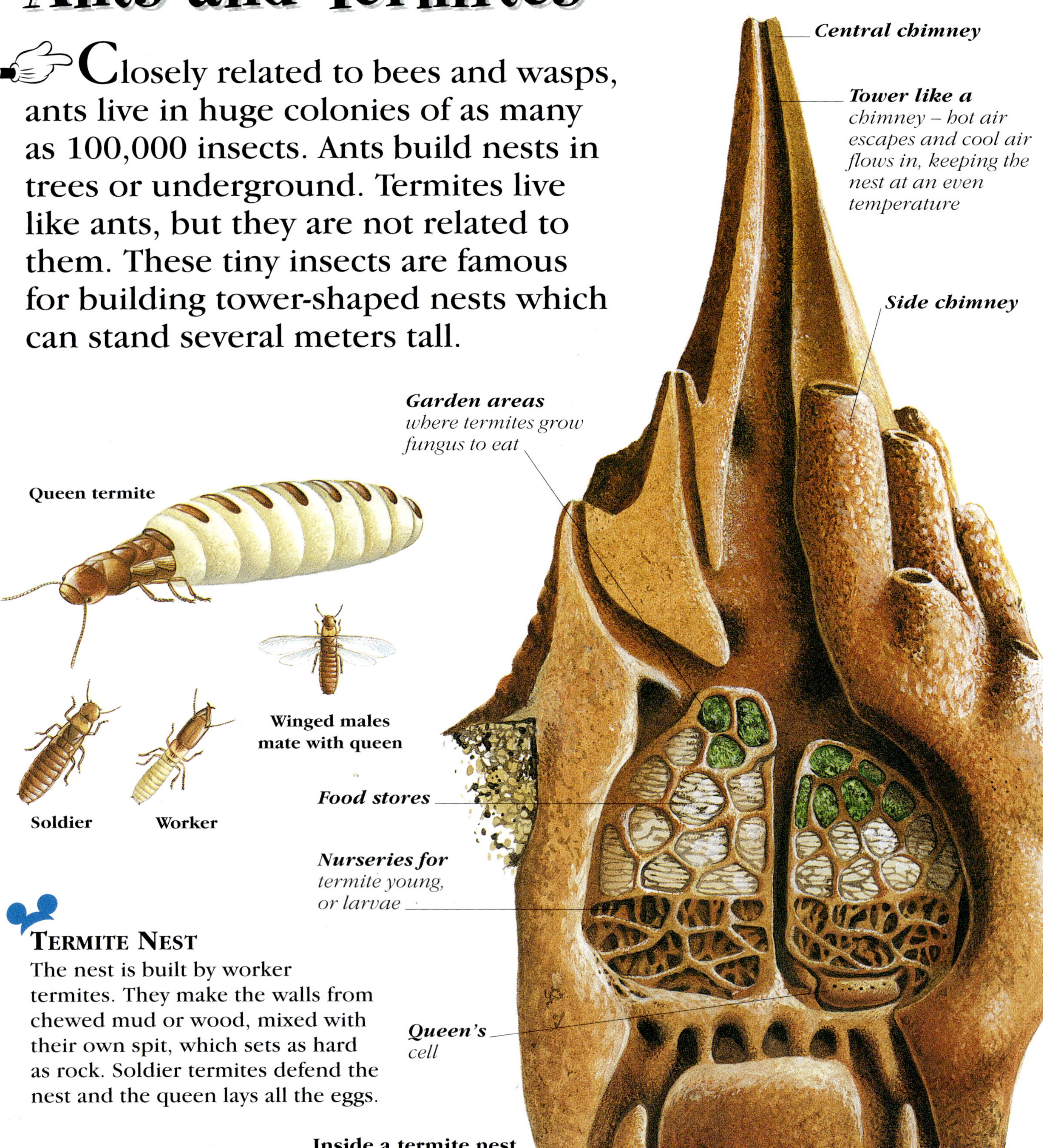

Inside a termite nest

Termite Nest

The nest is built by worker termites. They make the walls from chewed mud or wood, mixed with their own spit, which sets as hard as rock. Soldier termites defend the nest and the queen lays all the eggs.

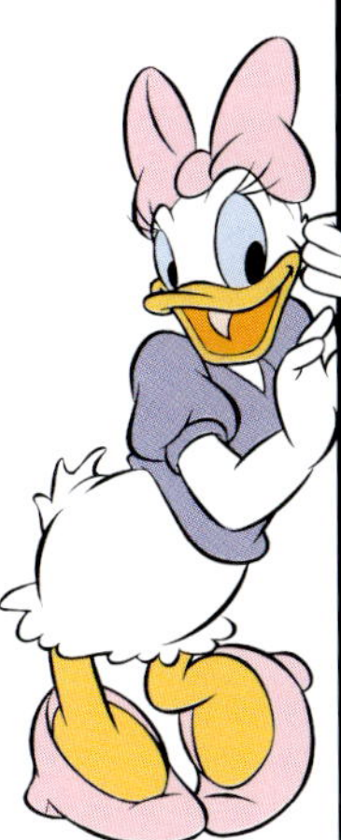

Amazing Facts

★ **Some honeypot ants are used as living storage jars. They are fed with so much nectar that their bodies swell. When food is scarce, other ants stroke the "honeypots" to make them release their stores.**

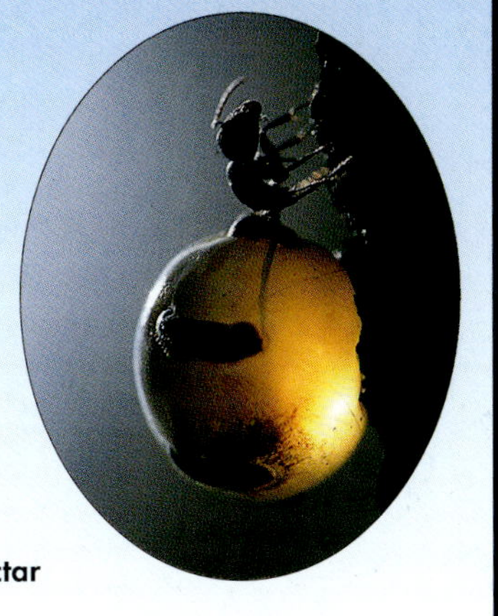

Honeypot ant swollen with nectar

Marching Ants

Unlike other ants, army ants do not live in a nest. They march across the forest floor in huge armies made up of thousands of ants. They swarm over insects, snakes, and other small creatures, devouring them with their large jaws.

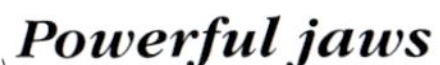

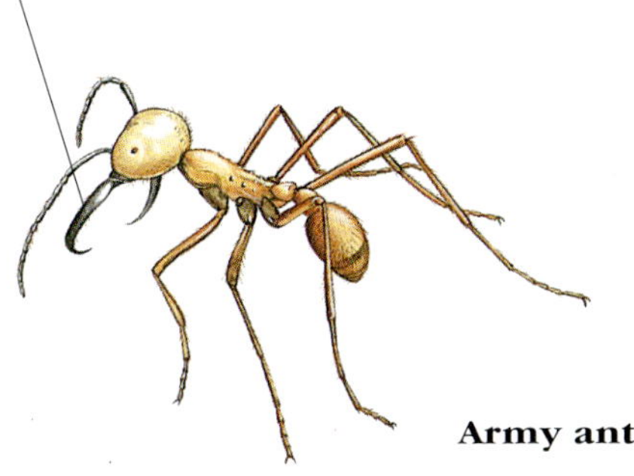

Army ant

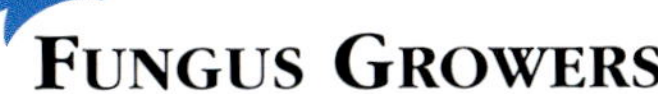

Fungus Growers

Leafcutter ants cut out pieces of leaves and carry them back to the nest underground. They grow fungus on the piles of rotting, chewed-up leaves and use the fungus as food.

Ants carrying pieces of leaf back to the nest

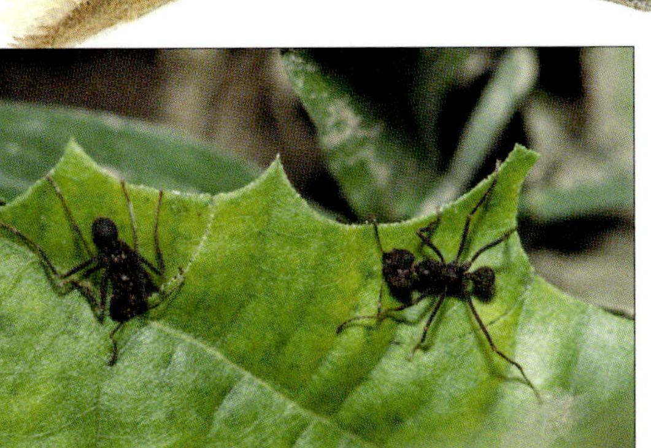

Leafcutter ants cutting pieces of a leaf with their strong jaws

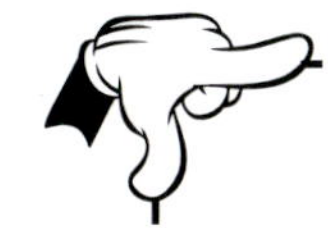

Find Out More
PLANT LIFE:
Ant plants, Seed dispersal

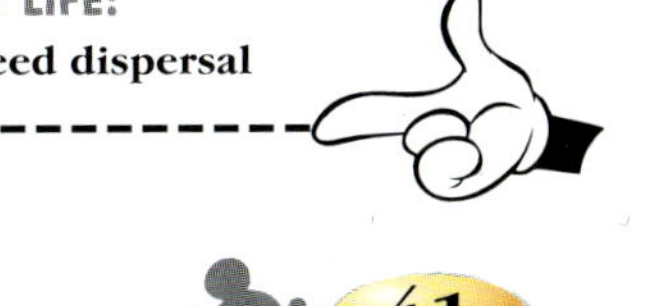

Insect Defenses

Many other animals catch and eat insects. But insects have special ways of protecting themselves so they do not always get caught by predators.

Some have weapons, such as sharp stings, for injecting poison into their enemies. Strong colors, such as red and black, warn an enemy that an insect is poisonous or nasty to eat. Some insects protect themselves by camouflage, or blending into the background. Others avoid attack by looking like something else. The clearwing moth is harmless, but it looks just like a stinging wasp. This fools its enemies into leaving it alone.

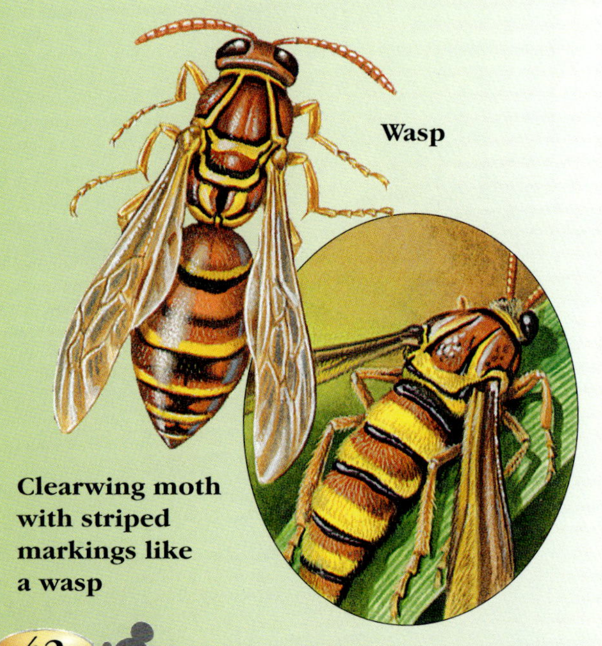

Beetle Bombs

If an enemy gets too close, a bombardier beetle shoots out a cloud of burning, poisonous gas. It makes the gas inside its abdomen from a mixture of two harmless chemicals. As these mix, they explode with a bang.

Antennae

***Cloud of** poisonous gas*

***Stinging hairs cover** the caterpillar's body*

Tussock moth caterpillar

Fearsome Fur

Many kinds of caterpillars are covered with stinging hairs and spines. They make a very painful mouthful and birds soon learn to leave them alone. Such caterpillars can also cause a nasty rash in humans.

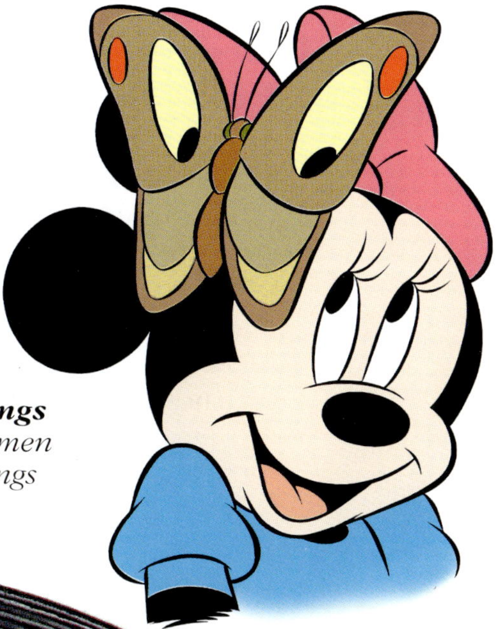

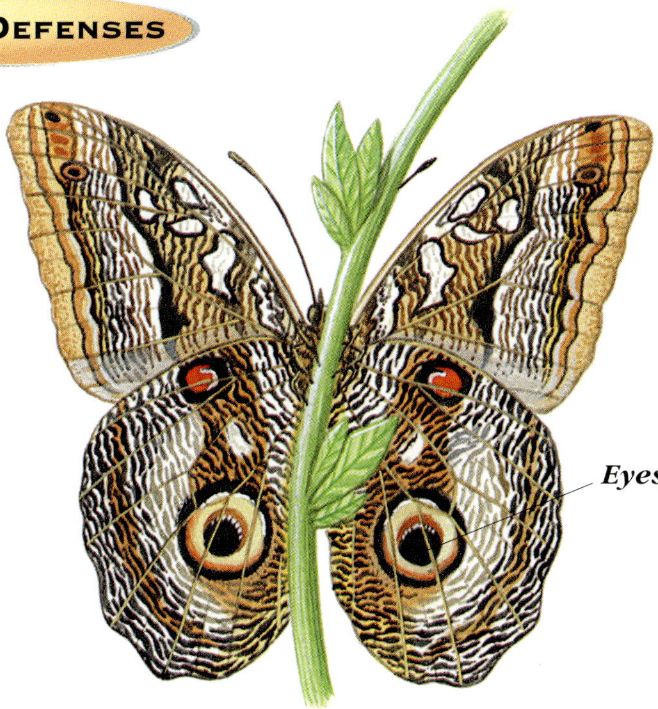

Tough front wings protect the abdomen and the back wings

Abdomen

The beetle can turn the tip of its abdomen to fire poisonous gas at its attacker

Three pairs of legs

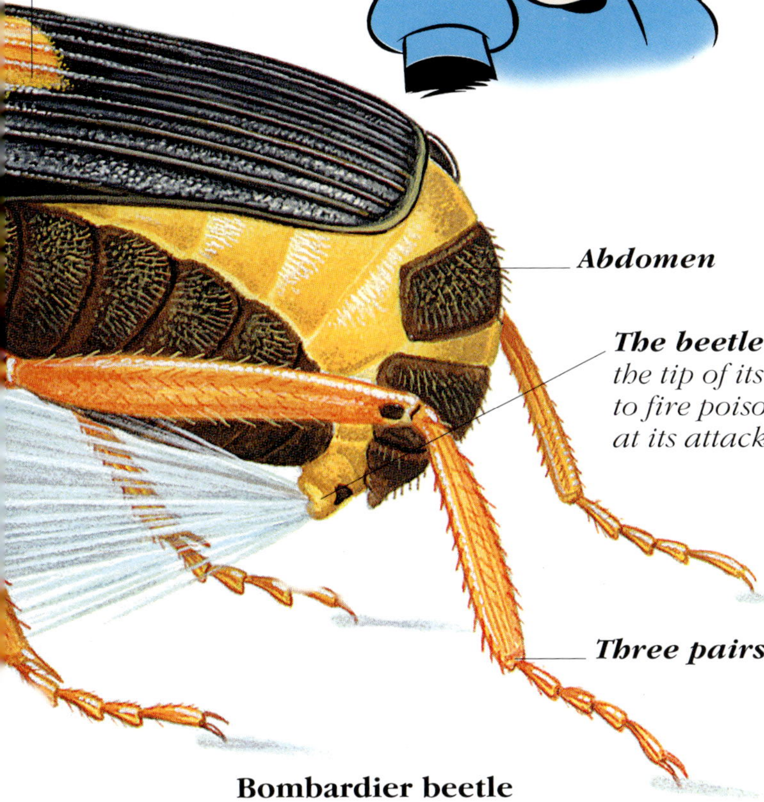

Bombardier beetle spraying gas

Eyespots

Owl butterfly

WARNING EYES

Some butterflies and moths have markings on their wings that look like large staring eyes. These make their enemies think that they are bigger and scarier than they actually are.

WASP STING

A wasp sting is long and hollow for injecting poison into an attacker. It can be pulled out of the victim and used again and again.

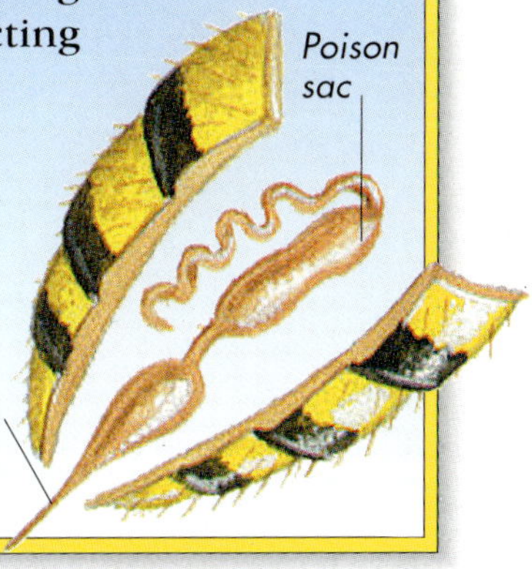

Poison sac

Sting

Close-up of sting inside the abdomen

A BAD TASTE

The toxic oil beetle's bold coloring warns hunters that it tastes horrible. Its body contains a powerful poison, which can paralyze predators. It causes blisters on human skin and a painful burn like a nettle.

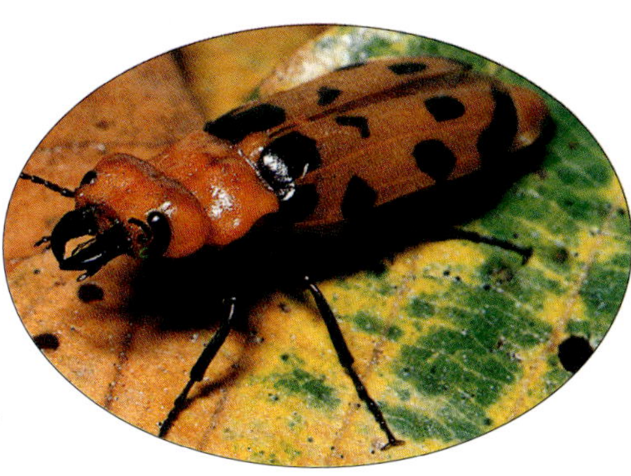

Toxic oil beetle

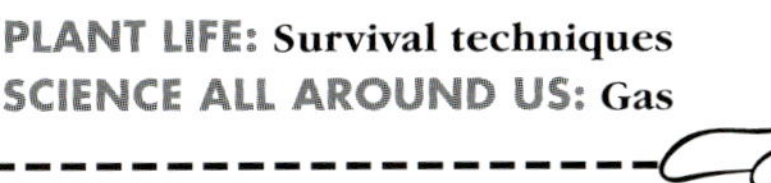

FIND OUT MORE
PLANT LIFE: Survival techniques
SCIENCE ALL AROUND US: Gas

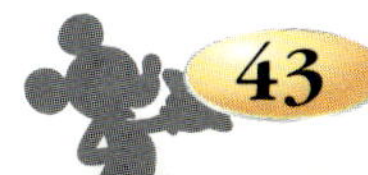

Insects and Humans

Humans often think of insects as a nuisance. Farmers call many insects pests because they destroy crops. Other insects bite or sting us, and spread diseases. But not all insects are harmful to humans. In fact, many are extremely helpful and valuable. Without insects to carry pollen from one flower to another, for example, most plants would not be able to grow and humans would have nothing to eat.

Plant Pollinator

Tiny grains of pollen are made by the male parts of a flower. The pollen must reach the female parts so seeds can form from which new plants grow. As insects such as flies and bees feed on a flower, they get dusted in pollen. The pollen brushes off onto the female parts of the next flower they visit.

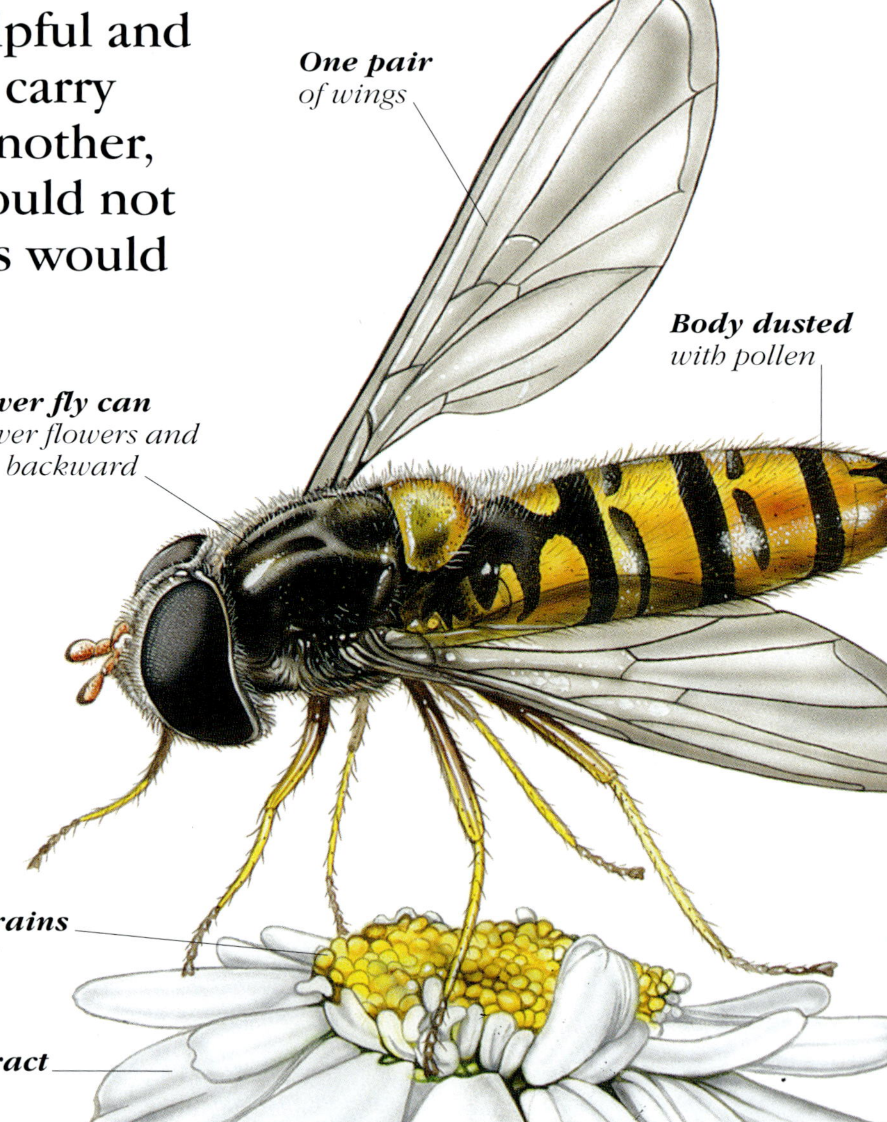

Hover fly landing on a flower

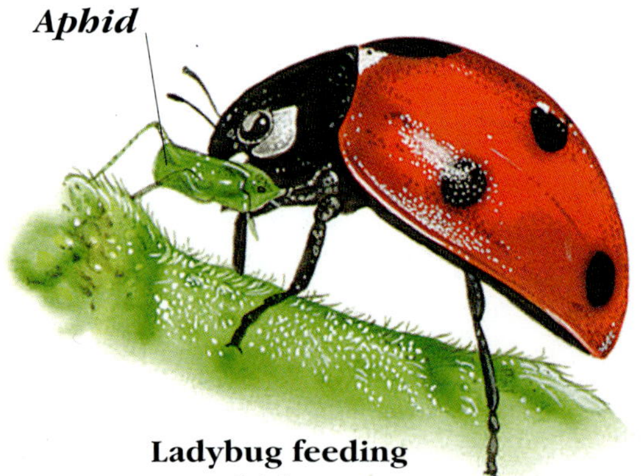

Ladybug feeding on aphid

Pest Control

Brightly colored ladybugs provide natural pest control. They eat tiny green bugs, called aphids, that swarm over plants in gardens and fields.

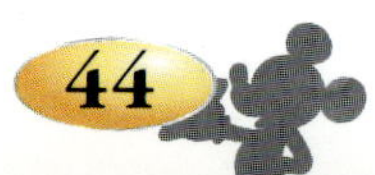

SILK SPINNERS

Silk is made by the caterpillars of the silkworm moth. It comes from the cocoons that the caterpillars spin around their bodies as they turn into pupae. The silken thread can be woven into a beautiful, shiny material.

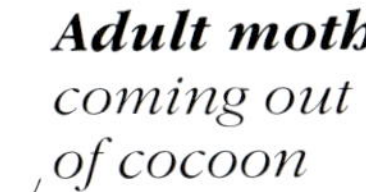
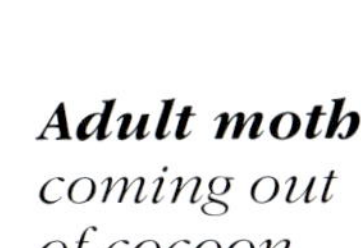

Adult moth *coming out of cocoon*

Silk cocoon that *formed around the caterpillar's body*

Silk for making *cloth is usually unwound before the moth hatches*

Silkworm moth and cocoon

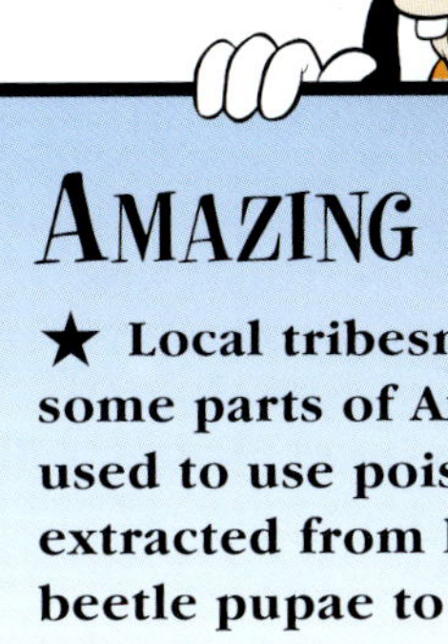

AMAZING FACTS

★ **Local tribesmen in some parts of Africa used to use poison extracted from leaf beetle pupae to tip their hunting arrows.**

HONEYBEE PRODUCTS

The honey you eat comes from a honeybee's hive. The bees feed honey to their newly hatched grubs, or larvae. The cells of the hive, the honeycomb, provide us with beeswax.

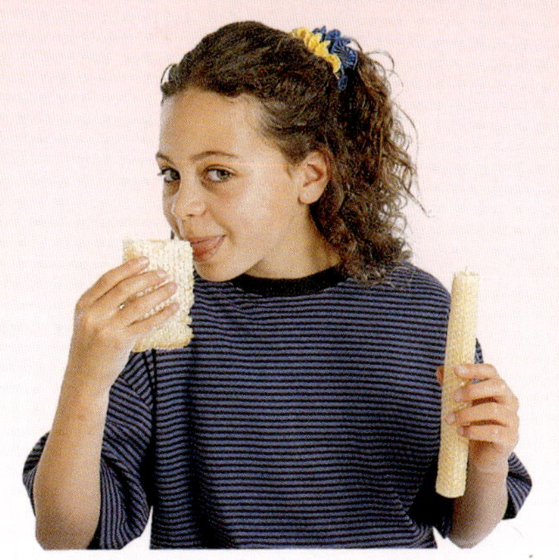

Hive cells can be seen in delicious honeycomb and a beeswax candle

INSECTS AS FOOD

There are many kinds of insects that are tasty and good to eat. These include fat, juicy grubs and big caterpillars. Deep-fried locusts make a particularly nourishing dish.

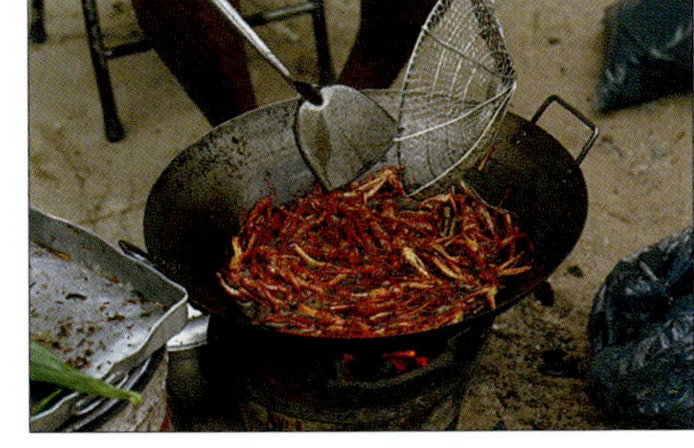

Fried locusts in a Thai market

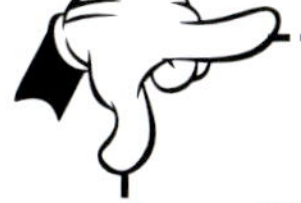

FIND OUT MORE
PLANT LIFE: **Pollination**
STORY OF THE PAST: **Silk Road**

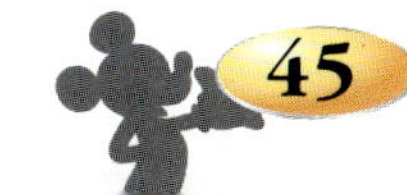

Web Spiders

Many spiders are famous for the silken webs that they spin as traps for insects. The silk is made inside the spider's body. It is squeezed out through tiny nozzles, called spinnerets, at the spider's rear. At first, the silk is liquid, but it hardens in the air. A web takes about an hour to spin. Then the spider waits for an insect to fly into its trap.

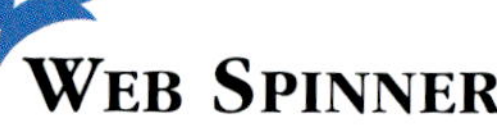

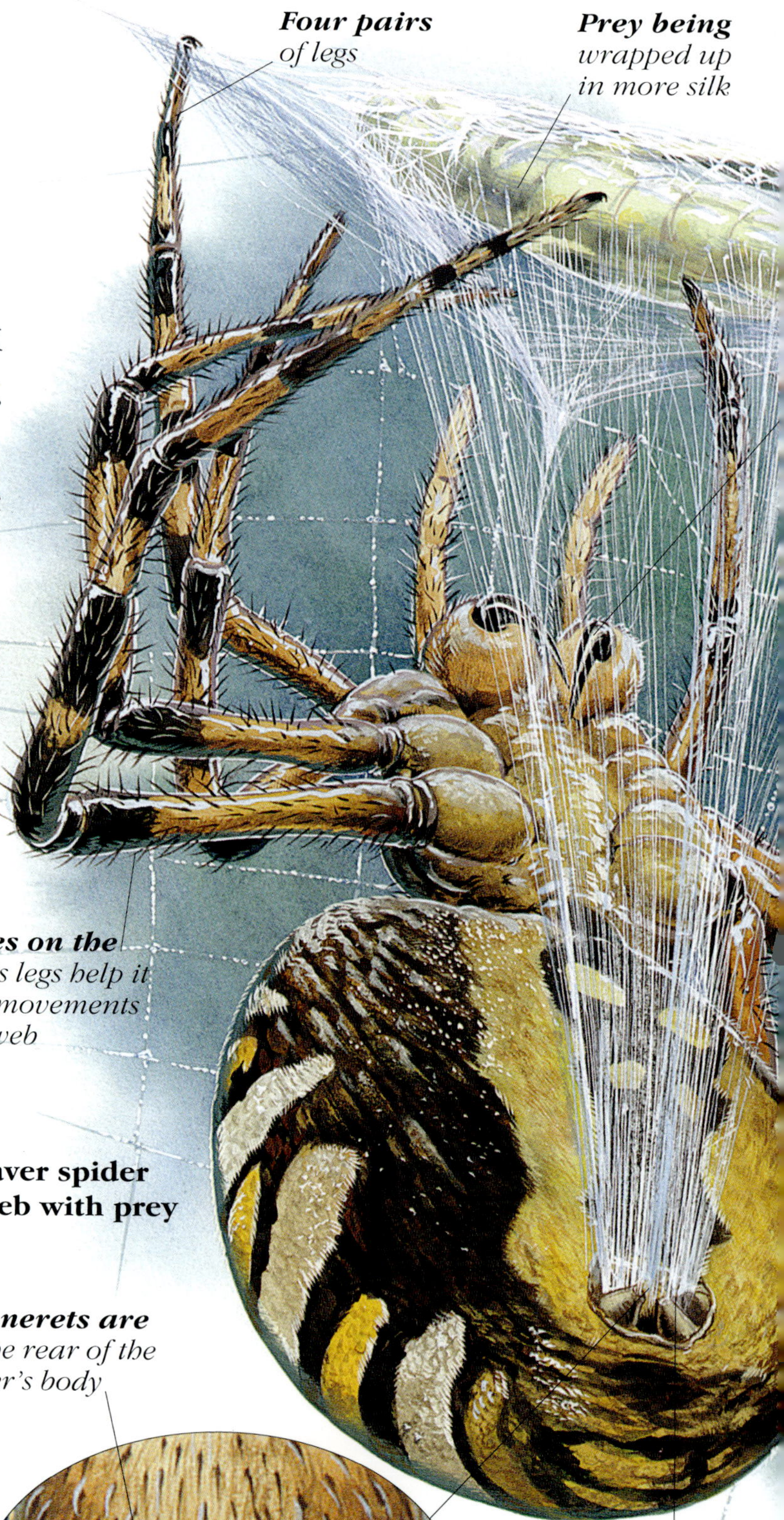

WEB SPINNER

Orb weaver spiders spin the wheel-shaped webs often seen in houses and gardens. They spin two types of silk. A strong, nonsticky thread is used for the framework of the web, and the center spiral is made from a sticky silk that traps the prey.

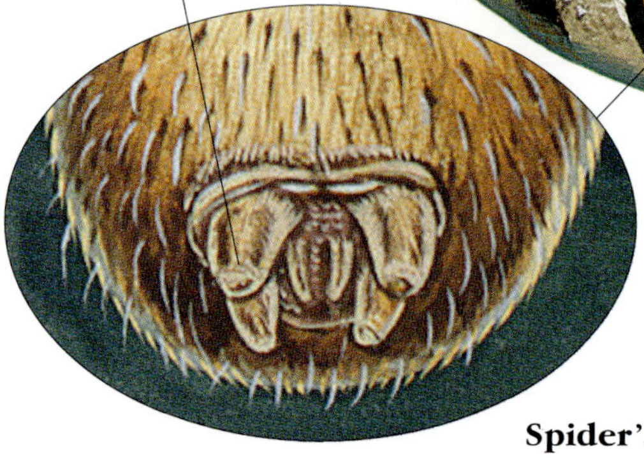

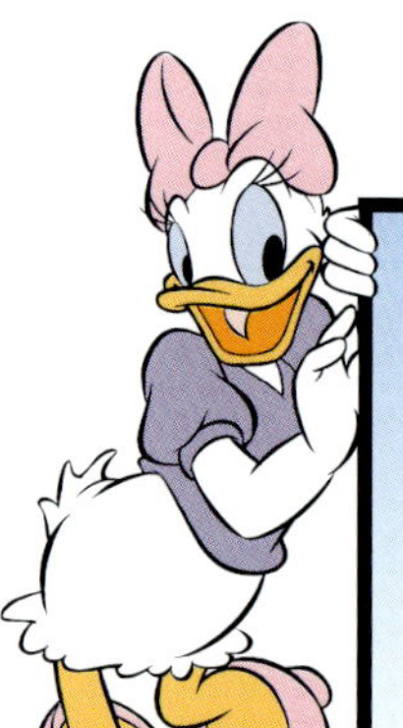

AMAZING FACTS

★ **Spider silk is very fine but strong. In fact, it is three times stronger than a piece of steel wire of the same thickness.**

Four pairs *of legs*

Prey being *wrapped up in more silk*

Bristles on the *spider's legs help it to feel movements on its web*

Orb weaver spider on its web with prey

Spinnerets are *on the rear of the spider's body*

Silk coming *from the spinnerets*

Spider's spinnerets

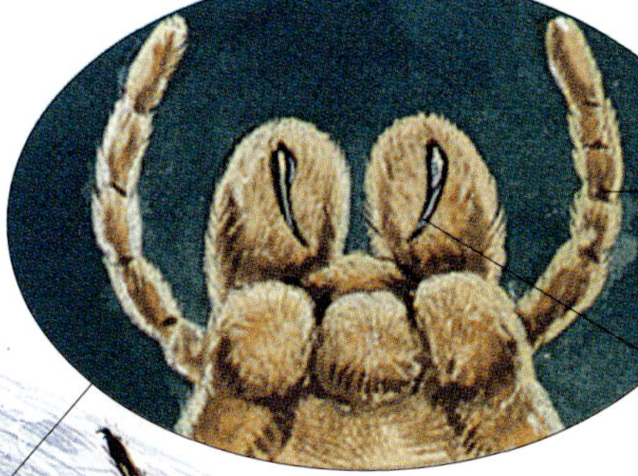

Pedipalps used *for signaling to mates*

Fangs for *seizing prey*

Spider's mouthparts

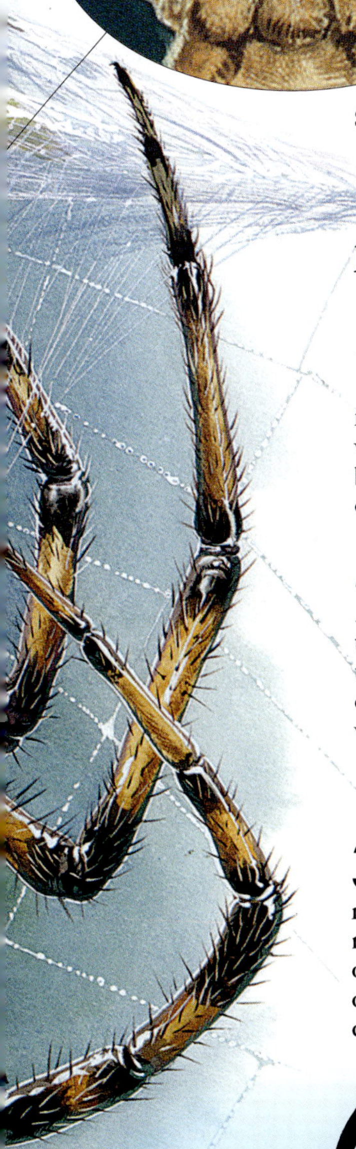

Flat Web

The sheet-web spider spins a flat web, like a sheet, among leaves and hides away underneath it. The web is held in place by long threads. When an insect hits the threads, it falls onto the web and is quickly grabbed by the spider.

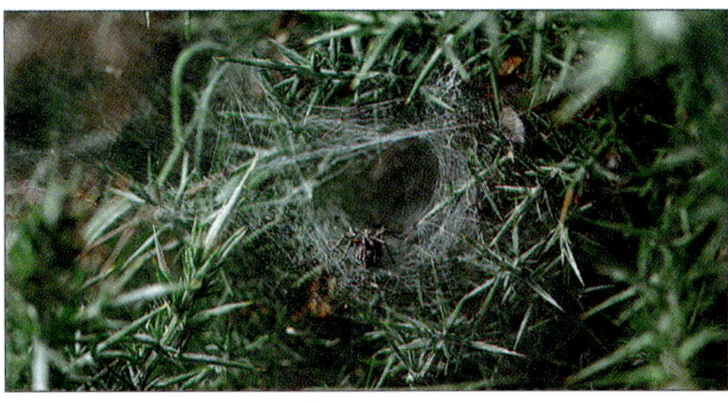

Sheet-web spider lying in wait for prey

Making a Web

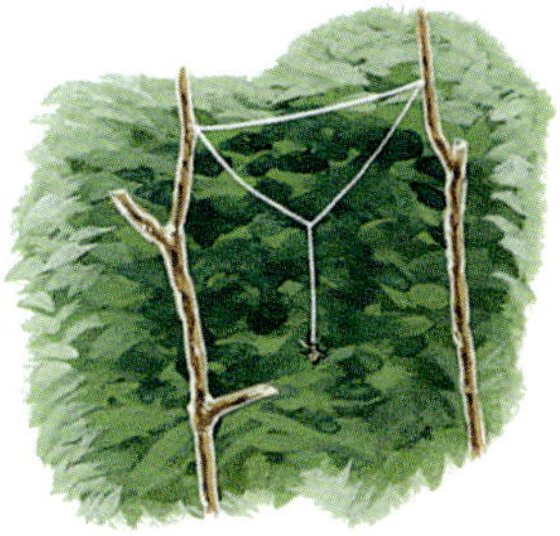

1 **First the spider** spins a Y-shaped framework of silk, which is supported between two twigs or stems.

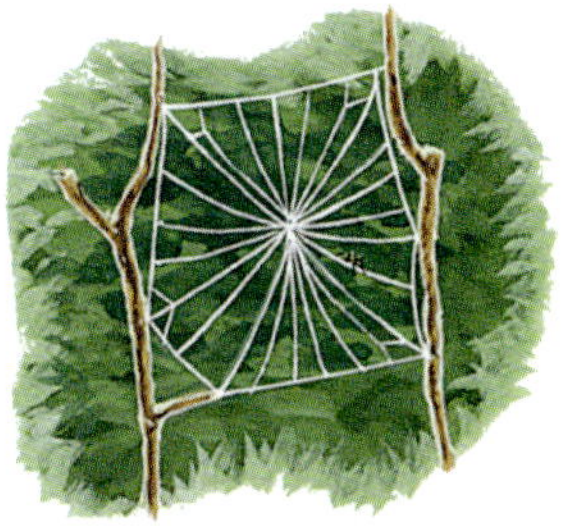

2 **Then it adds** more spokes to the Y, going from the center to the edges, to secure the web in place.

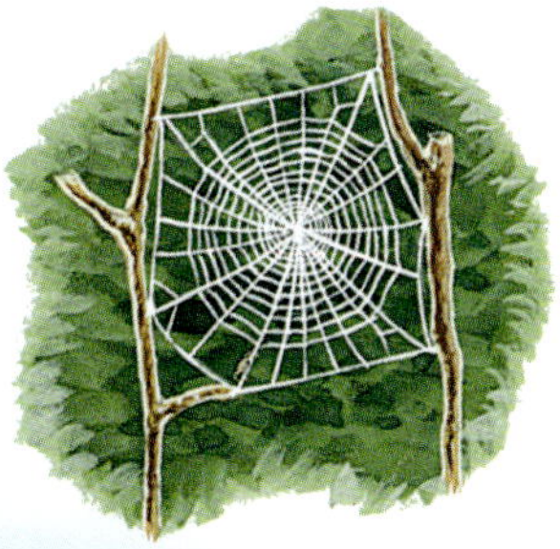

3 **Finally, the** spider spins round and round to make a sticky spiral of silk in the center of the web. Prey is caught on the spiral.

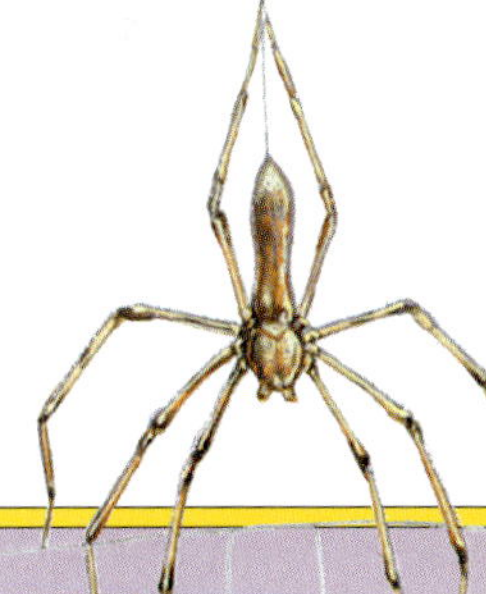

Ogre-faced spider with web

Spider Trap

The ogre-faced spider spins a small, strong web. The spider hangs by a thread of silk from a twig, holding its web out in front, like a net. When an insect comes close, the spider throws its net over the prey, then takes it away to eat.

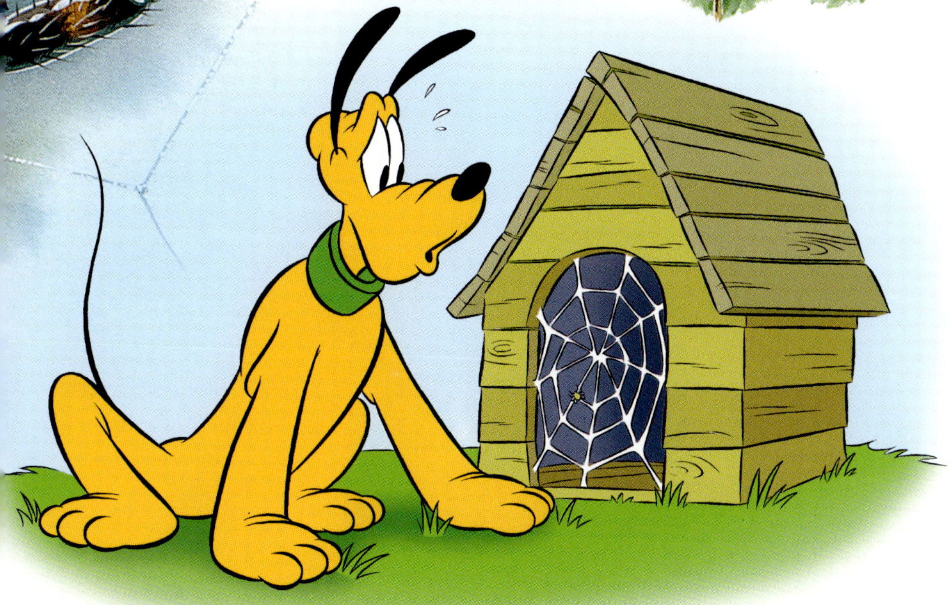

FIND OUT MORE

GREAT INVENTIONS: Spinning wheel

REPTILES AND AMPHIBIANS: Fangs

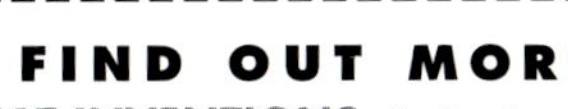

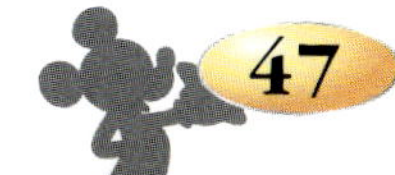

All Kinds of Spiders

All spiders can make silk, but not all of them spin webs to catch their food. Some are fast runners and chase after other creatures on the ground. Others build traps and tunnels and take prey by surprise. Many spiders use poison to paralyze and kill their prey, but only a few have a bite that is dangerous to humans.

HIDING UNDER A TRAPDOOR

The trapdoor spider makes a burrow with a hinged lid at the top, like a trapdoor. The spider waits until it senses an insect passing by. Then it opens the door, rushes out, and drags the prey back into its burrow to eat in safety.

Silk hinge

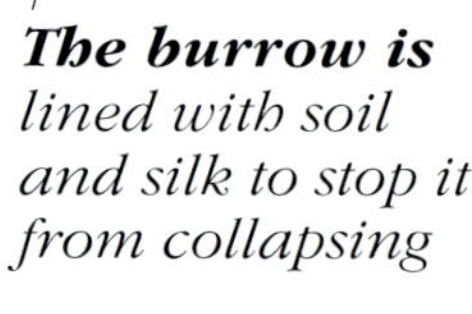

The burrow is *lined with soil and silk to stop it from collapsing*

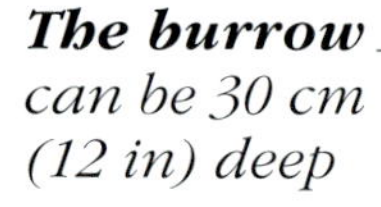

The burrow *can be 30 cm (12 in) deep*

Trapdoor spider's burrow

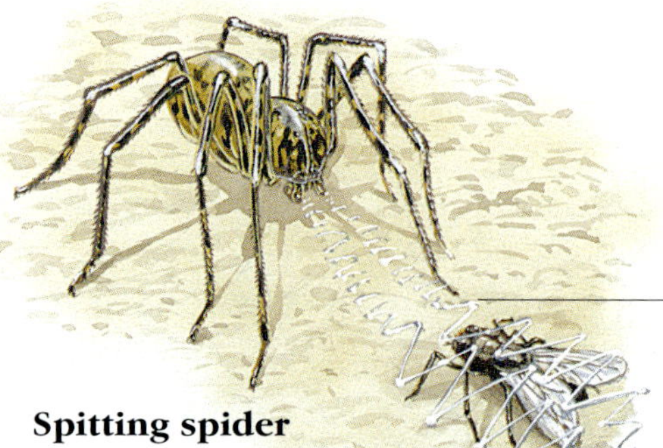

Sticky silk *threads*

Spitting spider

STICKY NET

When a spitting spider gets close to its victim, it spits out two sticky silk threads from its mouth. These fall like a net over the prey, pinning it to the ground before it has a chance to escape. The spider kills its victim with a bite and eats it.

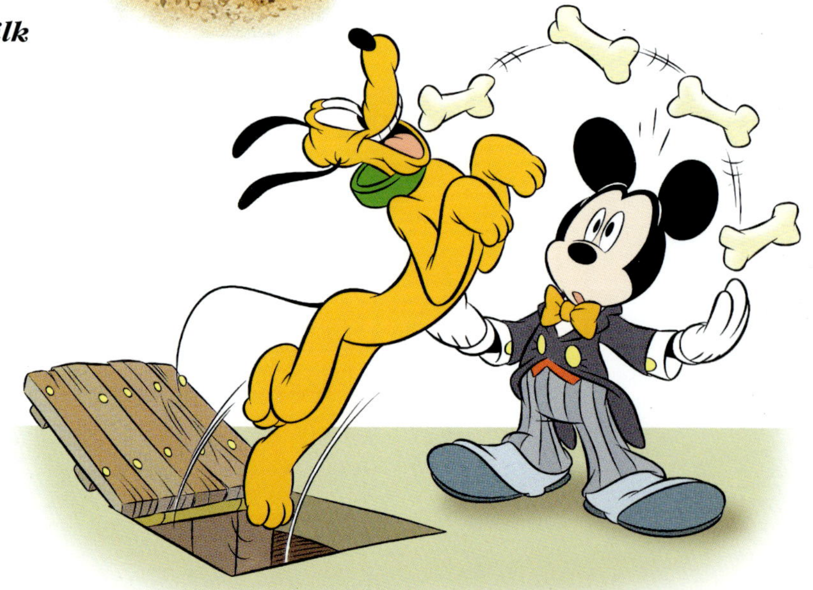

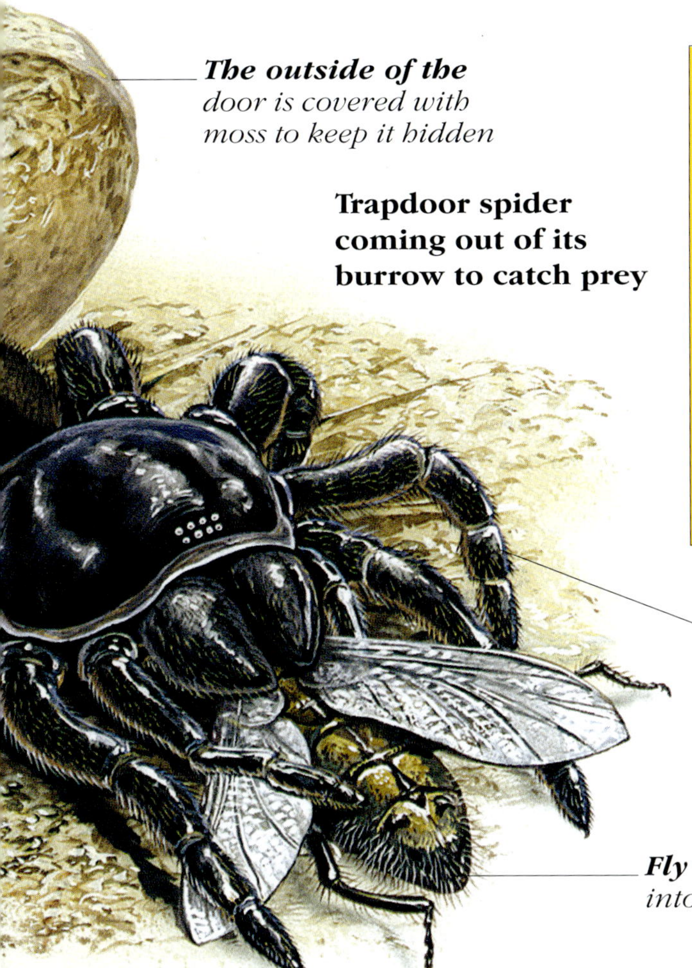

Trapdoor spider coming out of its burrow to catch prey

SPIDER-HUNTING WASP

Even spiders have enemies. The female spider-hunting wasp paralyzes spiders with her sting and puts them in an underground nest. She lays an egg in the nest and seals it up, leaving the spiders as food for her young when it hatches.

Spider-hunting wasp and prey

FUNNEL TRAP

The funnel-web spider makes a web shaped like a funnel, which leads into a burrow. Strands of silk are laid across the entrance. If a prey animal passes, it disturbs the strands and the spider rushes out for the kill. Its poisonous bite can even kill humans.

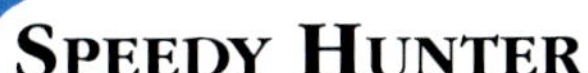

SPEEDY HUNTER

The wolf spider does not make a web. Unlike most spiders, it has good eyesight and lies in wait, watching for prey. Once it spots a victim, the spider runs after it and seizes it in its strong jaws.

Australian desert wolf spider

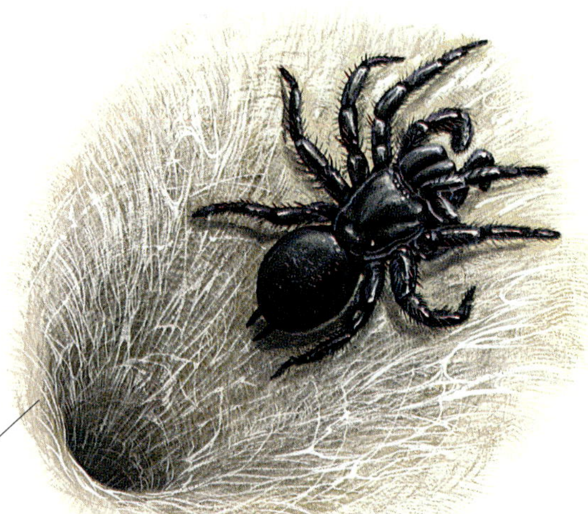

Funnel-web spider at the entrance to its burrow

AMAZING FACTS

★ Baby spiders use long strands of fine silk as parachutes to travel long distances through the air. This is called ballooning.

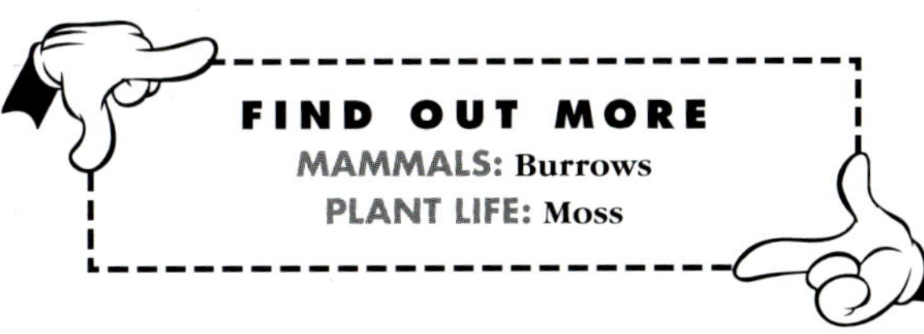

FIND OUT MORE
MAMMALS: Burrows
PLANT LIFE: Moss

Camouflaged Creatures

Some kinds of insects and spiders are specially colored, patterned, or shaped to help them hide from their predators. This is called camouflage. Staying hidden also allows insects to take their own prey by surprise.

Many insects and spiders that live in trees or bushes are colored green or brown so they are camouflaged by their surroundings. Others disguise themselves by looking like something else, such as leaves, flowers, thorns, or twigs. This makes them very hard for other creatures to see.

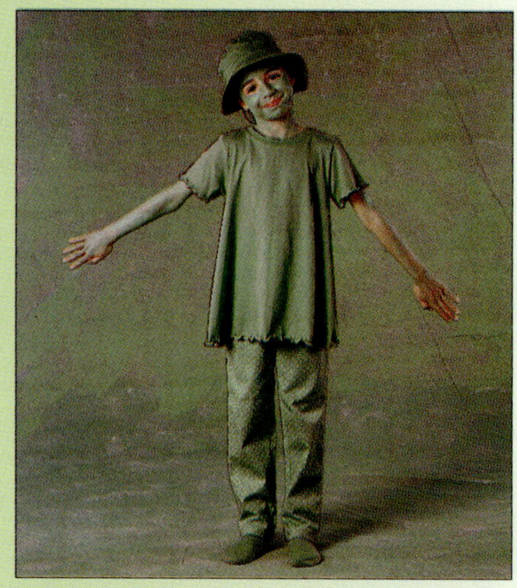

Green clothes and face paints work like camouflage to blend in with a green background

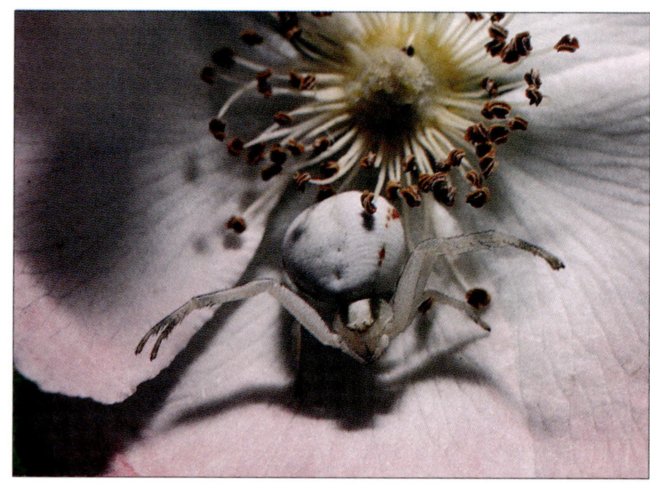

Crab spider camouflaged on a flower

HIDDEN SPIDER

Tiny crab spiders match the colors of the flowers they live on. A spider sits quite still, pretending to be a harmless flower petal, until an insect comes to visit. Then it pounces. Some spiders can even change color to match different flowers.

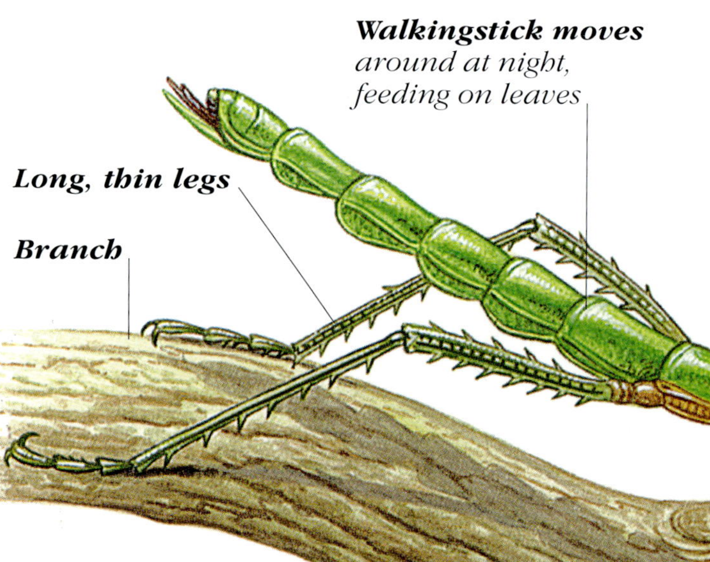

INSECT OR TWIG?

With its long, thin body, a walkingstick can look like a twig of the branch it rests on. It even sways slightly in the breeze like a real twig. These camouflaged insects are hard for predators to see.

Walkingstick camouflaged on a branch

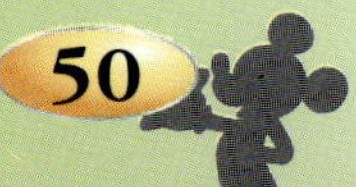

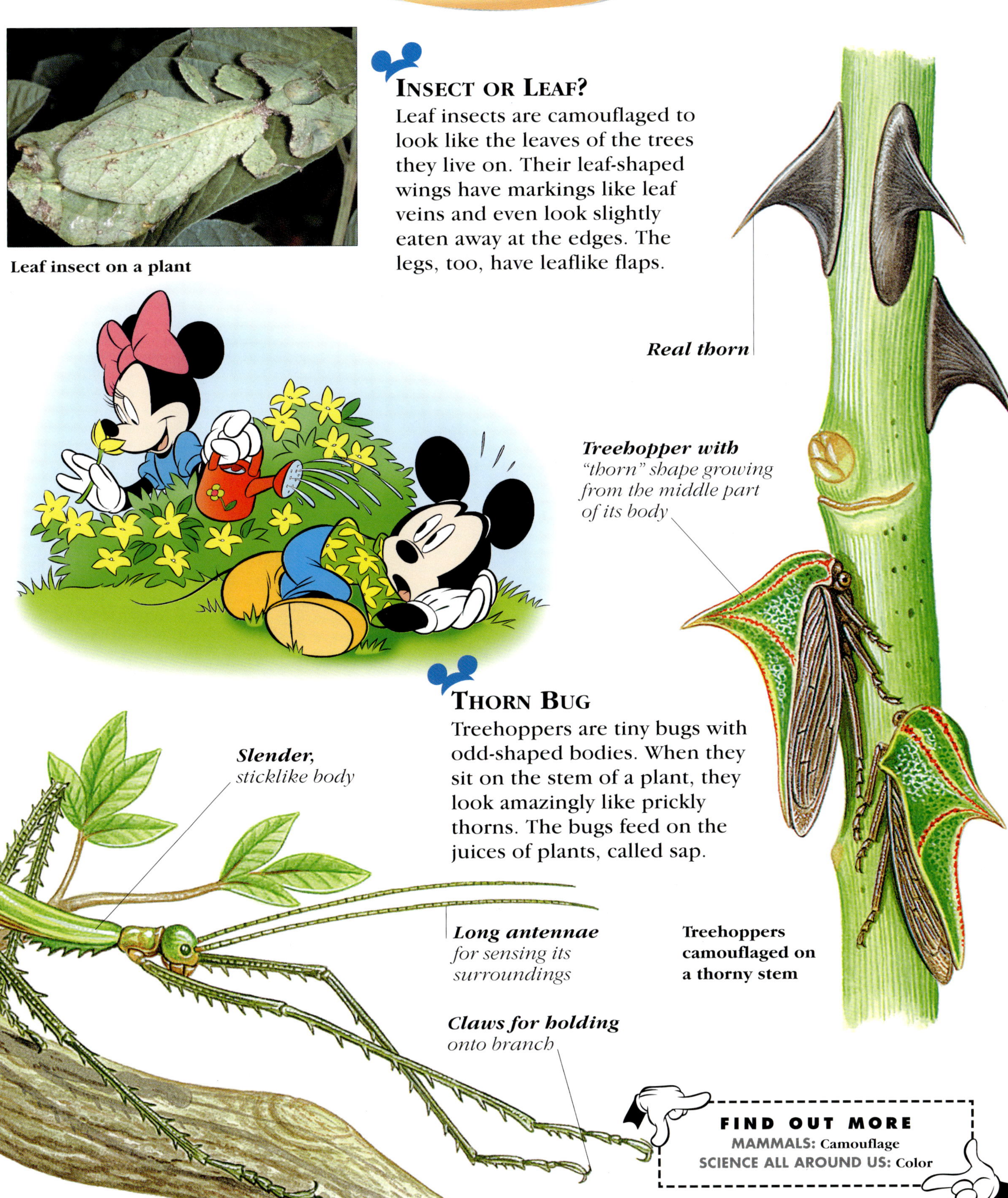

Leaf insect on a plant

Insect or Leaf?

Leaf insects are camouflaged to look like the leaves of the trees they live on. Their leaf-shaped wings have markings like leaf veins and even look slightly eaten away at the edges. The legs, too, have leaflike flaps.

Thorn Bug

Treehoppers are tiny bugs with odd-shaped bodies. When they sit on the stem of a plant, they look amazingly like prickly thorns. The bugs feed on the juices of plants, called sap.

Treehoppers camouflaged on a thorny stem

FIND OUT MORE
MAMMALS: Camouflage
SCIENCE ALL AROUND US: Color

Scorpions, Ticks, and Mites

Scorpions, ticks, and mites all belong to a group of invertebrates called arachnids. Like their spider relatives, they have eight legs and do not have wings or antennae. Scorpions have stingers at the end of their bodies, which they use to kill their prey. All ticks and some mites are parasites. They live on other animals, feeding on their blood or skin.

AMAZING FACTS

★ The huge African emperor scorpion measures 18 cm (7 in) – as long as a banana.

NIGHT HUNTER

The deadly desert scorpion spends the day hiding under stones or in holes in the sand. At night, it comes out to hunt for prey. It catches insects and spiders with its huge pincers and then swings the stinger over its body to kill them.

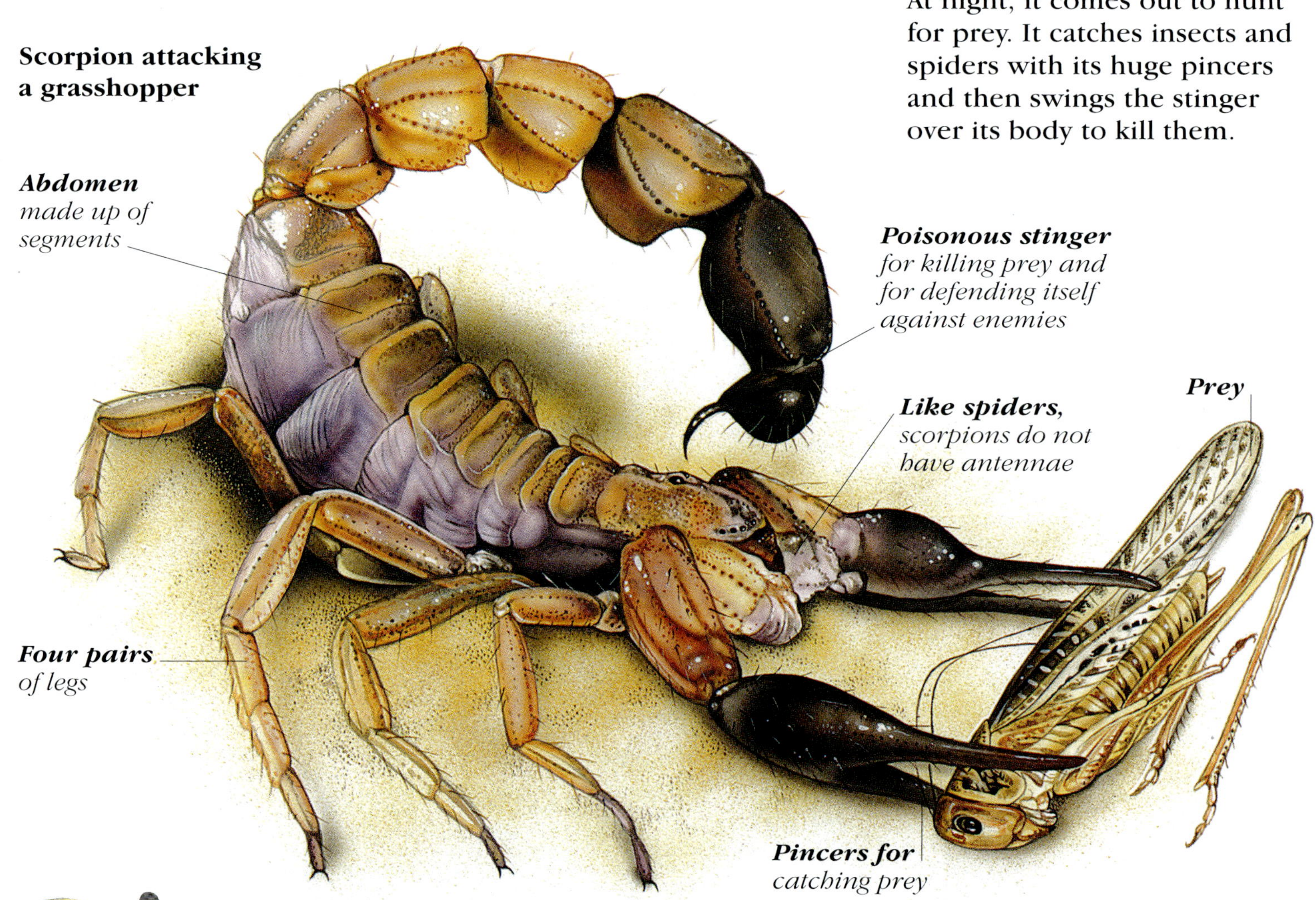

Scorpion attacking a grasshopper

Red velvet mite

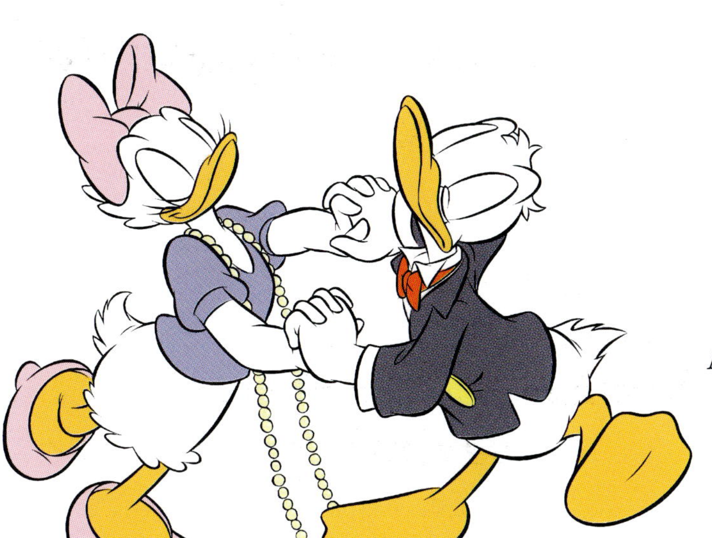

COLORFUL MITE

The body of the red velvet mite looks like it is covered in soft velvet. Adult velvet mites feed mostly on insect eggs. Their young live as parasites on insects, spiders, scorpions, and small mammals.

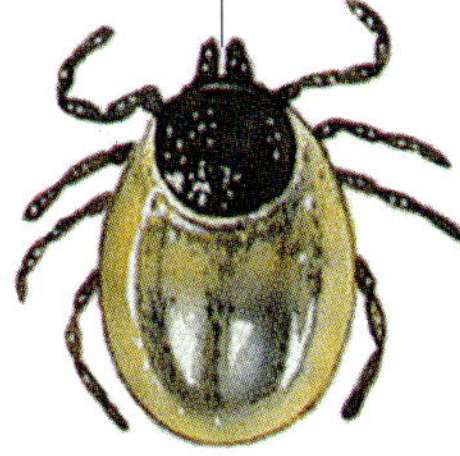

Tick swollen with blood after feeding

FEEDING TICKS

Ticks are parasites. They feed on the blood of birds, reptiles, and mammals such as cows and horses. They dig their mouthparts into their victim's flesh and can hang on for several days while they feed.

COURTSHIP DANCE

Before they mate, scorpions perform a long, slow dance. The male and female link pincers, then they dance to and fro, sometimes for several hours on end.

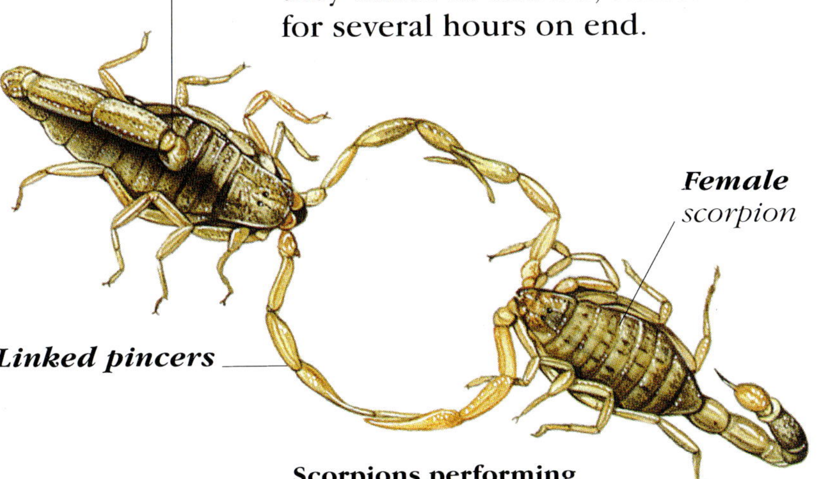

Scorpions performing a courtship dance

FALSE SCORPIONS

Pseudoscorpions and whip scorpions are not true scorpions, although they are closely related. They use their large pincers for attacking prey, but they do not have poisonous stingers.

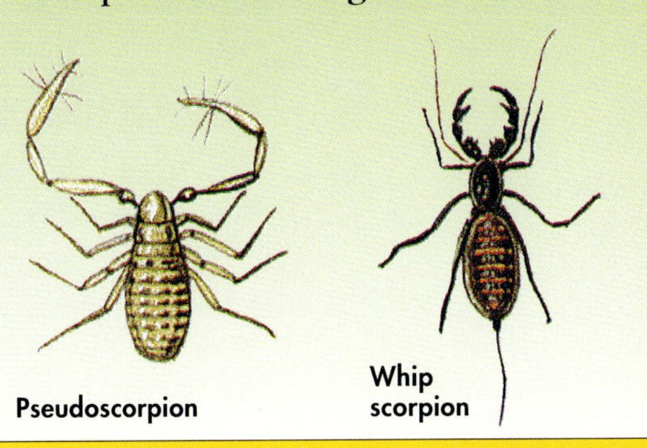

FEMALE AND YOUNG

Baby scorpions ride around on their mother's back for a few weeks until they are big enough to look after themselves. They cling on with their legs and pincers.

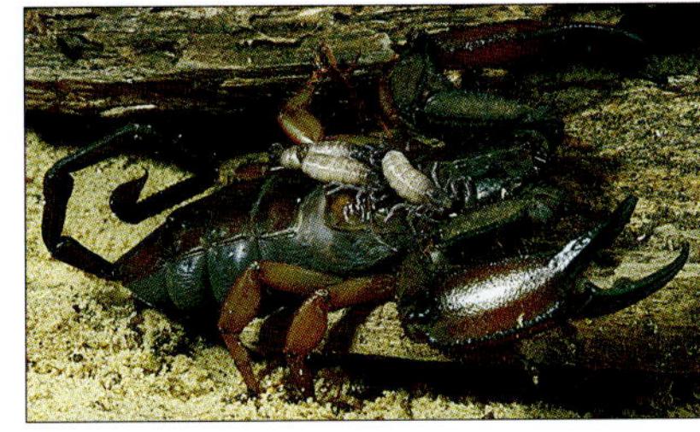

Female scorpion with babies

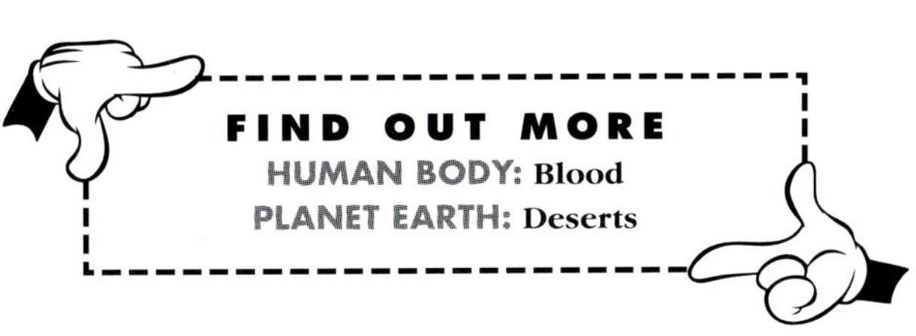
FIND OUT MORE
HUMAN BODY: Blood
PLANET EARTH: Deserts

These Aren't Insects or Spiders

Even though some of the creatures on these two pages may look like insects, none of them are. They belong to many other different groups. But like insects and spiders, these creatures are all invertebrates, so they do not have bony skeletons inside their bodies.

MOBILE HOME

Snails belong to a group of animals called mollusks. They have a soft body and a hard shell for protection. The snail always carries its protective home with it and can hide inside if in danger. Other types of mollusks include winkles and limpets.

Shell to protect *the snail's soft body*

PROTECTIVE SHELL

Crabs belong to a group of animals called crustaceans. Most crustaceans live in the sea. They include shrimp, lobsters, and barnacles. Crabs have thick shells to protect their soft bodies. They use their large claws for catching food.

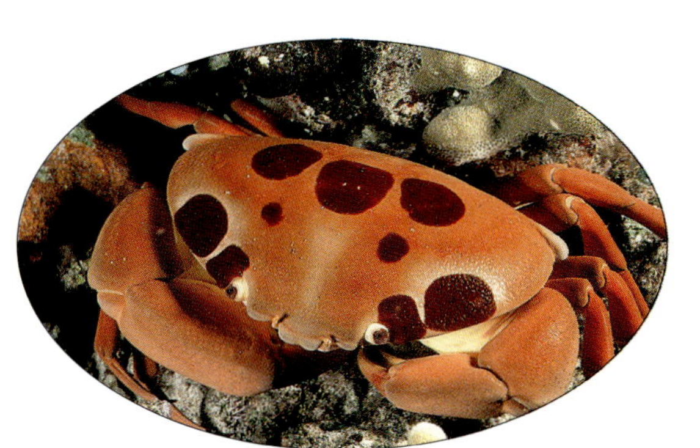

Hawaiian crab

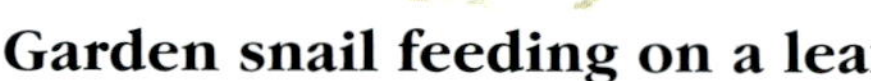

Garden snail feeding on a leaf

FAST RUNNERS

Centipedes have bodies divided into 15 or more parts called segments. Each segment has a pair of legs. Centipedes run after their prey, such as snails and worms. They kill their prey with a poisonous bite.

Pair of legs is *attached to each body segment*

Common centipede

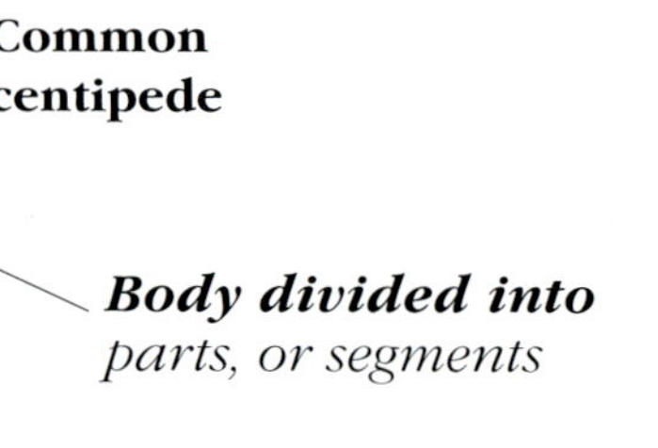

Body divided into *parts, or segments*

AMAZING FACTS

★ **The largest known snail is the African giant snail. It weighs about 900 g (2 lb), and its shell measures up to 27 cm (10½ in) long.**

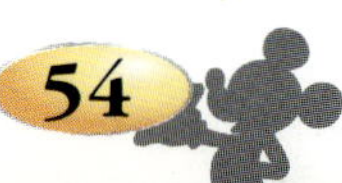

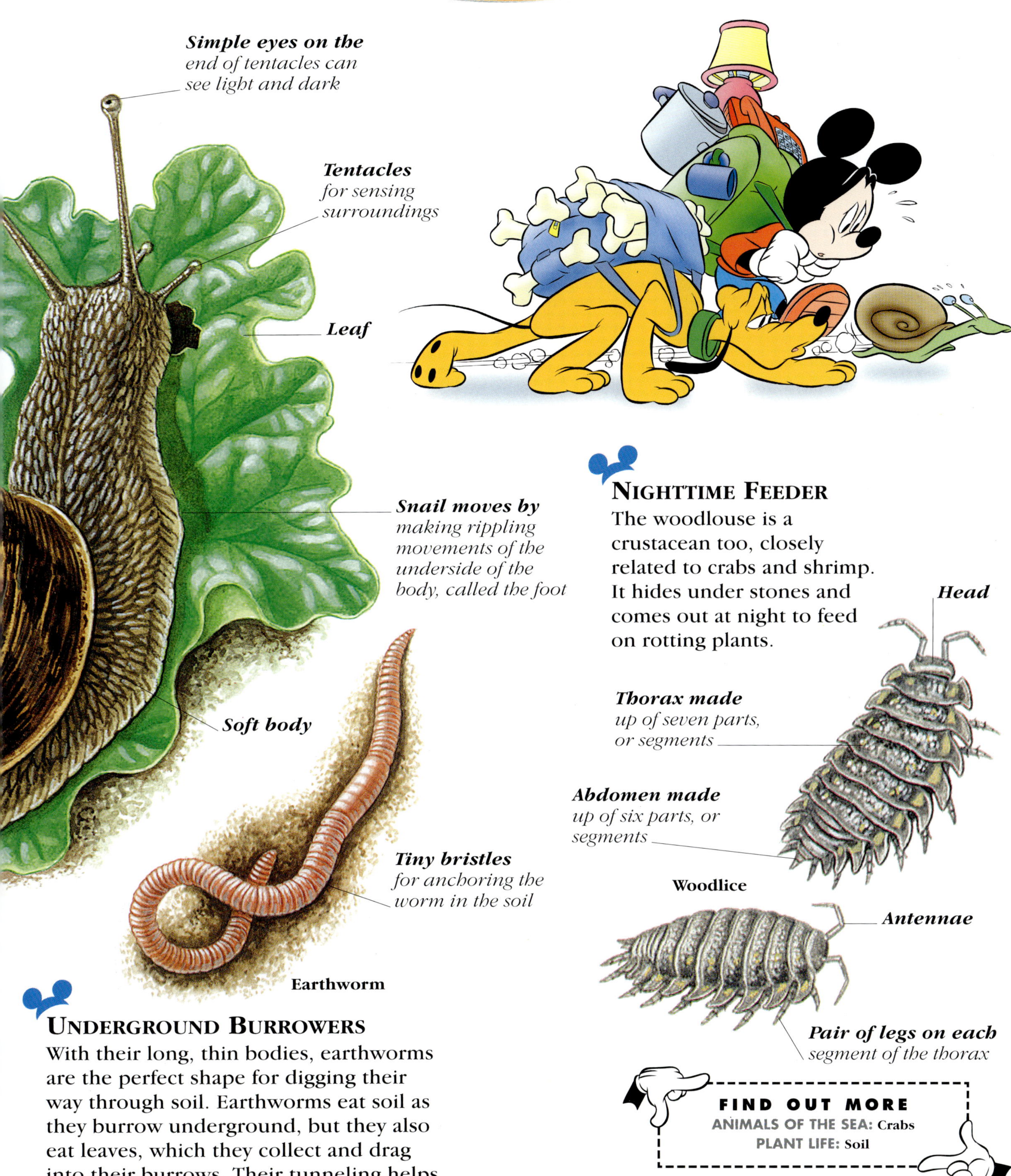

NIGHTTIME FEEDER

The woodlouse is a crustacean too, closely related to crabs and shrimp. It hides under stones and comes out at night to feed on rotting plants.

UNDERGROUND BURROWERS

With their long, thin bodies, earthworms are the perfect shape for digging their way through soil. Earthworms eat soil as they burrow underground, but they also eat leaves, which they collect and drag into their burrows. Their tunneling helps to open up and improve the soil.

FIND OUT MORE
ANIMALS OF THE SEA: Crabs
PLANT LIFE: Soil

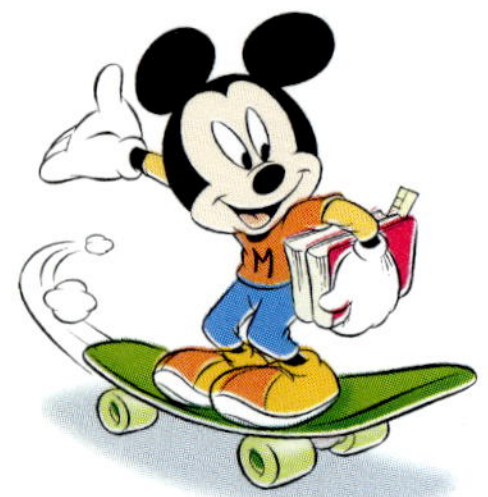

Glossary of Key Words

Abdomen: The lower part of an insect's or arachnid's body, behind its head and thorax.

Adapt: To change. Over many years, some animals have changed to suit different environments. For example, the legs of some insects have changed so that they can be used for swimming.

Antennae: A pair of feelers on an insect's head. They help the insect to smell, touch, and taste.

Arachnid: The name given to spiders and their relatives.

Bacteria: Tiny living organisms.

Bug: An insect with long, tubelike mouthparts that can pierce and suck.

Burrow: An underground home.

Camouflage: Special colors and patterns that help an animal blend in with its surroundings.

Caterpillar: The young of a butterfly or moth when it has changed from an egg into a larva.

Cell: In a bees' or a wasps' nest, a wax compartment that is used to store food and eggs.

Cocoon: A silk case that some insects spin around their bodies as they turn into pupae.

Colony: A group of the same type of animal living in the same place.

Compound eyes: Eyes that are made up of many tiny lenses.

Crustacean: An animal with a soft body and a hard, protective shell.

Exoskeleton: A hard casing on the outside of an insect that supports and protects it.

Eyespots: Moth and butterfly wing markings that look like eyes.

Fangs: A spider's pointed mouthparts, used to inject poison.

Fossil: The remains or the impression of a plant or animal preserved in rock.

Fungus: A special kind of living thing, such as a toadstool or mold, that feeds on rotting matter.

Halteres: Two knobs on a fly's back that help it balance as it flies.

Hatch: To come out of an egg.

Hive: A honeybees' nest, or the box in which they build their nest.

Host: An animal that a parasite lives and feeds on.

Invertebrate: An animal without a backbone or internal skeleton.

Iridescent: Shining with rainbow colors.

Larva: A stage in an insect's life between an egg and an adult. A larva looks very different from the full-grown adult form.

Lens: A piece of transparent material that bends light rays as they enter the eye.

Mating: When a male and female get together to produce young.

Membrane: A thin skin that covers or connects parts of an animal's body.

Metamorphosis: The changes an insect's body goes through as it turns from an egg into an adult.

Molting: In an insect, the process of shedding, or losing, a skin as the insect grows.

Mouthparts: An insect's mouth and jaws, which are adapted for sucking, biting, or chewing.

Nectar: A sweet liquid that is produced by many flowers.

Nymph: The young of a damselfly, dragonfly, or grasshopper.

Organ: A body part that has a special job, for example an ear, which is used for hearing.

Paralyze: Make unable to move.

Parasite: An animal that lives and feeds on other living creatures.

Pedipalps: The two armlike limbs at the front of a spider's mouth, used for touching and mating.

Pest: An animal that is destructive or a nuisance.

Pincers: Front claws that are used for catching and eating food.

Pollen: Tiny, powdery grains made by the male parts of flowers so the flowers can produce seeds.

Predator: An animal that hunts and kills other animals for food.

Prey: Animals that are hunted and eaten by other animals.

Proboscis: The long, tubelike mouthparts of some insects.

Pupa: The stage in an insect's life when it changes from a larva into an adult. Also, the hard case a caterpillar builds around its body when changing into an adult.

Sap: The juice found in the stems and leaves of plants.

Scale: A small, flat piece of hair or hardened skin, that overlaps other scales on an insect's body.

Silk: A natural fiber that spiders and insects produce in the form of strong, fine threads.

Swarm: A very large group of insects, such as locusts or bees.

Thorax: The second part of an insect's body, between its head and abdomen. In spiders and other arachnids, the head and thorax are joined.

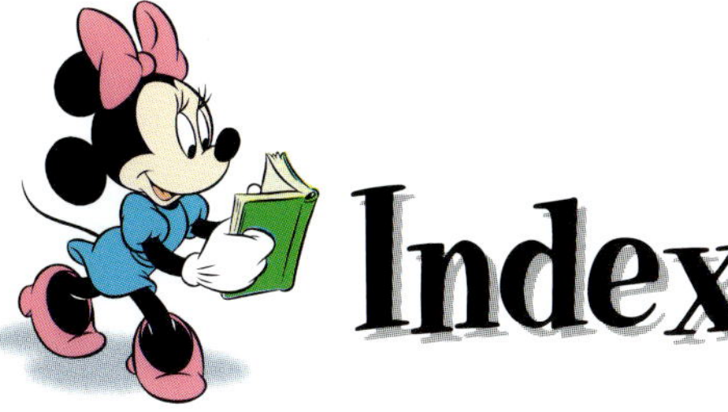

Index

(*see* **Famous Places** for a full index to your complete set of books)

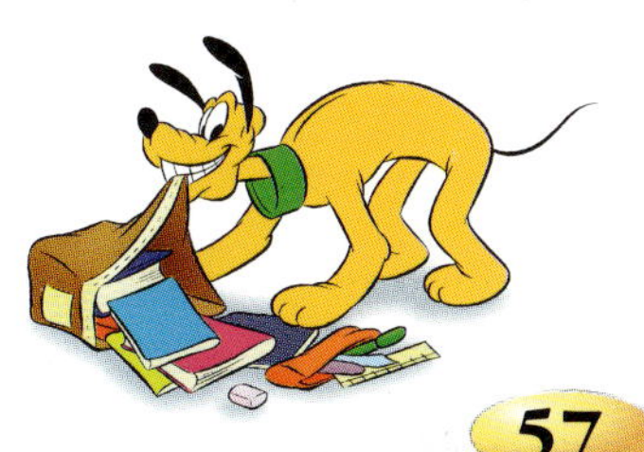

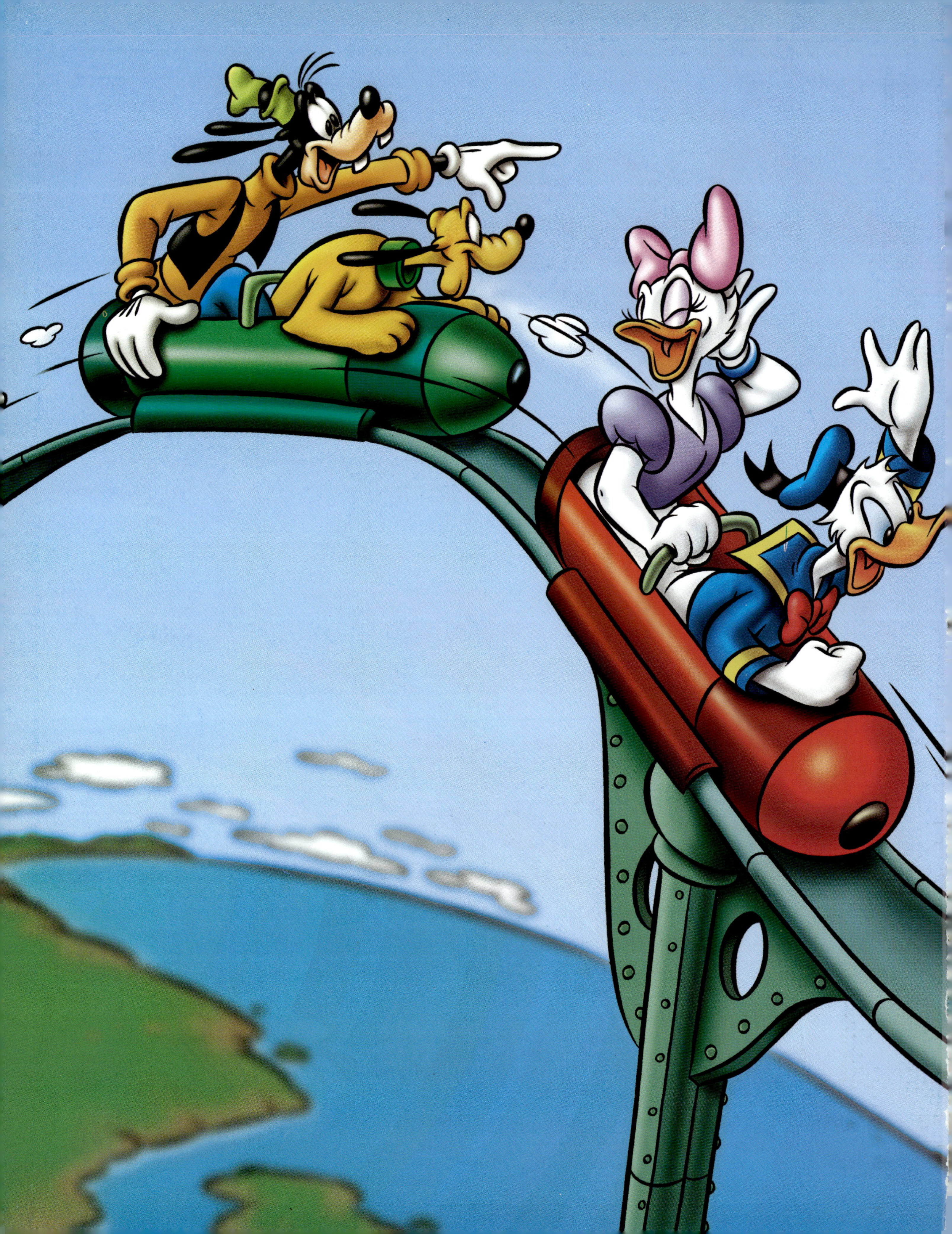